Committing to Action

Socially Just Leadership Education

A Volume in Contemporary Perspectives on Leadership Learning

Series Editor

Kathy L. Guthrie
Florida State University

Contemporary Perspectives on Leadership Learning

Kathy L. Guthrie, Series Editor

Committing to Action

Socially Just Leadership Education

editors

Kathy L. Guthrie
Florida State University

Vivechkanand S. Chunoo
Florida State University

Brittany Devies
Florida State University

≡IAP

INFORMATION AGE PUBLISHING, INC.
Charlotte, NC • www.infoagepub.com

Library of Congress Cataloging-in-Publication Data

CIP record for this book is available from the Library of Congress
http://www.loc.gov

ISBNs: 978-1-83708-594-1 (Paperback)

978-1-83708-593-4 (Hardcover)

978-1-83708-595-8 (ebook)

978-1-83708-562-0 (ePub)

CONTENTS

FOREWORD

Darren E. Pierre

"The ache for home lives in all of us, the safe place where we can come as we are and not be questioned."—Dr. Maya Angelou.

I remember when I first heard the aforementioned quote, I was in San Francisco, California at Glide Memorial Church. I was in the throes of writing my statement of purpose for applications to various doctoral programs. For me, a statement of purpose is a nebulous document, and as one who struggles with things not being black and white, I found the process of crafting that particular piece of writing stressful and arduous.

It was on an uneventful Sunday at Glide where my statement of purpose—and the force that drives my career in higher education became clear. The choir was singing, and behind them were images and inspirational quotes, including Angelou's quote on home. As soon as I saw the quote on the screen, it was a lightbulb moment, where I could name my purpose and passion for service within higher education and, more specifically, leadership education and development. At Glide, I recognized my goal as an educator which is to curate spaces where students can feel a sense of "home" on college and university campuses: where they can come as they are and not be questioned.

For the queer student in college, who is finding agency in crafting their identity outside of hegemonic norms, I hope for them to find home. For the first-generation college student, whose family comes from a working-class background, I hope for them to find home. For the female identified

Committing to Action: Socially Just Leadership Educations, pp. xi–xiii
Copyright © 2025 by Information Age Publishing
www.infoagepub.com

college student, who is finding themselves in a gendered major (that is a byproduct of a gendered-based society), I hope for them to find home. Regardless of the stripes or patterns of tapestry that describe a person's identities, I desire for all students to feel a sense of community, belonging, of *home*.

I suspect my passion around this notion of home is from my own personal sense of not fitting in. I now look back on my college experience: a member of a fraternity, student body president, accomplished in numerous ways—many would argue, but with all the accolades, and positional titles of "leadership," I rarely considered or classified myself as a leader. In many ways, I fell suspect to the temptation of the "Great Man Theory" of leadership—the belief that a leader was physically strong, male, White, straight—in other words not me. Over time, I have learned the preconceived notion of leadership I carried was a myth. I have spent my career through presentations, writings, and research trying to dismantle my own mis-informed archetypes of leadership so that others can see within themselves, things that have taken me decades to see within myself.

For people like me, this book, *Committing to Action* serves as good company for the leadership journey. Drs. Kathy Guthrie, Vivechkanand Chunoo, and Brittany Devies have elevated the conversation on inclusive and diverse narratives of leadership. Picking up where *Changing the Narrative* and *Shifting the Narrative* left off, this timely piece speaks to what is needed to approach leadership in contemporary times. The chapter authors of this book attempt to answer the call of not only leadership for what, but also leadership for whom. The critical question of the "who" in leadership learning, education, and development is more important now than ever before. As a leadership ambassador, promoter, and educator, I am accountable to ask (and answer) the question, "Who is involved in leadership?"—and just as important, who is not.

There is a need to discern how the socially constructed identities we carry, and historical legacies of power and privilege, have determined the diverse ways leadership is described, experienced, and enacted in society. Our journeys, identities, and differences matter, because each of them explains how we come to the table of leadership. Those journeys, identities, and differences should be celebrated and seen as an asset rather than a liability in the collective goal of fostering space for leaders fashioned to elevate the human condition.

Works like the one you are about to read honor the fact to talk about leadership without a conversation on identity is lacking, is limited and, in the context of leadership learning, education, and development, is a form of malpractice. So, I take this book as a resource, as a leadership educator committed to do work that expands the arena in which leadership learning, education, and development occurs. I carry gratitude in abundance for works like *Committing to Action* because I believe they are essential in the ongoing pursuit to cultivate the opportunities for students of all stripes and patterns to find their "home" that sacred place where people can come as they are and not be questioned.

AUTHOR BIO

Dr. Darren E. Pierre (he/him) is a Senior Lecturer in the Office of Global Engineering Leadership in the A. James Clark School of Engineering and holds an appointment as an affiliate assistant professor in the College of Education at the University of Maryland-College Park (UMD). He is a thought-leader within student affairs and leadership education. Darren is a 2023 ACPA Diamond Honoree recipient.

ACKNOWLEDGMENTS

No book is constructed in isolation, especially when it is focused on collective voices coming together to move forward and take action. It takes countless conversations, listening, thinking, reflection, and learning to build upon each other's ideas and concepts into something worthy of others reading and, hopefully, learning. When we think about all the individuals who have taken us up on engaging in the tough conversations about leadership and social justice, those who have taught us, and not only modeled what socially just leadership education is, we probably could write a book on just those lessons.

If someone had told us nine (!) years ago when we started the first socially just leadership education book that we would end up editing two more by now, we likely would not have believed them. In the time since we have started, we could not be prouder of how so many of you have taken these ideas and adapted them in incredible and unpredictable ways. What started as a complaint about resources we could not find has turned into the most spectacular journey filled with new experiences, relationships, and ideas we could not have foreseen at the start. We are more grateful than ever to be on this journey together, with all of you, and moving more rapidly than ever toward a brighter and fairer future for all.

Kathy continues to sit in a place of complete gratitude. I am beyond thankful I get to do this work and continually learn from so many awe-inspiring people. To V., thank you for being one of my people for over 10 years now. I am so deeply thankful you are back at FSU for so many reasons. One is so I can see your smiling face in person more. Brittany, you are such a gift to me and the whole field of leadership education. I am so

Committing to Action: Socially Just Leadership Educations, pp. xv–xvi thankful you jumped into this project with both feet and I continue to be in awe of you. Team Guthrie, I am nothing without you. Brian, you have always been the love of my life, and I do not take you for granted. Kinley, you are one of the kindest and coolest humans and I feel lucky I get to be your mom. Ahsoka, you are seriously the best dog. You have added to Team Guthrie in ways I could not have imagined.

V is grateful for the team in the LLRC at Florida State University; for their community, camaraderie, and love. I would also like to thank my colleagues and friends from across the country (and around the world)—both new and long-standing, for hearing out the ideas that sounded impossible until we made them happen. Eternal gratitude to you who saw the grand piano under the dollar store tablecloth.

Brittany is beyond thankful for her friends and mentors, Kathy and V., for inviting her into the work and conversation that is *Committing to Action*. You both are my guiding lights and sense of stability in our collective, critical work. I am eternally grateful for my brilliant colleagues, peers, and students at both the University of Maryland, College Park and Florida State University; my time at both places and spaces contributed immensely to this work. Above all, I sit in deep gratitude for my family (Mike, Julie, and Marcus), partner (Ryan), and friends who continue to love me unconditionally in the writing process.

Kathy L. Guthrie, Vivechkanand S. Chunoo, & Brittany Devies
February 2024

CHAPTER 1

ALIGNING INTENTION AND IMPACT

Our Commitment to Socially Just Leadership Education

**Vivechkanand S. Chunoo,
Kathy L. Guthrie, and Brittany Devies**

Wars in Ukraine and Gaza. Eroding faith in elected and appointed officials at all levels. A global climate crisis. The wonderful and terrifying rise of artificial intelligence. Developing nations struggling to find a place in the world, while superpowers horde wealth and resources. Nothing is so constant as change, and with it, heightened demand for individuals who can lead, guide, navigate an increasingly complex world. Subsequently, it falls to the leadership educators among us to craft the individuals who will not only change our world but save it from the brink of disaster; a position that has become all too familiar for far too many. These are the risks and responsibilities we face as we commit to socially just leadership learning.

One of the biggest challenges of integrating social justice with leadership education is proving that it works. Many of us are routinely required to produce evidence that what we do, and how we do it, matters. Beyond the anecdotal, we have more evidence than ever on how socially just leadership learning yields positive results; for our students and the wider world. We are proud to showcase the work of our colleagues in research, assessment,

Committing to Action: Socially Just Leadership Educations, pp. 1–8
Copyright © 2025 by Information Age Publishing
www.infoagepub.com

and evaluation who, collectively, are generating the data and information to verify what we have always been saying, and presenting it in ways that uplift (and not shame) those seeking to incorporate their wisdom into our efforts. As their ambassadors, we thank them for trusting us, and this platform, for their labor. We hope their stories inspire you to do what you can in your context.

Empiricism, however, is only one part of our story. No single volume can encompass all the socially just leadership scholarship that exists. Thus, we continue to amplify as many voices as we can, with special attention to those omitted in the past. In addition, we revisit some topics covered in our previous books as scholarly engagement in these areas has evolved rapidly in a very short time. *Committing to Action: Socially Just Leadership Education* both continues and accelerates the trajectory of what was started in *Changing the Narrative: Socially Just Leadership Education* (Guthrie & Chunoo, 2018) and carried forward in *Shifting the Mindset: Socially Just Leadership Education* (Guthrie & Chunoo, 2021).

Committing to Action can also serve as a starting point for social justice-oriented leadership educators. We hope you find within its pages useful recommendations, helpful suggestions, and a source of light in the darker moments. Whether this is where you join us, or if you have been with us all along the way, your impact has never been more important. Only by sharing the best of what each of us has to offer can we find the route to success. Our roadmap for the journey ahead starts in the next section.

CONVERGING SOCIAL JUSTICE AND LEADERSHIP EDUCATION

Several notable resources useful to the pursuit of socially just leadership learning have been created since our last outing in this vein. While a comprehensive review of even these selected examples would be beyond the scope of this introduction, their utility cannot be overstated. Perhaps most prominently, Komives and Owen's (2023a), *A Research Agenda for Leadership Learning and Development through Higher Education,* helpfully aggregated and interrogated what we think we know about leadership education in general, and leadership education research in particular, while challenging researchers and practitioners to apply social justice frameworks to their research, assessment, and evaluation projects. Specifically, this text pushed for equity-minded research agendas (Komives & Owen, 2023b), advocated for social justice as the beating heart of leadership education (Chunoo & Guthrie, 2023), extolled the virtues of liberatory pedagogy in leadership learning (Rocco & Beatty, 2023), and illuminated pathways toward liberatory leadership scholarship (Owen & Komives, 2023). While robust experience with socially just and/or critical approaches is not required prior to engaging with these authors and editors, they nonetheless drive us toward deeper innovation and creativity in leadership scholarship across contexts.

Tremendously important socially, just leadership literature has been generated by the *Contemporary Perspectives on Leadership Learning* series (the line to which this text also belongs) in recent years. For example, Beatty and Guthrie (2021) had taken to operationalizing the culturally relevant leadership learning model; a sorely needed addition to any leadership educators' toolkit. Also, Guthrie and Priest (2022) helped us move toward critical hope through their recommendations on navigating complexities in leadership learning. Moreover, vital lessons on engaging Black men in leadership learning have been provided (Beatty & Ford, 2023). Likewise, women's narratives around socially just leadership development has served as Teig and colleagues' (2023) sharp focus. Meanwhile, Rosch and colleagues (2023) helpfully provided guidance on how to conduct research in leadership education, with an orientation around socially just outcomes and processes. For the social justice-oriented leadership educator, there has never been a more well-resourced time to commit to this work.

The *New Directions for Student Leadership* (NDSL) series has also recommitted to advancing socially just and critical frames in recent years. The year 2021 saw scholarship related to: intersections of leadership learning and social class (Guthrie & Ardoin, 2021); the use of inventories to augment durable leadership growth (Shankman & Gigliotti, 2021); a keen focus on marginalized institutional environments in advancing racial equity (Whitney & Collins, 2021), as well as admonitions for protecting leadership education during times of tumultuous change and transition (Chung et al., 2021). In 2022, NDSL focused on engineering students' leadership learning experiences and contexts (Kendall & Rottmann, 2022); the use of games as leadership pedagogy (Egan & Banter, 2022); leadership development research and assessment methods (Rosch & Hastings, 2022); and Breen and Gleason's (2022) emphasis on leader development in graduate and professional school contexts. In the current year of 2023, additional scholarship in social action, leadership, and transformation (Puente et al., 2023); deep leadership identity development (Owen, 2023); leadership learning for environmental sustainability (Satterwhite et al., 2023) and applications of theories and models toward socially just leadership program construction and curriculum design (Rocco & Pierre, 2023) shine as examples of continued commitments to converging social justice and leadership learning.

Not to be outdone, developments in 2024 will carry on the legacy of what has been established. In addition to this text, the *Contemporary Issues* series will add texts on the theoretical foundations of leadership learning, case studies in cultural relevant leadership learning, the role and identities of leadership educators, the theory and practice of leadership, and leading in global contexts. The editorship of *New Directions for Student Leadership* is very excited to be working on issues related to intentional emergence in leadership education, applications of the leadership learning framework (Guthrie & Jenkins, 2018), facilitating leadership development in training contexts, and the use of pop culture in leadership learning. Furthermore, the *International Leadership Association's Guiding Principles* (2009) are being revised to account for the global context where leadership occurs. Taken together, it is quite clear the moral trajectory of leadership learning is growing and converging on social justice.

COMMITTING TO ACTION

In collaboration with our contributors, we are taking this opportunity to reconfirm and redefine our commitment to socially just leadership education in action. Later, in this extended introduction in Chapter 2, Adrian Bitton levels sharp criticism of our field while also highlighting how far we have come alongside a detailed analysis of how far we have left to go. Attendant to these remarks, Josh Taylor in Chapter 3 uncovers significant taken-for-granted assumptions about race and how leadership learning occurs. Our main body of writing, however, is organized into three parts.

New to readers of either *Changing the Narrative* and/or *Shifting the Mindset* is a section focused on empirical derivations of socially just leadership education. Next, we include an area on identity development in our continued pursuit of robust representation in leadership learning. Our final major section underscores methods of realizing our commitment through actions each of us can take. Every chapter is intended to be imminently useful regardless of having read any of the others here, the order in which you approach them, and whether you have read any of the other texts in this subseries or not.

Committing to Empirically Based Action

Our section on empirical socially just leadership education evidence showcases the early work of four emerging scholars. In Chapter 4, Michael Daniels's grounded theory study provides evidence of his Black men's leader identity development model (BMLID). Ana Maia's Presidential Fellows Program provides a backdrop for her model for fostering culturally relevant leadership development (FCRLD) in Chapter 5. Laura Irwin, in Chapter 6, problematizes leadership education's perceived boundaries toward the incorporation of social justice. Completing this area in Chapter

7, Vivechkanand S. Chunoo uses his own mixed methods study of cultural responsiveness as an example of systemic inquiry in leadership education. Taken together, these studies serve as both content and process for leadership educators seeking empirically based and evidence-supported socially just leadership education, with implications for how we might all go about documenting our impact.

Committing to Identity Development

In Chapters 8 through 15, our contributors contend with significant intra- and inter- personal elements of leader and leadership identity development. In Chapter 8, Derrick Pacheco takes us from the beach to the palm trees to better understand Caribbean-American student leadership development. Next, Challen Wellington critically interrogates issues of size, weight, and shape by asking if leadership is for every body type in Chapter 9. Desi leadership and the interactions of southeast Asian identity, culture, and language center Chapter 10 by Ravi Bhatt.

In Chapter 11, Adam Kuhn uses the environmental dimensions of the culturally relevant leadership learning model to add to our enlightenment around queer student leadership learning. Laura Vaughn, in Chapter 12, keenly deconstructs and reconstructs important assumed-to-be-true factors in socially just leadership education for international students studying in the United States. High-achieving students and the importance of attending to their unique experiences in leadership learning is the focus of Amy Haggard in Chapter 13.

Advancing from the foundation established by Farinella (2018) in *Changing the Narrative: Socially Just Leadership Education*, Lisa Jackson extolls the virtues of foster youth as peer leaders in Chapter 14. Continuing in this optimistic thread, Darius Robinson closes our section on identity in Chapter 15 with his discourse on critical hope and its unique applicability to Black students' leadership development. With these chapters, we hope to reignite conversations about students we have discussed in the past while continuing to represent as many, and as diverse, experiences of socially just leadership education as we can.

Making Action-Oriented Commitments

Chapters 16 through 21 comprise our section on action-oriented commitments to socially just leadership education. Brittany Devies's inquiry into leadership learning for capacity and efficacy development yielded important implications for the creation and maintenance of women-only and/or predominantly women spaces, which we are proud to underscore, in Chapter 16. In Chapter 17, Holly Henning frames academic advising spaces, relationships, and dynamics as avenues for socially just leadership education. Similarly, mentorship of Black students is addressed as a way of developing leaders and social justice agents simultaneously by Johnnie Allen, Jr. in Chapter 18, Ashley Archer Doehling depicts social justice peer educators as leadership educators-in-training, in Chapter 19, by leveraging the integrated model for critical leadership (Dugan, 2017).

To help us bounce back from the challenges and fatigue associated with socially just leadership education, Gen Ramirez extolls the virtues of resilience—while honoring our commitments, in Chapter 20. Chapter 21, by Antonio Ruiz-Ezquerro, demonstrates the power of tabletop games as socially just leadership pedagogy. Concluding with Chapter 22, we share some of our ongoing perspectives on doing the work of socially just leadership teaching and learning across contexts.

DOING THE WORK

Shifting the Mindset concluded with the bold assertion that, "Action is long overdue for justice, fairness, and equity" (Guthrie & Chunoo, 2021, p. 278) for socially just leadership educators and their students. *It still is.* At a time when even more of us, our rights, and our future are at risk, committing to socially just action has become a moral imperative. It is no longer a question of "if'" each of us will be affected by injustice; rather, they are questions of "when," "how," and "who will come to our aid?" Perhaps, by offering each other assistance in these trying times, we will each not need to look as hard for help when it is our turn to receive it. *Committing to Action* is our offer of support.

REFERENCES

Beatty, C. C., & Ford, J. R. (2023). *Engaging black men in college through leadership learning.* Information Age Publishing.

Beatty, C. C., & Guthrie, K. L. (2021). *Operationalizing culturally relevant leadership learning.* Information Age Publishing.

Breen, J. M., & Gleason, M. C. (Eds.). (2022). Developing leaders in graduate and professional school settings. *New Directions for Student Leadership, 2022*(176). Wiley.

Chung, J., Gleason, M., Guthrie, K. L., Navarro, C. D., Priest, K. L., Pierre, D. E., Cummings Steele, M., & Weng, J. (Eds.). (2021). Leadership education through complex transitions. *New Directions for Student Leadership, 2021*(172). Wiley.

Chunoo, V. S., & Guthrie, K. L. (2023). Social justice as the heart of leadership education. In S. R. Komives, & J. E. Owen (Eds.), *A research agenda for leadership learning and development through higher education* (pp. 39–58). Information Age Publishing.

Dugan, J. P. (2017). *Leadership theory: Cultivating critical perspectives.* Jossey-Bass.

Egan, J. D., & Banter, J. N. (Eds.). (2022). Games in leadership learning. *New Directions for Student Leadership, 2022*(174). Wiley.

Farinella, J. J. (2018). Foster care youth alumni to collegiate leaders: How non-traditional family structures impact leadership development. In K. L. Guthrie, & V. S. Chunoo (Eds.), *Changing the narrative: Socially just leadership education* (pp. 193–209). Information Age Publishing.

Guthrie, K. L., & Ardoin, S. (Eds.). (2021). Leadership learning though the lens of social class. *New Directions for Student Leadership, 2021*(169). Wiley.

Guthrie, K. L., & Chunoo, V. S. (2018). *Changing the narrative: Socially just leadership education.* Information Age Publishing.

Guthrie, K. L., & Chunoo, V. S. (2021). *Shifting the mindset: Socially just leadership education.* Information Age Publishing.

Guthrie, K. L., & Jenkins, D. M. (2018). *The role of leadership educators: Transforming learning.* Information Age Publishing.

Guthrie, K. L., & Priest, K. L. (2022). *Navigating complexities in leadership: Moving toward critical hope.* Information Age Publishing.

International Leadership Association. (2009). *Guiding questions: Guidelines for leadership education programs.* http://www.ila-net.org/Communities/LC/GuidingQuestionsFinal.pdf.

Kendall, M. R., & Rottman, C. (Eds.). (2022). Student leadership development in engineering. *New Directions for Student Leadership, 2022*(173). Wiley.

Komives, S. R., & Owen, J. E. (2023a). *A research agenda for leadership learning and development through higher education.* Edward Elgar.

Komives, S. R., & Owen, J. E. (2023b). An equity-minded research agenda for leadership learning and development in higher education. In S. R. Komives, & J. E. Owen (Eds.), *A research agenda for leadership learning and development through higher education* (pp. 3–24). Information Age Publishing.

Owen, J. E. (Ed.). (2023). Deepening leadership identity development. *New Directions for Student Leadership, 2023*(178). Wiley.

Owen, J. E., & Komives, S. R. (2023). Advancing liberatory leadership scholarship. In S. R. Komives, & J. E. Owen (Eds.), *A research agenda for leadership learning and development through higher education* (pp. 273–294). Information Age Publishing.

Puente, M., Mitchell, T. D., Museus, S., Ting, M. P., & Chandler, K. (Eds.). (2023). Fostering social justice leaders through the social action, leadership, and transformation (SALT) model. *New Directions for Student Leadership, 2023*(177). Wiley.

Rocco, M. L., & Beatty, C. C. (2023). Pedagogical practices through the lens of liberatory pedagogy. In S. R. Komives, & J. E. Owen (Eds.), *A research agenda for leadership learning and development through higher education* (pp. 191–210). Information Age Publishing.

Rocco, M. L., & Pierre, D. (Eds.). (2023). Applying models and theories to program design and curriculum development. *New Directions for Student Leadership, 2023*(180). Wiley.

Rosch, D. M., & Hastings, L. J. (Eds.). (2022). Research and assessment methods for leadership development in practice. *New Directions for Student Leadership, 2022*(175). Wiley.

Rosch, D. M., Kniffin, L. E., & Guthrie, K. L. (2023). *Introduction to research in leadership*. Information Age Publishing.

Satterwhite, R., Sheridan, K., & McIntyre Miller, W. (Eds.). (2023). Teaching sustainability through leadership education. *New Directions for Student Leadership, 2023*(179). Wiley.

Shankman, M. L., & Gigliotti, R. A. (Eds.). (2021). Using inventories and assessments to enhance leadership development. *New Directions for Student Leadership, 2021*(170). Wiley.

Teig, T., Devies, B., & Shetty, R. (2023). *Rooted and radiant: Women's narratives of leadership*. Information Age Publishing.

Whitney, R., & Collins, J. D. (Eds.). (2021). Advancing racial equity in leadership education: Centering marginalized institutional contexts. *New Directions for Student Leadership, 2021*(171). Wiley.

CHAPTER 2

FOSTERING AN ETHOS OF JUSTICE

Socially Just Leadership Education

Adrian L. Bitton

Is higher education a marketplace good to be consumed or is it meant to be the free pursuit and exchange of ideas for the public good? As leadership educators, we are drawn to the aspirational nature and promising ideals of the latter; however, the realities of shrinking budgets, decreasing enrollments, and competing priorities often force our focus to the former as we navigate the burdens of doing our work authentically and meaningfully and under increased challenges. How does the shifting landscape of higher education affect student leadership learning at colleges and universities? To answer this question, and more, this chapter begins by acknowledging neoliberalism and examining how it has influenced both higher education and leadership education. Next, I discuss the current movement toward socially just leadership education and identifies current challenges. The chapter concludes by offering ideas for potential pathways forward toward enacting socially just leadership education within neoliberal higher education contexts.

THE EMBRACE OF NEOLIBERALISM

Neoliberalism is an ideology that promotes efficiency and productivity through competition; individualism; and free, unregulated markets

Committing to Action: Socially Just Leadership Educations, pp. 9–20

(Durako Fisher & Gilbert, 2023; Giroux, 2002; Slaughter & Rhodes, 2004). As an economic policy, neoliberalism gained popularity in the 1970s when the United States experienced economic stagnation and inflation. In the 1980s, then-President Reagan embraced neoliberal "logic" through policies of privatization, tax cuts, deregulation, and reducing funding of social welfare programs, including education. Giroux (2002) warned against neoliberalism and cautioned about the negative effects on our society when "politics are market driven and the claims of democratic citizenship are subordinated to market values" (p. 428). Despite these warnings, neoliberalism has steadily grown within our capitalist society, which also highly values efficiency and productivity. This alignment perpetuates the positioning of neoliberal tenets as "common sense" which means they are often less scrutinized. As a result, neoliberalism has flourished while simultaneously eroding public institutions, including higher education.

Neoliberalism in Higher Education Broadly and Leadership Education Specifically

Durako Fisher and Gilbert (2023) described four key characteristics of neoliberalism which have become embedded within higher education institutions: knowledge commodification and expectations of productivity, decision-making driven by efficiency and prioritizing economic outcomes, demands of political neutrality, and the treatment of students as rational consumers. There are countless examples of how these tenets shape colleges and universities today. As leadership educators, it is tempting to believe leadership education is insulated from the perils of neoliberalism. However, this is only a false sense of security. The next paragraphs will trace how neoliberalism has expanded its reach into leadership education.

Commodification and Productivity. As an emerging discipline, leadership education is particularly susceptible to knowledge commodification and expectations of productivity. Slaughter and Rhodes (2004), by coining the term *academic capitalism,* described how shifting from an industrial economy to a knowledge economy created new pathways to monetize knowledge production. Leadership scholars and educators are developing the leadership canon, legitimizing the field, and simultaneously generating revenue through initiatives such as authoring (text)books, leading research centers, and using their expertise for public speaking engagements and private consulting opportunities.

Furthermore, the interest in and commodification of leadership extends well beyond the higher education context. In 2010, the U.S. reportedly spent $12 billion in leadership programs (Ashford & DeRue, 2012). Less than a decade later, in 2019, leadership development and training was reportedly a $366 billion global industry with an estimated $166 billion spent within the United States (Westfall, 2019).

Efficiency and Outcomes. While the first neoliberal tenet focuses on productivity through increased revenue streams, the second tenet—decision-making driven by efficiency and prioritizing economic outcomes (Durako Fisher & Gilbert, 2023), aims to maximize limited resources. Educational reforms have led to steady declines in government funding such that federal and state funding now makes up a smaller percentage of a university's overall operating budget. Despite the market demand for leadership education and/or appeal of leadership development, leadership educators are increasingly asked to do more and/or maintain high levels of productivity with fewer financial resources. Even when relatively well-resourced, leadership faculty are limited and often occupy dual appointments. Similarly, student affairs leadership units are typically small in personnel size and have modest budgets in comparison to other departments.

To administrators who navigate resource scarcity and budgetary constraints inherent in the neoliberal university, leadership education can be perceived as expendable. It can be difficult to justify dedicating huge resources and funding to leadership departments when there are multiple and often competing priorities, such as the growing number of college students accessing food pantries on campus (Freudenberg et al., 2019) or the pressure to address campus sexual assaults (Harris et al., 2020). As a result, leadership educators are often asked to institute a variety of cost-saving measures such as increasing class sizes, merging curricular and co-curricular leadership areas with other academic or student affairs units respectively, and/or navigating hiring freezes or eliminated positions. The prioritization of economic outcomes often comes at the expense of leadership educators' morale and the student experience.

Some curricular and co-curricular leadership departments have sought alumni donations to financially support leadership programs and initiatives. Unlike funding the day-to-day costs associated with facilities management and university operations, university advancement divisions and alumni/donor relations departments can romanticize leadership and its heroic conceptualizations to solicit donations to fund specific initiatives such as endowed chairs in an academic department, a co-curricular leadership program, or a donor-named leadership scholarship for college students.

Political neutrality. On the surface, leadership education seems non-controversial and can appear to be politically neutral as neoliberalism demands. However, the movement toward socially just leadership education is a political stance that can have financial consequences for restricted donation practices widely used in higher education institutions. This brings us to the third tenet of neoliberalism, *demands of political neutrality*, which perpetuates the myth of knowledge as objective and/or neutral and education can (or should) be depoliticized (Durako Fisher & Gilbert, 2023).

Every day there are new legislative efforts aimed to depoliticize education by, ironically, controlling both the pedagogy and content taught within K–16 public education. Restrictions on how and when certain subjects are taught (e.g., identity development) or the outright banning of certain topics (e.g., critical race theory) within school and class curricula are in direct conflict with the direction of leadership education toward socially just leadership. This topic will be discussed in greater detail later below.

Rational consumerism. The fourth neoliberal influence on higher education is the treatment of students as rational consumers (Durako Fisher & Gilbert, 2023). The commodification of higher education has led to colleges and universities to compete for applications and enrollments. Colleges and universities have shifted to increasingly rely on a variety of return-on-investment strategies, such as job placement rates and earning potential in payroll dollars, to justify the value of their academic credentialing and tuition cost. Many universities use leadership education and personal leadership development as a way to appeal to students during the admission process and throughout their actual college experience.

For example, during campus visits and informational interviews, admission counselors often discuss the leadership development opportunities available through participation in university clubs and organizations or tell students about academic leadership programs related to their intended major(s) or future career aspirations. Similarly, academic advisors, faculty, and other higher education professionals often present academic leadership studies options (e.g., leadership majors, minors, and certificate programs) to students using neoliberal appeals (e.g., students who hold additional leadership credentialing have advantages in competitive job markets and/or are more appealing applicants for highly ranked graduate programs).

These four tenets are inextricably linked to one another and magnify the impact of neoliberalism on both higher education institutions and leadership education. The following section adds additional layers of complexity to the content of leadership education based upon the oppressive societal ideologies of imperialism, White supremacy, capitalism, and patriarchy.

A Legacy of Multiple Interlocking Systems of Oppression

Contrary to the narrative of neutrality and the neoliberal aim to depoliticize leadership, leadership, as both a construct and a practice, are political. The lack of definitional clarity around leadership "allows those with power to decide which interpretations of leadership matter most" (Liu, 2021, pp. 8–9). As a result, dominant assumptions and associations of leadership have developed over time based upon the larger historical and societal context of imperialist, White supremacist, capitalist, and patriarchal ideologies within the U.S. (Liu, 2021). These oppressive ideologies complement the tenets of neoliberalism highlighted above and have influenced the content of leadership education by serving as the basis of foundational and early theories within the leadership studies canon (e.g., The Great Man theory, mid-1800s to early 1900s; Dugan, 2017; Northouse, 2010).

For example, Anglo-American values such as utilitarianism, pragmatism, and individualism infused leadership theories and practices, which were then asserted as part of a universal worldview (Liu, 2021). There are parallels between this example and neoliberalism. The Anglo-American values of utilitarianism, pragmatism, and individualism are similar to the neoliberal values of productivity, efficiency, and competition. Furthermore, their assertion as part of the universal worldview employs a similar strategy as neoliberalism's positioning as "common sense" logic. The ideologies of imperialism, White supremacy, capitalism, and patriarchy are strengthened and reinforced through their relationship to neoliberalism as demonstrated in Figure 2.1.

Figure 2.1

Ideological Reinforcement for Neoliberalism

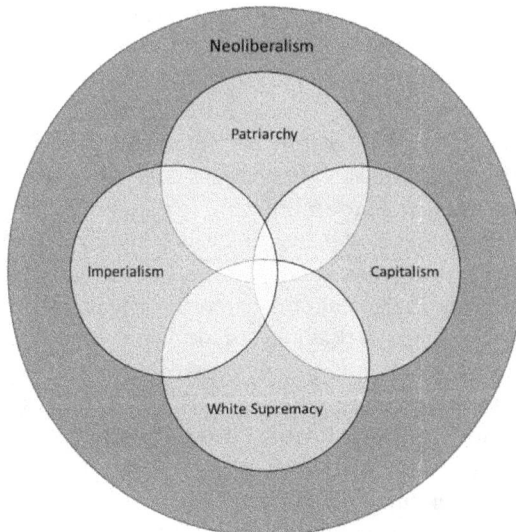

The ties between neoliberalism and (academic) capitalism combined with the fact that many colleges and universities have mission statements that express a goal of producing globally- and civically-engaged leaders (Devies & Guthrie, 2022; Guthrie & Chunoo, 2018) has resulted in a proliferation of both co-curricular and leadership development programs and academic leadership studies programs. As such, leadership can and has been embedded within almost every aspect of the college experience. Academic programs seek to develop leaders in their field (Komives & Guthrie, 2015). Recent analysis by Guthrie et al. (2019) reported over 1,500 academic leadership programs within the United States. Student Affairs professionals advise and support student leaders through their participation in collegiate organizations and university programs (e.g., orientation leaders, residence assistants). Employers seek to hire college graduates with leadership skills (Seemiller, 2014).

Like the current perspective of conceptualizing student development theory as a series of waves that have built upon itself over time (Abes et al., 2019), leadership approaches have evolved in much the same way. Early approaches of leadership (first wave) were leader-centric, focused on an individual leader's traits, qualities, and behaviors (Northouse, 2010). In response to the social, political, and religious movements of the 1970s, second wave approaches of leadership theories were more values-driven, relational, democratic, and participatory in nature and took into account the ways in which leadership is socially constructed (Burns, 1978; Dugan, 2017; Northouse, 2010). Now leadership educators, scholars, and researchers are incorporating critical perspectives into the teaching, learning, and research of leadership in order to illuminate how leadership has and can be oppressive as well as leadership's potential as liberatory in the pursuit of social justice. This is another large paradigmatic shift, or third wave, within leadership education (Dugan & Humbles, 2018; Osteen et al., 2016).

Although the above progression is chronological, it does not necessarily reflect how leadership within higher education is currently being taught, learned, or practiced. There are many co-curricular leadership programs and academic leadership courses that still utilize first-wave, leader-centric approaches and focus on identifying and developing specific traits, behaviors, or skills that have been coded as leadership (Guthrie et al., 2013). Over time, the social construction of leadership through reinforcement of certain traits, behaviors, or skills has resulted in a "mythical leader" archetype. There is a danger of creating a dominant narrative, or a "story most often told" (Dugan, 2017, p. 59) about leaders and leadership for not only are these traits, behaviors, and skills mapped onto leadership, but they are also associated with, or mapped onto, certain social identities.

For too long leadership educators have not acknowledged how social identities are mapped onto leader and leadership. Whether explicitly stated or not, the dominant narrative of leaders as *cisgender, heterosexual, White, male, Christian, and upper-class,* has real consequences for who identifies (or is identified) as a leader, who has access to leadership opportunities, and who engages in leadership development programs. Previous studies have shown students with minoritized identities are more likely to embrace the term (and identity) of activist rather than the term (and/or identity) of leader (Linder et al., 2020). The rejection of the term *leader* could be linked to traditional conceptualizations of leader as those who hold power and authority, and oftentimes, associated with corruption, dominance, and oppression (Guthrie et al., 2013). Moreover, *leader* is not only an identity or label that can be claimed, it can also be granted onto other people (DeRue & Ashford, 2009). Administrators and educators often associate student activists in a negative light, labeling them troublemakers (Linder et al., 2020). Their behaviors are often viewed as a disruption when other students who exhibit the exact same behavior are coded as leaders(hip).

For example, behaviors of White student leaders might be described as passionate, assertive, and visionary, whereas students of color exhibiting identical behaviors are more likely to be described as angry, aggressive, and unrealistic (K. Obear, personal communication, March 4, 2022). This same double standard gets replicated across other social identities as well (e.g., the double bind refers to this same phenomenon in the context of gender and leadership). Incorporating this lens allows for more nuanced considerations about social identity group differences in students' engagement in leadership programs and classes.

THE TIME FOR SOCIALLY JUST LEADERSHIP EDUCATION IS NOW

The issues mentioned above, combined with the "seemingly unending disruptions of a global health pandemic, racism and civil unrest, economic and social injustice, political polarization, flailing educational systems, natural disasters, and more" (Chung et al., 2021, p. 5) result in a call for socially just leadership education which has never been clearer. Leadership educators increasingly recognize the imperative to reconcile the gap between what we *say* we value in leadership and what our practices *demonstrate* we value in leadership. That includes analyzing and critiquing how previous attempts of inclusivity and best practices have been counterproductive to the goal of socially just leadership education. For example, Wiborg's (2020) dissertation on whiteness in leadership education, details how the framing of "anyone can be a leader" actually advances hazardous colorblind notions of leadership, without taking into consideration how one's social identities can influence their access to and experience with leadership development opportunities.

Leadership educators and scholars are advancing this third wave toward socially just leadership education by coalescing around shared research agendas (e.g., Inter-association Leadership Education Collaborative [ILEC] 2016 Collaborative Priorities and Critical Considerations for Leadership Education; National Leadership Education Research Agenda 2020–2025 by Andenoro and Skendall; ACPA & NASPA's (2015) leadership competencies; Komives and Owen's (2023) *A Research Agenda for Leadership Learning and Development through Higher Education*). They are also developing new resources with the publication of socially just leadership education articles (e.g., multiple special issues of *New Directions for Student Leadership)* and books (e.g., Dugan's *Leadership Theory: Cultivating Critical Perspectives* [2017], Guthrie & Chunoo's *Changing the Narrative* [2018] and *Shifting the Mindset* [2021]).

A review of these publications provides two key insights regarding the shift to socially just leadership. First, current research regarding socially just leadership is largely conceptual in nature and describes aspects of how power, privilege, and oppression are embedded within leadership education (Bertrand Jones et al., 2016; Dugan, 2017; Wiborg, 2020). These elements are important and illuminate how leadership has and can be oppressive. However, socially just leadership education is not just an ideological perspective; rather it necessitates advancing leadership as liberation toward justice.

Second, it is important to acknowledge that most socially just leadership learning literature is written from the educator's point of view (Andenoro & Skendall, 2020; Guthrie & Chunoo, 2018, 2021; Guthrie & Jenkins, 2018). As a result, the body of socially just leadership literature emphasizes pedagogy and/or leadership learning. However, in order to truly infuse equity and justice within leadership education, we need to know more about what students believe about leadership and themselves and how students understand the relationship between social justice and leadership.

POTENTIAL PATHWAYS FORWARD

The Interconnectedness of Leadership and Social Justice

One of the most promising pathways involves disrupting the false dichotomy between social justice (and/or activism) and leadership. Today, college students arrive on campus with more advanced conceptualizations of social justice than students in previous decades (Seemiller & Grace, 2017). Culturally, this generation grew up during a time when same sex marriage was legal, a Black man was the President of the United States, and the Black Lives Matter (#BLM) and #MeToo movements were highly visible. These cultural markers contribute to Generation Z deeply held convictions and morality regarding power, privilege, and oppression, their courage in tackling these deeply complex and entrenched social issues, and their openness to imagining new possibilities and ways of being.

Although students are coming to college with more exposure, knowledge, and beliefs about social justice issues, many do not associate leadership and social justice with one another. The harmful ideologies embedded in foundational leadership theories and the enduring, dominant narrative of leadership as authoritative power to command and control are in direct conflict with their moral and ethical ideals and aspirations for justice and equity. In particular, Generation Z's disillusionment with political leadership is understandable given the ways leadership can, and is often, used as an exclusionary way to consolidate power, perpetuate systemic violence, and harm members of marginalized communities. Every day, new legislation is proposed, passed, and enacted that has significant and negative consequences for those most oppressed within our society (e.g., laws that ban trans-affirming healthcare and limit bodily autonomy, bans on books and topics within education, policies that reinforce environmental racism and draconian immigration practices).

The unique challenge of fusing leadership and social justice together also requires leadership educators to critically examine how their own mindset and socialization regarding leadership aligns or conflicts with the activist tactics and change strategies that have been successful in social (justice) movements. Doing so, opens a whole new set of possibilities for both leadership, social justice, and socially just leadership education.

Holistic Student Leadership Development

Another pathway requires a shift in the approach to developing socially just leaders. As leadership education has evolved within higher education, much of the focus has been leadership development, particularly, developing one's identity as a leader. The leadership identity development (LID) model has been a driving force over the last 20 years (for more information, see Owen, 2023) that has shaped a considerable volume of leadership development programming. However, critiques of the model and extant research on its relevance for certain student populations have identified limitations. Leadership (identity) development cannot exist as an independent endeavor, especially considering the issues of (in)justice that affect who is identified as a leader and/or self-identifies with leader as an identity. Rather, leadership development is a reflection of an intersectional process that occurs between cognitive, moral, and identity development.

Anchoring socially just leadership education within these mutually reinforcing aspects of human development creates a more holistic approach that addresses the interest and needs of Generation Z college students and provides more opportunities for growth and developing a socially just orientation toward leadership.

CONCLUSION

Neoliberalism is the prevailing ideology that shapes our higher education institutions. As leadership educators, it is important to acknowledge how the neoliberal tenets (knowledge commodification and expectations of productivity, decision-making driven by efficacy and prioritizing economic outcomes, demands of political neutrality, and students as rational consumers) can also be applied to leadership education. The context of the neoliberal university combined with the evolution of leadership and leadership education makes the call for socially just leadership education even more imperative.

Postcolonial perspectives stress the importance of reclaiming language and decolonizing the mind (Liu, 2021). It requires a radical shift in our thinking and sociological imagination in order to envision and enact new possibilities for a more just and equitable world. When leadership and social justice are positioned as inextricably linked and mutually reinforcing as two components of a braided rope—neither functions optimally without the other. If the purpose of leadership, and the goal of social justice, is to create a more just and equitable world, then they can only be realized through integrated socially just leadership. Only through redeeming and reimagining leadership will we have any hope of achieving this goal. This is the world I want to live in, this is the society I hope future generations inherit and cultivate, and socially just leadership education is the work I'm committed to learning and pursuing in community.

REFERENCES

Abes, E. S., Jones, S. R., & Stewart, D.-L. (2019). *Rethinking college student development theory using critical frameworks*. Stylus.

ACPA & NASPA. (2015). Professional competency areas for student affairs practitioners. https://www.naspa.org/images/uploads/main/ACPA_NASPA_Professional_Competencies_FINAL.pdf

Andenoro, A. C., & Skendall, K. C. (2020). National leadership education research agenda 2020-2025: Advancing the state of leadership education scholarship. *Journal of Leadership Studies, 14*(3), 33–38. http://dx.doi.org/10.1002/jls.21714

Ashford, S. J., & DeRue, D. S. (2012). Developing as a leader: The power of mindful engagement. *Organizational Dynamics, 41*(2), 146–154. http://dx.doi.org/10.1016/j.orgdyn.2012.01.008

Bertrand Jones, T., Guthrie, K. L., & Osteen, L. (2016). Critical domains of culturally relevant leadership learning: A call to transform leadership programs. In K. L. Guthrie, T. Bertrand Jones, & L. Osteen (Eds.), *Developing culturally relevant leadership learning.* (New Directions for Student Leadership, No. 152, pp. 9–21). Jossey-Bass. https://doi.org/10.1002/yd.20205

Burns, J. M. (1978). *Leadership.* Harper & Row.

Chung, J., Gleason, M., Guthrie, K. L., Navarro, C. D., Priest, K. L., Pierre, D. E., Cummings Steele, M., & Weng. J. (2021). Leadership education through complex transitions. *New Directions for Student Leadership, 2021*(172), 5–10. http://doi.org/10.1002/yd.20463

DeRue, D. S., & Ashford, S. J. (2009). *On becoming a leader: A process of claiming and granting identity* (Submission 13851 accepted for the 2009 Academy of Management Annual Meeting).

Devies, B., & Guthrie, K. L. (2022). What mission statements say: Signaling the priority of leadership development. *Journal of Higher Education Policy and Leadership Studies 3*(1), 91–107. http://dx.doi.org/10.52547/johepal.3.1.91

Dugan, J. P. (2017). *Leadership theory: Cultivating critical perspectives.* Jossey-Bass.

Dugan, J. P., & Humbles, A. D. (2018). A paradigm shift in leadership education: Integrating critical perspectives into leadership development. *New Directions for Student Leadership, 2018*(159), 9–26. http://doi.org/10.1002/yd.20294

Durako Fisher, L. E., & Gilbert, C. (2023). Centering the humanity of student activists: Pedagogy as resistance to neoliberalism in US higher education. In *Emancipatory Human Rights and the University* (pp. 89–104). Routledge.

Freudenberg, N., Goldrick-Rab, S., & Poppendieck, J. (2019). College students and SNAP: The new face of food insecurity in the United States. *American Journal of Public Health, 109*(12), 1652–1658. https://doi.org/10.2105/AJPH.2019.305332.

Giroux, H. A. (2002). Neoliberalism, corporate culture, and the promise of higher education: The university as a democratic public sphere. *Harvard Educational Review, 72*(4), 425–463. http://dx.doi.org/10.17763/haer.72.4.0515nr62324n71p1.

Guthrie, K. L., & Chunoo, V. S. (Eds.). (2018). *Changing the narrative: Socially just leadership education.* Information Age Publishing.

Guthrie, K. L., & Chunoo, V. S. (Eds.). (2021). *Shifting the mindset: Socially just leadership education.* Information Age Publishing.

Guthrie, K. L., & Jenkins, D. M. (2018). *The role of leadership educators: Transforming learning.* Information Age Publishing.

Guthrie, K. L., Bertrand Jones, T., Osteen, L., & Hu, S. (2013). *Special issue: Cultivating leader identity and capacity in students from diverse backgrounds. ASHE Higher Education Report. 39*(4). Jossey-Bass.

Guthrie, K. L., Batchelder, J. M., & Hu, P. (2019). *Examining degree types of academic leadership programs in the United States.* Leadership Learning Research Center, Florida State University.

Harris, J. C., Cobian, K. P., & Karunaratne, N. (2020). Reimagining the study of campus sexual assault. In L. Perna (Ed.), *Higher education: Handbook of theory and research, 35*, 229–275. Springer. https://doi.org/10.1007/978-3-030-11743-6_12-1

Inter-association Leadership Education Collaborative [ILEC]. (2016). *Collaborative priorities and critical considerations for leadership education.* https://www.leadershipeducators.org/resources/Documents/ILEC%20Final%20Report%20.pdf

Komives, S. R., & Guthrie, K. L. (2015). Series editors' notes. In J. E. Owen (Ed.), Transforming leadership development for significant learning. *New Directions for Student Leadership, 2015*(1), 7–18. http://dx.doi.org/10.1002/yd.20120

Komives, S. R., & Owen, J. E. (2023). *A research agenda for leadership learning and development through higher education.* Edward Elgar.

Linder, C., Quaye, S. J., Lange, A. C., Evans, M. E., & Stewart, T. J. (2020). *Identity-based student activism: Power and oppression on college campuses.* Routledge.

Liu, H. (2021). *Redeeming leadership: An anti-racist feminist intervention.* Bristol University.

Northouse, P. G. (2010). *Leadership: theory and practice* (5th ed.). SAGE.

Osteen, L., Guthrie, K. L., & Bertrand Jones, T. (2016). Leading to transgress: Critical considerations for transforming leadership learning. *New Directions for Student Leadership, 2016*(152), 95–106. http://dx.doi.org/10.1002/yd.20212.

Seemiller, C. (2014). *The student leadership competencies guidebook: Designing intentional leadership learning and development.* Jossey-Bass.

Seemiller, C., & Grace, M. (2017) *Generation Z leads: A guide for developing the leadership capacity of Generation Z students.* Self-published, CreateSpace.

Slaughter, S., & Rhoades, G. (2004). *Academic capitalism and the new economy: Markets, state, and higher education.* The Johns Hopkins University Press.

Westfall, C. (2019, June 20). Leadership development is a $366 billion industry: Here's why most programs don't work. *Forbes.* https://www.forbes.com/sites/chriswestfall/2019/06/20/leadership-development-why-most-programs-dont-work/?sh=640bac8161de.

Wiborg, E. R. (2020). *A critical discourse analysis of leadership learning* (Publication No. 28022412) [Doctoral dissertation, Florida State University]. ProQuest Dissertations and Theses Global.

CHAPTER 3

DISCOVERING CATALYST POINTS

Reframing Social Justice Leadership for (White) Students

Joshua Taylor

B. Brown (2018) argued leaders often "armor up" instead of being vulnerable (p. 134). This form of armored leadership results in avoiding topics like diversity and equity. Avoidance of these topics is counterproductive because it maintains the status quo, which is damaging to members of historically oppressed groups in society. I have worked with numerous White students who have told me that they will not talk about race because they are afraid of "saying the wrong thing." This is an armored response; a reply caused at least in part by an educational environment that promotes being right over learning to get it right. In the learning process, failure is an important and often necessary step. Educators cannot expect students to know the 'right' words or have all their thoughts worked out immediately. Students may need space and time to deconstruct a previously held worldview that devalues or dehumanizes specific groups. Socially just and antiracist leadership development is messy because we all inevitably get it wrong countless times before we approach getting it right. Therefore, one central question for socially just leadership educators committed to action is, "How do we create brave spaces for vulnerability in leadership education so students can remove the armor and engage?" While there are many pressing needs for leadership educators to address and nuanced

Committing to Action: Socially Just Leadership Educations, pp. 21–33
Copyright © 2025 by Information Age Publishing
www.infoagepub.com

contexts where leadership educators must engage, this chapter will specifically examine how leadership educators working with White students, a population who demonstrates resistance and often seeks to avoid conversations about diversity and equity, can discover and leverage catalyst points toward change.

CATALYST POINTS

Socially just leadership educators artfully create entry points for students to engage in socially just and antiracist leadership. Some entry points trigger students' resistance; they cue students to armor up, resulting in students entrenching themselves in ideologies that perpetuate injustices enacted toward historically marginalized groups (Taylor & Manning-Ouellette, 2022). However, other entry points serve as catalysts for change. When educators masterfully guide students toward socially just or antiracist leadership engagement and the students lean into the discomfort, the educators have created a "catalyst point." Catalyst points are experiences that navigate past resistance and accelerate critical analysis, which leads to change.

Harro (2000) proposed a similar idea in work on cycles of socialization and liberation. Harro (2000) stated, "As people come to a critical level of understanding of the nature of oppression and their roles in this systemic phenomenon, they seek new paths for creating social change and taking themselves toward empowerment or liberation" (p. 618). Harro (2000) suggested the "waking up" phase could begin with either a critical incident or a slow process of gradual evolution (p. 619). Either way, it is the process of coming to a "critical level of understanding" that initiates all the growth and change that follows. To augment Harro's framework of the "waking up" phase, catalyst points are specific moments, experiences, conversations, or realizations that serve as entry points to the "waking up phase" that skillfully avoid triggers to resistance and ignite awareness, understanding, and action.

POSITIONALITY

My experiences as a leadership educator are shaped by my social identities as well as the context in which I lead. I hold several historically advantaged social identities. I am a middle-aged, heterosexual, White, cis male. As I interact with socially just leadership issues on a daily basis, I have opportunities to keep conversations and actions at the forefront of system-wide priorities. My identities allow me to see some aspects of socially just leadership development extremely clearly, while there are other aspects that I often do not see initially. In my position, I work to listen broadly and hear voices different from my own, but I am limited by my own experiences and network.

This chapter focuses specifically on White student leaders because of the unique challenges of engaging White students in socially just and antiracist leadership work. Without a doubt, I see this opportunity for leadership growth because of my own positionality. Furthermore, at my core, I am an educator, so I see the world through the eyes of students. It is a great honor when students share pieces of their stories with me, and through those stories I have heard the heartbreak of when leadership—whether parents, peers, teachers, or institutions—have not led equitably. I have also seen the life that is breathed into people whenever leadership is just. Thus, while socially just leadership work is always a process of learning, that learning can never paralyze leadership educators. I believe we must act and continue to call others to action. I am grateful for the voices in my life that continue to challenge me and call me to analyze and act so that I am modeling a way to lead justly. As Harro (2000) stated, "Liberation is the practice of love" (p. 624). May we all lead and love well.

REFRAMING THE INVISIBILITY OF WHITENESS

One challenge White student leaders face when asked to commit to antiracist leadership action is that Whiteness itself is often a taboo topic. In an interview with a White student leader, he divulged that his fraternity banned any mention of race in their chapter GroupMe because of the possibility of conflict (Taylor, 2023). Another student leader stated they consciously avoid discussions about race or gender identity out of fear of offending someone (Taylor, 2023). Thus, a major barrier for White student leaders developing the leadership skills necessary to lead in socially just ways is a lack of understanding due to censored discourse. However, leadership educators, instead of seeing this as an insurmountable obstacle, can reframe this challenge as a possible catalyst point when they are aware of it. These same student leaders expressed a desire to discuss race in contexts where they can process experiences and beliefs (Taylor, 2023). These vulnerable dialogues create space for students to deconstruct beliefs, race-based assumptions, and worldviews that often curtail socially just leadership action. Thus, White student leaders are identifying a vacuum that needs to be filled with candid and intentional dialogue that leads to action.

The First Rule of Fight Club Is: You Do Not Talk About Fight Club

In 1999, the movie *Fight Club* captured audiences with the compelling story of an unfulfilled soap salesman, numb to the world around him, who starts a fight club as a way of escaping the monotonies of life. As new characters join the fight club, Tyler, one of the main characters, gives the rules to the group: "The first rule of fight club is: you don't talk about fight club" (Fincher, 1999). White students tend to operate from a similar unspoken rule; they do not talk about being White. In one recent study, 16 of the 18 White student leader participants (88.89%) stated they did not think about their identity as a White person while leading (Taylor, 2023). Racially White student leaders often do not see race as significant because it has never been salient for them.

Studies consistently demonstrate how White people struggle to recognize or articulate the significance of their Whiteness (Foste, 2019; McDermott, 2020). In pioneering work about adolescent ethnic identity development, Phinney (1989) was forced to exclude the data collected from White student participants because "ethnicity was not an identity issue to which [the white participants] could relate" (p. 41). Phinney (1989) observed, "They did not think of themselves as having an ethnicity other than simply 'American'" (p. 41). Phinney's (1989) conclusion that participants often interpreted the term 'ethnicity' as only referring to minority groups is consistent with McKinney's (2013) findings. When McKinney asked students to write a racial autobiography that delved into their experiences as White people, one student concluded, "I could tell my life story without mentioning my race" (McKinney, 2013, p. 1). From this data, McKinney (2013) posited "most whites do not think about being white unless they are asked to do so" (p. 2). Therefore, when socially just leadership educators do ask students to think about race, McKinney's (2013) research suggests that most White student leaders have not started processing how their race affects their leadership work.

The Invisible Power of Whiteness

Another way of conceptualizing the influence of Whiteness and its power is to think of Whiteness like gravity; it is an invisible force always acting on everyone and everything, regardless of whether a person acknowledges the force. Consequently, Whiteness, due to its invisibility, is often assumed. Flagg (1997) highlighted the practice that identification of race is usually reserved for historically minoritized peoples, not for White people. McDermott (2020) writes, "When Americans think about race, 'white' is often the furthest thing from their minds. To have a race is to be Black, Asian, Latina\o or American Indian" (p. 1). Using the previous analogy, a person does not often mention that gravity was keeping them on the ground while walking; it is assumed or normative. However, one would mention a feeling of weightlessness in an anti-gravity simulator because of the juxtaposition from the norm. Similarly, among White people with whom race is often invisible, unmentioned, and assumed, race is usually only mentioned when referring to a person from a racially minoritized community.

Moreover, the presence of White fragility further complicates the lack of racial awareness among White people. DiAngelo (2018) described White fragility as an "insulated environment of racial privilege ... [where] ... whites both expect racial comfort and become less tolerant of racial stress" (p. 100). Whiteness' invisibility upholds the insulation DiAngelo (2018) described due to a lack of critical analysis and discourse about Whiteness. Beatty et al. (2021) highlighted that when race is overtly stated and the insulation of Whiteness is broken, especially when race is examined with a critical lens, White people can experience racial stress that can trigger anger, fear, guilt, defensiveness, and resistance.

LISTENING FOR CATALYST POINTS: "I DIDN'T SEE ANYTHING THAT HAD TO DO WITH RACE"

In one research inquiry, I asked White student leaders to bring pictures of what leadership looks like to them in college for a focus group discussion (Taylor, 2023). Gwen shared a picture of a pallet of food at a food bank. There were no people in the picture. Gwen believed service was essential for leadership. I asked how race played a part of the interaction, and she stared at me confused before saying, "I don't think I really saw anything out of the ordinary.... Like, no racism. I didn't see anything that had to do with race." After more conversation about the experience and service, Gwen mentioned the volunteers were White, and the staff of the foodbank was mostly White. Then, she paused and said that the people receiving the food were mostly Black. I then asked, "So, how did race play of part of this leadership experience?" Flustered, she said, "Well, I never thought about it until just now" (Taylor, 2023).

"I Never Thought About [Race] Until Just Now"

While Gwen's story could be another example of how White student leaders often do not see race as salient, I saw something slightly different in this story. Gwen's revelation that she never thought about race as a salient element of her leadership work was an invitation; this was a catalyst point. Gwen cared deeply for the service in which she was engaged. She wanted to lead in a way that made a difference and helped others. Because of her desire, her racial unawareness and colorblind approach were an entry point for learning and growth. Whatever resistance may have been present was successfully navigated in the context of the focus group with her own exploration and critical analysis.

Furthermore, Gwen's story was not unique in the study. From the 18 White student leader participants, 14 ascribed to some variation of a colorblind approach to race (Taylor, 2023). Whether leadership educators and scholars like it or not, the colorblind approach is a dominant theory in use concerning how to overcome racism. When another participant was asked how race plays a part of his leadership decisions, Johnny stated, "I never think about it. I don't see color" (Taylor, 2023). Johnny revealed that, to him, not seeing color was the way to avoid being racist. He explained, "That's the goal, isn't it? For race to not matter. For race to not limit a person because of someone else's hate?"

Reframing Colorblind Approaches as Catalyst Points

One way of critically understanding the colorblind approach is to regard it as another way of ensuring the invisibility of Whiteness. Since Whiteness is not talked about, White student leaders struggle to see how race is a salient part of their leadership work (Mahoney, 2016). McDermott (2020) succinctly encapsulates the deficiencies of the colorblind approach, writing, "'Not seeing color' can mean not seeing inequality" (p. 18).

While criticisms of the colorblind approach are valid, it is also important to recognize the pervasiveness of this ideology. Consequently, socially just leadership educators can shift our mindsets to leverage the colorblind approach as an opportunity to create a catalyst point. In interviews with White student leaders, those who expressed a colorblind approach also frequently self-identified as allies or stated that diversity, equity, and inclusion (DEI) work was important to them (Taylor, 2023). Thus, there is a common ground that can serve as the catalyst point leading to more developed critical thinking. When students want to disrupt racism as a leader, and they want to be allies for racial justice, that agreement is the start of the catalyst point. Now the conversation can shift to ways in which minimizing race ignores the reality of racial injustice, and by ignoring the injustice, leaders perpetuate the beliefs and systems that inflict the injustices.

THE DISCONNECT BETWEEN PEOPLE AND SYSTEMS

It is difficult for students and other leaders to differentiate between people and systems. Student leaders tend to respond in empathetic and tremendously helpful ways whenever a social injustice occurs at an individual level—a hungry student sitting next to them in class, a trans student who needs a safe living environment who is a part of their sorority, a Black classmate who shared her story of experiencing racial discrimination or racial violence, a gay friend whose parents just disowned him for coming out. However, social injustices are often perpetuated through invisible systems which are difficult to identify and demonstrate causality. While student leaders may lead in empathetic, socially just, and antiracist ways in one-on-one interactions, many of these same students profess antithetical positions when faced with systemic issues. Thus, when looking at the systems that cause injustices, student leaders tend to armor up (Brown, 2018) and become defensive and resistant instead of engaging in meaningful dialogue and just leadership actions.

Admittedly, it is difficult for the general public, and even for some advanced scholars, to identify how invisible forces operate in systems of power. Thus, the difficulty in analysis leads many to deny the reality or effects of structural racism. Consequently, many scholars have engaged in critical theory work to detail exhaustively the effects of structural or systemic oppression as a way of unmasking the hidden structural powers (see, Alexander, 2010; Haney-López, 2006; Kendi, 2006; McDermott, 2020; McGhee, 2021; Wilkerson, 2020). Unfortunately, many of the systems at the core of these critical analyses have become politicized in ways that spark strong resistance from many, especially those who benefit from them. Thus, the central challenge to analyzing systems is navigating student resistance to reach a catalyst point, leading to growth and development.

Clear (2018) argued people do not "rise to the level of [their] goals" but "fall to the level of [their] systems" (p. 28). This concept has proven a good catalyst point for basic systems analysis. The culturally relevant leadership learning model (CRLL; Bertrand Jones et al., 2016; Guthrie et al., 2017) is another resource for teaching student leaders the skill of systems analysis. By teaching students to see systems, leadership educators can overcome the grand challenge of student leaders rarely identifying systems in general, or seeing how social systems perpetuate injustice specifically.

Helping Student Leaders See Systems

A few years ago, I met with Darcy, a student in a leadership class I taught who was a part of the leadership team for the largest student-run campus event. Darcy stated her goal was for all students to be involved in the event, but I noticed significant frustration. She said many students were not involved at all, especially multicultural Greek students and students outside the Greek system. Darcy, because of the trust we had built, allowed me to ask some difficult questions, culminating in, "Who is on your leadership team?" Her response indicated every student was a White female from a historically White sorority. Darcy then quickly made the connection between why the goals of the leadership team were completely unattainable and the lack of compositional diversity in the leadership team.

Yet, the team was not entirely the fault of the students. There was a system in place for how the team was selected. That system did not foster representation from diverse members of the student body. Year after year, the same student organizations dominated by the same social identities were represented on the leadership team, and the same groups were excluded from representation on the team. Those defending the system would say students of color were not applying for the positions and every student had an equal chance and a fair opportunity. However, these arguments are just examples of how leaders fail to recognize the effects of systems. While the goal was participation by all, the system only allowed for participation from a select few.

Using Systems Analysis as Catalyst Points

When I had this conversation with Darcy, I was just learning about CRLL (Bertrand Jones et al., 2016; Guthrie et al., 2017). If this conversation happened today, I would have Darcy use the CRLL model to analyze the leadership system in which she was operating, and unbeknownst to her, also perpetuating. Darcy would have been able to identify historical legacies of inclusion/exclusion, and the compositional diversity of the leadership team, and then make connections to the psychological and behavioral functioning of her organization, as well as understand how all of these factors impacted in-group and out-group dynamics through the organizational dimension. Using the CRLL model for systems analysis gives leadership learners and educators a lens to see the mechanisms that are actively influencing their leadership work. For many students, this is a revelation.

Furthermore, this experience is a strong reminder to leadership educators; we create and uphold systems. Students are in a system for a few years, and they have the power to make some changes, but we must critically analyze the systems we create and uphold, striving for equitable systems that create opportunity, not hidden barriers.

OPPORTUNITIES TO CREATE CRITICAL EXPERIENCES

Socially just leadership educators create opportunities for action by helping students see and trust stories and experiences beyond "the stories most often told" (Dugan, 2017, p. 59). Foste (2019) demonstrated how White student leaders, wittingly or unwittingly, often seek to protect and reproduce the status quo. The systems already in place have benefitted those student leaders who currently enjoy leadership opportunities; thus, it can be challenging to commit to actions to critically analyze and disrupt those very systems. Subsequently, to move student leaders who benefit from the status quo to action, there must be an increase in empathy. Brown (2018) encouraged leaders to develop empathy through vulnerability in leadership while still maintaining healthy boundaries. Vulnerability breaks down barriers, but getting to that culture of vulnerability in which a student leader can shift their understanding is challenging.

Taylor and Manning-Ouellette (2022) argued for the importance of giving language to students leaning into discomfort and not retreating from difficult conversations. They suggested it is imperative to create brave spaces where student leaders can speak honestly to, and wrestle mightily with, their own cognitive dissonance, with the end goal of learning how to see things from another's perspective. This process of empathy building is organic, not programmatic. However, leadership educators can create a catalyst point for this organic growth by creating experiences in which students can place themselves in another's shoes.

Intentional Immersive Experiences as Catalyst Points

Every summer, I offer a short-term study abroad course for student leaders. On one of these experiences, the class went to a Nazi concentration camp. A professor from a local university talked to the students about the atrocities that happened during World War II and took students through the gas chambers and barracks of the camp.

In organized small group discussions following the concentration camp experience, one student, Barbara, mentioned that the concentration camp, which the professor specifically named as a work camp, resembled the American racial slavery system. Barbara mentioned how both were based on race or ethnicity, both were fueled by prejudice and hatred, and both led to economic advantages for the dominant group. Barbara's comparison led to some strong resistance and criticism from other students; however, when I encouraged the group to keep analyzing Barbara's argument, the entire group eventually agreed that the comparison was valid. Whatever seemingly insurmountable barriers may have been present previously crumbled as they remembered the gas chambers and the barracks. In one reflection, Jonathan, a member of Barbara's group wrote that he did not like the comparison because he always thought of America as a hero, but he clearly saw how America had dehumanized, exploited, and massacred Black people to enrich the dominant, or White, group.

Later discussions, fueled by this initial experience at a concentration camp, would start a process of reanalyzing modern experiences of Black Americans and reconsidering previously held assumptions. In assignments, students applied their growth to their own leadership decisions, finding examples of how they were not leading inclusively. This experience was a catalyst point for each student, and while students explored different aspects of critical analysis—some focusing on the treatment of the LGBTQ+ community in World War II and beyond, some focusing on race, some on economic equity—every student was able to connect their experience visiting the concentration camp to their leadership work through a socially just leadership lens.

Constructing Experiences as Catalyst Points

Whenever possible, socially just leadership educators should strive to give their students experiences that allow them to view the world from another's perspective. Tours of museums, guest speakers who lived through historic moments, study abroad experiences, or moments for students to share life stories are critical for growing empathy. A. C. Brown (2018) described a transformative college student leader experience that was a turning point for her in which Black and White students traveled together from Chicago to tour plantations and a lynching museum. The discussions that followed were full of emotion and frustration. However, at one point, a White female student addressed the group and said, "I don't know what to do with what I've learned … [but] doing nothing is no longer an option for me" (p. 58). This is the opportunity that awaits leadership educators who are able to construct experiences and use them as catalyst points; it is the opportunity for students to commit to action.

Student resistance is inevitable; it is a natural human response to change. However, resistance manifests differently when students are in the field and face-to-face with the problems. It is no longer a theoretical concern. Whenever leadership educators can humanize an issue, resistance wanes. Therefore, creating space for the meaningful sharing of stories through trusted relationships as a part of intentional experiences is a primary catalyst point.

CONCLUSION

The catalyst point is that point of entry from which a person begins the critical analysis necessary to reshape their worldview. Sometimes these catalyst points are epiphanic experiences, and other times they are the start of an avalanche, something that seems unremarkable in the moment— a new friendship, a peer sharing a lived experience in contrast to one's own experiences, or a moment of service handing food to a hungry fellow student—but the avalanche has begun, and the momentum is not easily stopped. The art of creating catalyst points is in navigating individual and group resistance. Catalyst points can only occur whenever resistance is skillfully managed. Therefore, socially just leadership educators artfully craft catalyst points for students as an act of initiating the liberatory leadership actions that follow.

Handled astutely, conversations about Whiteness can be a catalyst point for White students. It can start the process of seeing an issue in a new way. Handled poorly, this conversation can lead to entrenched thinking that triggers students into a fight-or-flight response (Taylor & Manning-Ouellette, 2022). The invisibility of, and the silence surrounding, Whiteness among people struggling to see systems are classic challenges in socially just leadership development. Yet, socially just leadership educators reframe these pervasive challenges as opportunities for catalyst points. Furthermore, leadership educators have the tremendous opportunity to create experiences that increase empathy. These three approaches, reframing colorblind approaches, using systems analysis, and constructing experiences, create catalyst points for students that result in commitments to leadership action. By upholding the common goal of creating a just world for people of all races, where race does not limit opportunities for anyone, socially just leadership educators can navigate through resistance to catalyst points. Then, when students begin analyzing the challenges of the invisibility of Whiteness and the ways in which not seeing color minimizes inequity, students can experience that moment of exclaiming, "I never thought about race [like that] until now."

REFERENCES

Alexander, M. (2010). *The new Jim Crow: Mass incarceration in the age of colorblindness.* New Press.

Beatty, C. C., Manning-Ouellette, A., & Wiborg, E. R. (2021). Addressing White fragility in leadership education. In K. L. Guthrie, & V. S. Chunoo (Eds.), *Shifting the mindset: Socially just leadership education* (pp. 257–270). Information Age Publishing.

Bertrand Jones, T., Guthrie, K. L., & Osteen, L. (2016). Critical domains of culturally relevant leadership learning: A call to transform leadership programs. In K. L. Guthrie, T. Bertrand Jones, & L. Osteen (Eds.), *Developing culturally relevant leadership learning* (New Directions for Student Leadership, No. 152, pp. 9–21). Jossey-Bass. https://doi.org/10.1002/yd.20205

Brown, A. C. (2018). *I'm still here: Black dignity in a world made for Whiteness.* Convergent.

Brown, B. (2018). *Dare to lead: Brave work. Tough conversations. Whole hearts.* Random House.

Clear, J. (2018). *Atomic habits: An easy & proven way to build good habits & break bad ones.* Penguin.

DiAngelo, R. (2018). *White fragility: Why it's so hard for white people to talk about racism.* Beacon Press.

Dugan, J. P. (2017). *Leadership theory: Cultivating critical perspectives.* Wiley.

Fincher, D. (Director). (1999). *Fight Club* [Film].

Flagg, B. (1997). *Was blind, but now I see: White race consciousness and the law.* University Press.

Foste, Z. (2019). Reproducing Whiteness: How White students justify the campus racial status quo. *Journal of Student Affairs Research and Practice, 56*(3), 241–253. https://doi.org/10.1080/19496591.2019.1576530.

Guthrie, K. L., Bertrand Jones, T., & Osteen, L. (2017). The teaching, learning, and being of leadership: Exploring context and practice of the culturally relevant leadership learning model. *Journal of Leadership Studies, 11*(3), 61–67. https://doi.org/10.1002/jls.21547.

Haney-López, I. (2006). *White by law: The legal construction of race.* New York University Press.

Harro, B. (2000). The cycle of liberation. In M Adams (Ed.), *Readings for diversity and social justice* (pp. 618–625), Psychology Press.

Kendi, I. X. (2006). *Stamped from the beginning: The definitive history of racist ideas in America.* Avalon Publishing Group.

Mahoney, A. D. (2016). Culturally responsive integrative learning environments: A critical displacement approach. In K. Guthrie, T. Bertrand Jones, & L. Osteen (Eds.), *Developing culturally relevant leadership learning* (New Directions for Student Leadership, No. 152, pp. 47–59). https://doi.org/10.1002/yd.20208

McDermott, M. (2020). *Whiteness in America.* Polity Press.

McGhee, H. (2021). *The sum of us.* One Word.

McKinney, K. D. (2013). *Being White: Stories of race and racism.* Routledge.

Phinney, J. S. (1989). Stages of ethnic identity development in minority group adolescents. *Journal of Early Adolescents, 9*(1-2), 34–49. https://doi.org/10.1177/0272431689091004

Taylor, J. K. (2023). *Lenses for leadership: How white student leaders make meaning of the intersection of race and leadership* [Unpublished dissertation manuscript]. Department of Higher Education and Student Affairs, Oklahoma State University.

Taylor, J. K., & Manning-Ouellette, A. (2022). Finding growth zones: Socially just leadership learning, developmental readiness, and zones of proximal development. *Journal of Leadership Studies*, *16*(3), 1–5. https://doi.org/10.1002/jls.21823

Wilkerson, I. (2020). *Caste: The origins of our discontents*. Random House.

PART I

EMPIRICAL EVIDENCE ON SOCIALLY JUST LEADERSHIP EDUCATION

CHAPTER 4

MISEDUCATED

Socially Just Leadership Education and Black Men's Leader Identity Development

Michael Daniels

Building our future starts with acknowledging our past, and this country's past is rife with attempts to erase any meaningful contributions of Black men from existence. This sad reality only strengthens the need for leadership educators to include the experiences of Black men in their curriculum. More importantly, to effectively strive towards social justice, educators must ensure Black men are represented in the information they are learning. When we strive for social justice in leadership education, educators intentionally center the identities of those who are misrepresented or absent from historical accounts of leadership. There may be no better way to both center Black men's experiences in leadership and support educators with the tools to better facilitate social justice leadership education than to provide a theory on Black men's leader identity development. First, I would like to situate this conversation within past discussions of socially just leadership education.

In *Changing the Narrative*, Guthrie and Chunoo (2018) stated "empowering diverse students to develop voice and agency across leadership environments is critical to socially just leadership education" (p. 2). Many authors align with the notion that the exploration of social identities, specifically those at the intersection of multiple identities, proves beneficial for the goal of socially just leadership education (Andenoro & Skendall, 2020; Haber-Curran & Tillapaugh, 2017; Inter-Association Leadership

Committing to Action: Socially Just Leadership Educations, pp. 37–49

Education Collaborative, 2016; Ospina & Su, 2009). To this end, more scholars are conducting research dedicated to exploring leadership at the intersections of identity, in particular, race and leader identities (Acosta & Guthrie, 2022; Apesin & Gong, 2018; Elliott et al. 2018; Shetty, 2020; Spencer, 2019; Torres, 2019). Researching the experiences of populations that are usually racially underrepresented in literature begins to challenge the stereotypical concepts of leadership development that often drive leadership education.

Challenging these concepts within leadership education literature is a direct act of social justice through counter-storytelling (Solórzano & Yosso, 2002). I believe more leadership educators are beginning to understand the dangers of omitting the experiences of historically oppressed populations. In *Shifting the Mindset*, Guthrie and Chunoo (2021) stressed the value of including experiences of students from diverse populations and included work in this book that assisted with "demystifying the nature of our students with the intent of broadening our individual and collective horizons on who we teach, how they show up, and what really matters in their leadership learning" (p. 5). Now is the time for leadership educators to perform one of the singular most important acts of social justice: empowering Black men to develop their voices and agency in leading. This starts by acknowledging Black men's experiences as unique from any other group of leaders. Particularly, leadership educators can utilize a leadership theory created explicitly for Black men, based on the experiences of Black men, to support their leadership development.

Guthrie and Chunoo (2018) insisted, "socially just leadership education is more than informing students of injustices and leadership knowledge and skills, but providing them with tools toward empowerment and change in the world" (p. 4). In the spirit of moving from educators simply providing information to students, and instead, moving toward empowerment, this chapter highlights how leadership educators can educate others on Black men's experiences, as well as provide a meaningful educational experience for Black men directly. The three goals of this chapter are (1) to provide a brief overview of Black men's leader identity development (BMLID) model (Daniels, 2022). As a result of understanding BMLID, leadership educators can (2) explore ways systems, policies, and practices affect the external contextual influences within BMLID. Finally, leadership educators (3) will be able to identify strategies to implement that contribute to the empowerment of Black men developing their leader identity.

BLACK MEN'S LEADER IDENTITY DEVELOPMENT

Many leadership educators reference or utilize key theories of leadership development that do not center the experiences of Black men. This lack of representation of Black men within leadership theory, projected onto Black men during their experience of learning leadership, can lead to them feeling dissonance with their leader identities, especially related to the accepted behaviors and values of leaders (Daniels, 2022). The white-washing of leader and leadership development theories harm Black men by rendering their labor invisible, which is itself a hurtful tradition that dates back to the founding of the United States (Hotchkins & Dancy, 2015). Fewer Black men seeking leadership perpetuates the cycle of reduced representation of Black men in these roles to conduct research studies to help solve this problem (Harper & Quaye, 2007). With consideration of how valuable theory is to a person's leadership development, I recognized how essential producing a theory Black men can use in understanding their own self-image reflected in a theory. In addition to providing a useful tool for affirming Black men's experiences and supporting their authentic leader identity development, this theory is helpful for socially just leadership education.

Methodology

The purpose of this constructivist grounded theory study was to explore the experiences of undergraduate Black men in formal leadership roles at predominantly White institutions to understand their leader identity development process. As a result of studying these students' experiences, the intended outcome of this study was a leader identity development theory for Black men. The study was conducted across 10 four-year predominantly White institutions (PWIs) in the United States. There were 11 participants from 10 different institutions. All participants in this study identified as Black men. Participants' ages ranged from 18–24 years old. Class standing among participants ranged from junior to recent graduates (graduating from college within the previous year, at the time of data collection). The result of this study was the emergence of a substantive theory explaining the process of Black men's leader identity development. I have identified this substantive theory as *Black men's leader identity development (BMLID)*. BMLID encompasses the experiences that contribute to Black men's leader identity development, specifically within formal leadership roles at PWIs.

Findings

The categories represented within BMLID are: (1) a support system teaching lessons about leadership, (2) developing a sense of independence, humility, and/or appreciation as a result of hardships or challenge, (3) valuing opinions of peers and mentors who reflect similar racial identity,

(4) being identified as a leader by someone else before seeing oneself as a leader, (5) experiencing challenges resulting in self-reflection that can cause self-doubt or lead to perseverance, (6) asking for and accepting help, (7) developing confidence as leader as a result of feedback from others and outcomes in situations of active leadership, (8) navigating racist systems and practices while leading as a Black man, (9) experiencing feelings of pressure as a result of hypervisibility and lack of representation, (10) gaining a sense of self through learning, (11) losing confidence because of ridicule or isolation as a result of other's perceptions, and (12) leading by example. To demonstrate the relationship between each of the 12 categories, there are components I identify as *elements*. These 18 elements are crucial categorical properties of the theory for leader identity development of Black men. Though participants explained instances of their identity development that resulted in the 12 categories, the connection between each category is ambiguous without these 18 elements. These elements are present throughout the entire process and show up in different ways in each of the categories. The 18 elements are organized into three different groups, *external contextual influence*, *individual actions*, and *interactions*. Figure 4.1 represents the theory of Black men's leader identity development.

Figure 4.1

Black Men's Leader Identity Development Model

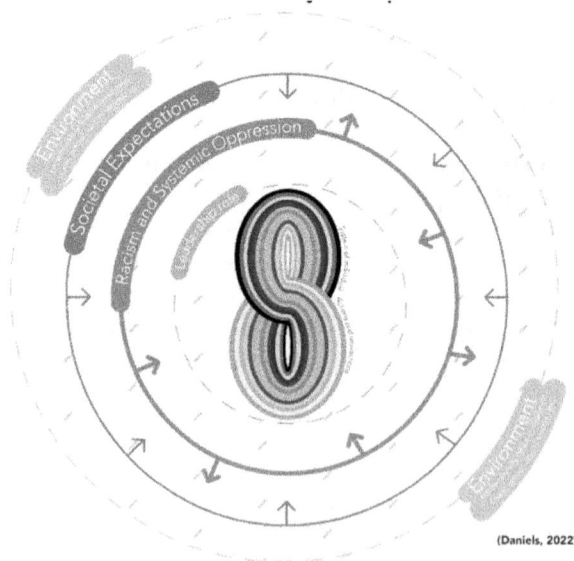

(Daniels, 2022)

Source: Reprinted with permission from Daniels, M. (2022).

This study allowed for deeper understandings about the experiences of Black men in formal leadership roles, and how they develop their leader identity. Several participants' accounts included insights on how Black men develop their leader identity. Central to all other findings, however, was the understanding of how the experiences of Black men at predominantly PWIs are unique and different than those of other students. These institutions are inherently designed to center the experiences of White students and, subsequently, further marginalize the experiences of non-White students (Mahoney, 2016). Dugan (2011) emphasized unpacking contextual influences in leadership development by paying more attention to dimensions of social identity. Many authors highlighted the racist and oppressive systems Black men in leadership face within PWIs (Collins et al., 2017; Druery & Brooms, 2019; Harper & Quaye, 2007; Harper et al., 2011; Hotchkins & Dancy, 2015; Oaks et al., 2013). Within my study, I learned how Black men's leadership experiences were influenced by different contexts, internal processes, and the interactions they have with other people. However, for the purpose of this chapter, I will explain how leadership educators can leverage strategies for socially just leadership education focusing on the external contextual influences to effect social change.

Using External Contextual Influences to Operationalize BMLID

Within BMLID, participants described four external contextual influences that contributed to their leader identity development process. These elements affected leaders, actively and passively, through people, systems, or expectations of behavior. The entire process was influenced by external contextual influences and each of the four elements were present throughout the entire leader identity development process of Black men. These four elements are: environment, societal expectations, racism and systemic oppression, and leadership roles. (1) *Environment*, the spaces, and places where the individual is in consideration to their development (e.g. predominantly White environment, home, school, sports team, etc.). (2) *Racism and systemic oppression*, prejudice, or discrimination against the person because they are Black, both overt, covert, and passive. This includes oppressive systems acting upon Black people within different environments. (3) *Societal expectations*: society's beliefs of what the individual should be doing or how they should be acting in certain situations or roles; this is related to their racial identity, their gender identity, or leader identity. (4) *Leadership role*, the position of leadership specifically, the responsibilities associated with the role including tasks, assignments, or expectations. Now that I have provided an overview of BMLID, with emphasis on the external contextual influences, I want to help socially just leadership educators use this theory with recommendations focusing on education, representation, and support.

RECOMMENDATIONS: PROBLEMATIZE CURRENT INSTITUTIONAL SYSTEMS, POLICIES, AND PRACTICES

Being a socially just leadership educator means using critical lenses to examine systems, policies, and practices influencing our work. Investigating what one 'knows' to be true from historical, cultural, and political perspectives provides a more comprehensive understanding of the issues impacting leader identity development of Black men. Far too often, educators accept situations as common practice and normalize behaviors, attitudes, and practices that are inherently oppressive and discriminatory. For example, have you ever questioned the requirements for certain leadership education experiences within your institution? Are these requirements creating barriers for certain types of populations? How are these experiences evaluating the learning or development of those participating? With this line of questioning, we start to identify fundamentally problematic practices within our system of educating leaders.

To aid in this critical analysis of systems, policies, and practices, I call upon the practice of problematizing, influenced by French philosopher, Michel Foucault (Harter, 2016). Defined as a line of inquiry, problematizing is a process of objects, in this case systems, inclusive of policies and practices, becoming problems by being characterized, analyzed, and treated as problems (Bacchi & Goodwin, 2016). Truly, being a socially just leadership educator means investigating systems, questioning practices, and interrogating policies to understanding how these systems, practices, and policies are inherently racist and oppressive. Next, we move into asking the tough questions others refuse to confront or choose to ignore. This is the impetus to how socially just leadership educators start to break down barriers and develop an inclusive environment that supports the development of all students. Only then can we dismantle systems, practices, and policies preventing Black men from having the full experience they deserve in developing their leader identity. Finally, we take the final step in coconstructing equitable systems and collaboratively implementing socially just practice with reference from several of the findings from my study.

Properly Educate Those Learning and Those Teaching

Coconstructing equitable systems begins by educating those who will (1) be within the environments, (2) perpetuate societal expectations, (3) enact racism, (4) create, or oversee, the leadership roles. This means identifying those who will likely engage with leaders in various settings such as advisors, coaches, or instructors. Within my study, multiple participants expressed how their experiences within their institution reinforced racism and systemic oppression. Daniel, a senior, responded to the question, how does your institution currently support your development as a leader?

> The university tailors everything to White students because they are the majority. You're not teaching me about skills that a black person needs in the professional field to be successful. You're teaching me about, "you can just go in there and try your hardest. You're just going to do the best you can." You know, that kind of myth of meritocracy, a lot of things were rooted in hard work and effort gets you to where you need to go and not acknowledging those systemic barriers that prevent people of color. And so all of these leadership things were catered to the majority population. So when it came to the minority population, it wasn't a puzzle piece fit for the type of leaders that we had to be generally and in a predominantly White space.

Daniel outlined the pervasive nature of miseducation within leadership education at his institution. Approaching leadership education with a prescriptive playbook only referencing literature or resources accounting for the needs of White students is deeply problematic. Instead, we need a comprehensive repertoire of resources that account for a variety of identities. Daniel's experience underscores the value of having a leader identity theory specifically for Black men.

Theory to practice within HESA graduate programs. These future leadership educators can be trained before entering these roles. Higher Education and Student Affairs graduate (HESA) programs are positioned to prepare socially just leadership educators prior to entering such roles. However, many neglect to share models and theories designed to serve Black men enrolled in postsecondary educational institutions. By sharing BMLID within courses that review student development theory or leadership theory, HESA faculty, and student affairs professionals, can begin construction of more equitable systems at the foundation of learning. Leadership educators can help HESA students learn how to use theory as a lens to view student development to inform their practice. Creating a curriculum that critiques leadership development theories offers emerging HESA practitioners a strong foundation in becoming socially just leadership educators. After identifying tenets of critical perspectives, Dugan (2017) offered tools of deconstruction and reconstruction to use when examining the bodies of theory in leadership As HESA students prepare to work with Black men, they can reference this theory as a guide to understanding Black men's leader identity development. Additionally, they can incorporate BMLID in program development, both in how they will engage with Black men, and, how they support the other educators and peers who will interact with Black men in a leadership education space.

Develop training and education for leadership educators. Another strategy is developing curriculum to train current leadership educators by providing BMLID as a theory to incorporate into practice, socially just leadership educators can enhance stocks of knowledge and start to unlearn understandings of leadership that are situated in hegemony (Dugan, 2017). The emphasis in this section is to highlight how societal expectations influence leader identity development and how leadership educators can problematize those expectations.

Multiple participants shared how coaches and advisors within their institution aided in their leader identity development. Derek, a student leader, and student athlete expressed how his football coach was able to help him develop through sharing a different approach towards leadership. He described how his football coach helped him embrace his less vocal leadership style which helped him to be more comfortable in his leader identity. Others in similar positions as Derek's football coach who can educate leaders must find ways to explore the nuances of Black men's leader identity. This practice, coupled with a holistic understanding of BMLID, provides leadership educators a pathway to properly educating Black men.

Dante, a senior at a large commuter college, shared another example of how leadership educators can use a critical lens to problematize prior knowledge and learning of Black men's leadership. Dante mentioned how his advisor of the men of color initiative created experiences to help him to challenge some of the stereotypes about masculinity he had been taught in other spaces. Dante expressed, "I think it's helped me break down a lot of toxic masculinity traits, [...] from not opening up, to asking for help." Both Derek and Dante shared examples of how leadership educators have successfully engaged with Black men to assist in their leader identity development. We can use these examples to create trainings for current leadership educators, noting the benefits of providing space for Black men to challenge stereotypes of how they were taught to show up as leaders who are Black and men.

Education for students. Lastly, moving from focusing on those who are educating Black men to the peers of Black men is crucial in creating an environment for BMLID to thrive. Participants within this study underscored the influence of peers on their leader identity. Multiple participants expressed how certain environments reinforced racism and systemic oppression through microaggressive behaviors and actions devaluing their experiences as Black men.

Derek shared how serving on the fraternity and sorority life council as the representative of his historically Black fraternity made him feel like his voice was being silenced by his White peers. He reflected on his experience stating,

> It's not very many black organizations. So we're just surrounded by White organizations who already don't know much about your fraternity or how y'all operate as a whole. You can feel like you don't have a voice. You speak about things, and it just goes in one ear and out the other and that can lead to some imposter syndrome. You think like, "maybe I'm not the type of leader I thought I was."

Derek's experience with his White peers is a perfect example of how lack of education can perpetuate systemic silencing of Black men's voices. This silencing causes doubt within Black men; and even more damaging, discourages them from leadership. If we, as socially just leadership educators, want to break the cycle of silencing Black men with the intention of removing them from history as valuable contributors to our society, we must begin with educating the people within the environment where the leadership education takes place.

Representation Matters

We often hear how the power of representation can contribute to students' sense of belonging (Strayhorn, 2018). However, we rarely hear how powerful representation is to the people themselves. In this study, participants shared both how the lack, and presence, of representation aided them in their development. Daniel shared how lack of representation impacted his experience at a PWI:

> There wasn't a lot of leaders that look like me. There wasn't that many black people in high power and they were, they were leaving the school because of how it treated like professionals. And so thinking about when I needed guidance on how to be a leader or a certain position, I may be the only black person on this committee. I may be the only black person who served in this position in the last five years.

This demonstrates the pervasive nature of systemic racism and its impact on multiple levels. Without representation in professional roles for Black men to seek guidance, there is a void in how they can feel supported as leaders. The disturbing fact is that Daniel mentions both the lack of Black professional staff he can go to within the university because of harmful treatment, and the significant lack of representation of Black people in certain roles over time. As socially just leadership educators, surveying the landscape for representation in current student leadership roles for students to see themselves and have someone to consult on matters related to their unique experiences as well as exploration the representation of professional staff who can mentor Black men who are developing as leaders.

Contrary to the oppressive behaviors of White peers, participants highlighted how support from their peers who were Black men was paramount in their leader identity development. Chris shared how one of his teammates began to mentor him and helped him develop his confidence as a leader stating, "He encouraged me to go out, just join groups at school and just be involved. On the field as a freshman, he allowed me to have a voice and encourage me to have a voice." Socially just leadership educators recognize the value of peer support in the development of Black men's leader identity development. However, to have support from other Black men, it is our responsibility to develop an environment that encourages representation of Black men.

Develop a System of Support

Expanding on lack of representation, one of the other categories relevant to addressing the influence of environment is providing support. I have already discussed the ways we can support Black men developing their leader identity through educating leadership educators and Black men's peers, increasing representation by addressing some of the systemic issues within PWIs, now I want to share ways to directly support Black men's leader identity development. Understanding Black men's leader identity development begins with understanding the role of support systems in their development; specifically, from the onset of how family, faith, and friends are a part of that development.

Overwhelmingly, Black men accredit the foundational development of their leader identity to the early influences from their family members, lessons from their faith, and interactions with their peers. This is important to note as leadership educators engage with Black men. By providing opportunities for them to develop their leader identity, we can carefully consider where the core of their leader identity may have started and find ways to tap into those experiences while building intentional opportunities to enhance their leader identity development. Moving from understanding the foundation of leader identity development, I want to share how leaders within my study expressed their support within college influenced their leader identity development.

Multiple participants discussed their experiences of support from both formal and informal leadership educators. Many participants expressed the value of support from leaders in their churches, sports teams, and college organizations. CJ, who was involved in youth organizations with his church growing up, shared how his pastor encouraged him when he connected with him in church. CJ stated how these interactions inspired him to continue to develop as a leader because he felt seen and supported. Another participant, Jim, mentioned having access to someone who look liked him made a difference in the trust he was able to develop in receiving support from a staff member. He also stated he was personally tapped by a director of the multicultural center for a leadership opportunity. Jim recalled, "He was like, 'I think this is something you should do. I think you'll do well with it, be a good bridge for these students.'" CJ and Jim's experiences reinforce how our Black men need support from the institution by way of staff who share the same racial background. Socially just leadership educators examine their environments to learn where mechanisms of support are present for Black men. More importantly, does your environment have systems of support comprised of sustainable approaches for inclusive leadership education to provide these leaders with sense of belonging through representation and relevant resources for learning?

CONCLUSION

Leadership educators are in the center of how others learn about leadership and can either break oppressive systemic understanding of knowledge or perpetuate those systems of oppression through their teachings. This position demonstrates the systems we are a part of and function within. Finding ways to interrogate these systems to assess the intentionally designed mechanisms that perpetuate oppression is the responsibility of any true socially just leadership educator. This responsibility, though inherently difficult, is the only way leadership education can dismantle these systems through social justice. The study that yielded BMLID provided a theory rooted in critical lenses. My hope is that this chapter helped you in your journey of developing your ability to deconstruct your formal knowledge of leadership theories and reconstruct your knowledge with BMLID as an example of using a critical lens to examine how racism, systemic oppression and societal expectations influence Black men. More importantly, using BMLID as a vehicle to educate others on ways to provide meaningful experiences for Black men to develop their leader identity. Empowering Black men to develop their leader identity needs to be the intention of any socially just leadership educator if their goal is to avoid repeating mistakes of the past and to build a better future.

REFERENCES

Acosta, A. A., & Guthrie, K. L. (2022). Haciendose un líder: Leadership identity development of Latino men at a predominantly White institution. *Journal of Hispanic Higher Education, 21*(1), 112–125. http://dx.doi.org/10.1177/1538192720932472

Andenoro, A. C., & Skendall, K. C. (2020). The national leadership education research agenda 2020–2025: Advancing the state of leadership education scholarship. *Journal of Leadership Studies, 14*(3), 33–38. https://doi.org/10.1002/jls.21714

Apesin, A., & Gong, T. (2018). The impact of freshmen college leadership experiences on their leader self-efficacy development in historically Black institutions. *Journal of Applied Research in Higher Education, 10*(3), 283–295. https://doi.org/10.1108/JARHE-10-2017-0121

Bacchi, C., & Goodwin, S. (2016). *Poststructural policy analysis: A guide to practice*. Springer.

Collins, J. D., Suarez, C. E., Beatty, C. C., & Rosch, D. M. (2017). Fostering leadership capacity among Black male achievers: Findings from an identity-based leadership immersion program. *Journal of Leadership Education, 16*(3), 82–96. https://doi.org/10.12806/v16/i3/r4

Daniels, M. A. (2022). *Leader identity development of Black men: A constructivist grounded theory study* [Doctoral dissertation, Kent State University].

Druery, J. E., & Brooms, D. R. (2019). "It lit up the campus": Engaging Black males in culturally enriching environments. *Journal of Diversity in Higher Education, 12*(4), 330–340. https://doi.org/10.1037/dhe0000087

Dugan, J. P. (2011). Pervasive myths in leadership development: Unpacking constraints on leadership learning. *Journal of Leadership Studies, 5*(2), 79–84. https://doi.org/10.1002/jls.20223

Dugan, J. P. (2017). *Leadership theory: Cultivating critical perspectives*. John Wiley & Sons.

Camacho, L., Jr., Elliott, K. C., & Salinas, C. (2018). No role models: The experience of Black and Latino men in a mentorship program at a two-year Hispanic serving institution. In J. McClinton, D. S. B. Mitchell, & T. Carr, et al., (Eds.), *Mentoring at minority serving institutions (MSIs): Theory, design, practice, and impact* (pp. 45–62). Information Age Publishing.

Guthrie, K. L., & Chunoo, V. S. (Eds.). (2018). *Changing the narrative: Socially just leadership education*. Information Age Publishing.

Guthrie, K. L., & Chunoo, V. S. (Eds.). (2021). *Shifting the mindset: Socially just leadership education*. Information Age Publishing.

Tillapaugh, D. & Haber-Curran, P. (Eds.). (2017). *New Directions for Student Leadership: No. 154. Critical perspectives on gender and student leadership*. Jossey-Bass.

Harper, S. R., & Quaye, S. J. (2007). Student organizations as venues for Black identity expression and development among African American male student leaders. *Journal of College Student Development, 48*(2), 127–144. https://doi.org/10.1353/csd.2007.0012

Harper, S. R., Davis, R. J., Jones, D. E., McGowan, B. L., Ingram, T. N., & Platt, C. S. (2011). Race and racism in the experiences of Black male resident assistants at predominantly White universities. *Journal of College Student Development*, *52*(2), 180–200. https://doi.org/10.1353/csd.2011.0025

Harter, N. (2016). *Foucault on leadership: The leader as subject*. Routledge.

Hotchkins, B. K., & Dancy, T. (2015). Black male student leaders in predominantly White Universities: Stories of power, preservation, and persistence. *Western Journal of Black Studies, 39*(1), 30–44.

Inter-Association Leadership Education Collaborative. (2016). *Collaborative priorities and critical considerations for leadership education*. Association of Leadership Educators. https://www.leadershipeducators.org/ILEC

Mahoney, A. D. (2016). Culturally responsive integrative learning environments: A critical displacement approach. In K. Guthrie, T. Bertrand Jones, & L. Osteen (Eds.), *Developing culturally relevant leadership learning* (New Directions for Student Leadership, No. 152, pp. 47–59). https://doi.org/10.1002/yd.20208

Oaks, D. A. J., Duckett, K., Suddeth, T., & Kennedy-Phillips, L. (2013). Leadership development and the African American male college student experience. *Journal of College and Character, 14*(4), 331–340. https://doi.org/10.1515/jcc-2013-0042

Ospina, S., & Su, C. (2009). Weaving color lines: Race, ethnicity, and the work of leadership in social change organizations. *Leadership, 5*(2), 131–170. https://doi.org/10.1177/1742715009102927

Shetty, R. L. (2020). *The leader identity of Black women in college: A grounded theory* [Doctoral dissertation, University of Georgia].

Solorzano, D. G., & Yosso, T. J. (2002). Critical race methodology: Counter-story telling as an analytical framework for education. *Qualitative Inquiry, 8*(1), 23–44. https://doi.org/10.1177/107780040200800103

Spencer, D., Jr. (2019). *"Like a unicorn": A narrative inquiry exploring the leadership experiences of undergraduate Black men* [Doctoral dissertation, The Florida State University].

Strayhorn, T. L. (2018). *College students' sense of belonging: A key to educational success for all students*. Routledge.

Torres, M. (2019). *Ella creyó que podía, así que lo hizo: Exploring latina leader identity development through testimonio* [Doctoral dissertation, The Florida State University].

CHAPTER 5

CONNECTING SOCIAL JUSTICE TO LEADERSHIP LEARNING

Applying Cultural Relevance to the Student Experience

Ana Maia

The call for intentionally designed college student leadership programs has only intensified in recent years (Guthrie & Jenkins, 2018; Komives & Sowcik, 2020). This includes creating meaningful leadership programs that directly address issues of inequality and promote social justice (Beatty et al., 2020; Chunoo et al., 2020). As socially just leadership educators, we must also prioritize critically attending to learners of traditionally marginalized groups and underserved identities.

The culturally relevant leadership learning (CRLL) model centers on the development of all students and views both students of dominant and non-dominant identities as assets to the learning environment (Bernard Jones et al., 2016; Chunoo & Callahan, 2017; Ladson-Billings, 1995). The CRLL model is also a helpful tool for social justice leadership educators (Guthrie & Chunoo, 2018). This approach focuses on students' individual and collective leadership identity, capacity, and efficacy development. It calls for educators to critically consider the five dimensions of campus climate—compositional diversity, psychological, behavioral, organizational/ structural, and the historical legacy of inclusion and exclusion (Hurtado et al., 1999; Milem et al., 2005).

Committing to Action: Socially Just Leadership Educations, pp. 51–62

STUDENTS' PERSPECTIVES ON CULTURALLY RELEVANT LEADERSHIP LEARNING

In 2022, I completed a qualitative study to address a substantial gap in the CRLL literature—a lack of empirical research showcasing how CRLL is instrumental in educating college students. Informed by students' perspectives, I explored meaningful experiences that contributed to how students developed leadership identity, capacity, and efficacy (Maia, 2022a). Through a critical constructivist lens, I collected in-depth data on students' collective and individual lived experiences.

All participants had completed their first year in a curricular and co-curricular leadership program at a four-year, private, comprehensive university (Maia, 2022a). Participants self-identified as holding at least one non-dominant (traditionally marginalized) social identity as central to their core (i.e., a Black, genderqueer, lower-middle-class student; or a Latina, first-generation college student). Even though I held multiple roles in relation to the participants (researcher, previous professor, and current program advisor), I developed a rapport with participants. Participants shared their leadership development journey in an hour-long individual interview, followed by a one-and-a-half-long focus group with three to four other participants. They also critiqued the study as part of a member-checking process.

THE MODEL FOR FOSTERING CULTURALLY RELEVANT LEADERSHIP DEVELOPMENT (FCRLD)

After in-depth coding analyses and an additional literature review, I summarized the findings in the model for fostering culturally relevant leadership development (FCRLD; see Figure 5.1; Maia, 2022a). The goal of this model was to provide leadership educators with a practical framework to facilitate students' culturally relevant leadership development. In the following sections, I will describe each element in the FCRLD and how educators can apply each of these concepts to develop a more robust, intentional CRLL experience for college students.

Leadership Identity, Capacity, and Efficacy

The ultimate goal of CRLL is to further students' individual and group-oriented growth. Like the CRLL framework, student leadership identity, capacity, and efficacy are at the heart of student leadership development. Leadership educators facilitate the development of students as leaders:

Figure 5.1

Model for Fostering Culturally Relevant Leadership Development (FCRLD)

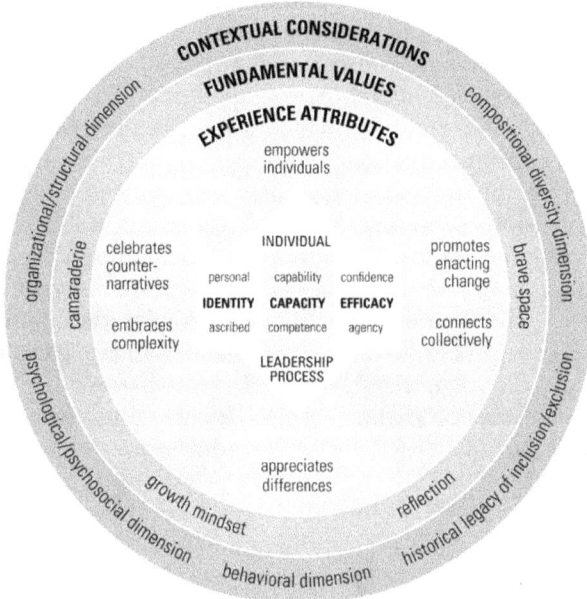

Source: Reprinted with permission from Maia, A. C. (2022a). *Educating culturally relevant leaders: Experiences in leadership identity, capacity, and efficacy development in college students.*

who they are in leadership processes (identity), their ability to lead independently as well as engage in collective leadership (capacity), and what they do as autonomous leaders and collaborative actors (efficacy) (Guthrie et al., 2021; Chunoo & French, 2021). For participants, these three concepts were intertwined and did not appear as distinct elements (Maia, 2022a). Furthermore, when we zoom out from the individual's experience, these three elements are influenced by the surrounding climate.

Contextual Considerations: Five Critical Dimensions

Before creating intentional leadership identity, capacity, and efficacy development experiences, socially just educators focus on the environment in which learning occurs. These *contextual considerations* are at the outermost layer of the model; all five are modeled after the CRLL. They include the five elements that affect the educational climate: *compositional diversity*, *historical legacy of inclusion/exclusion, behavioral, psychological/psychosocial*, and *organizational/structural dimensions* (Bertrand Jones et al., 2016). These critical dimensions affect student learning. Therefore, educators should consider such elements when designing socially just leadership development programs and experiences (Osteen et al., 2016).

For example, participants described how microaggressions and racism on campus affected their leadership development (Maia, 2022a). By understanding the *historical legacy of inclusion/exclusion* at the institution, socially just leadership educators are better equipped to prepare students to thrive as change-makers in such environments. Such educators ask, "How are systemic oppression, prejudice, and discrimination addressed through leadership learning? Are there leaders of underrepresented identities in positional roles (*compositional diversity dimension*)? Are diverse perspectives considered by those in power? Are the actions of traditionally marginalized folks perceived as leadership (*behavioral dimension*)? How about views on intergroup relations (*psychological/psychosocial dimension*)? Are students exposed to other ways of leading within the curriculum or co-curriculum (*organizational/structural dimension*)?" For additional similar queries, see Beatty and Guthrie (2021).

Socially just leadership educators consider how the five critical dimensions influence what educational content is chosen and delivered (*organizational/structural*); which students are selected or encouraged to participate in leadership learning (*compositional diversity*); the types of leadership behaviors (*behavioral*) and interpersonal actions (*psychological/psychosocial*) that are esteemed; and how to interrogate systemic inequality tied to learning (*historical legacy of inclusion/exclusion*) (Chunoo & French, 2021; Maia, 2022a). These five dimensions also influence how educators can espouse the FCRLD's *fundamental values* and best support students of traditionally underserved identities.

Fundamental Values

As socially just leadership educators craft intentional CRLL experiences, they focus on fundamentally enhancing the learning experience. The FCRLD's *fundamental values* entail creating a *brave space*, supporting a *growth mindset*, cultivating *camaraderie*, and encouraging *reflection*. To the participants, these elements were foundational to their learning experience (Maia, 2022a).

Brave Space

The brave space concept originated from Arao and Clemens' (2013) redefinitions of safe spaces for learning where no space is truly safe for our students. Instead, brave educators cultivate courageous environments for students to share their perspectives and to be boldly vulnerable while owning their social location. *Brave spaces* provide room for meaningful dialogue. They also allow for a community of respect and care to flourish. This includes setting the stage for students to engage in difficult dialogue surrounding contentious leadership topics and conversations on social justice issues. They also allow beliefs to be challenged in a supportive learning space (Guthrie & Jenkins, 2018; Maia, 2022b). Empirical studies like Brazill (2020) illustrated a space where students can share their stories of discrimination and prejudice. For the participants, this type of courageous disclosure facilitated students' personal growth and the group's collective connection (Maia, 2022a). It allowed for actionable leadership to take form through controversy with courage development and coalesce building, both major components of the social action, leadership, and transformation (SALT) model (Mitchell et al., 2023).

Educators start by declaring their intention in the initial interaction to create a *brave space*. From the students' perspective, this began by cocreating community agreements (i.e., ground rules) to hold one another accountable (e.g. using "I" statements, actively listening, considering others' lived experiences, and challenging oneself to grow; Maia, 2022a). As the educator, I shared my hope for establishing a respectful leadership community and that I would treat all participants as responsible adults. When facilitating sensitive and engaging activities where students disclose their political ideologies, educators need to take care to respect each opinion and not pass judgment.

Even though vulnerable sharing can lead to authentic conversations and deep learning, it can also be tricky to encourage. Issues can unexpectedly arise that violate the *brave space* ethos. It is important to approach students when they break the learning community agreements; intentionally or accidentally. This entails asking for clarification from a student's potentially disrespectful comment, facilitating an intent versus impact discussion, or checking in with a student one-on-one about their negative impact while cocreating a solution to address its effects in the group setting. If further distrust arises, educators can also examine the five *contextual considerations* to brainstorm how to address systemic issues alive in the learning space.

Camaraderie

Relationships matter to students engaging in CRLL. All participants disclosed how peer engagement and relationship building was important to their development (Maia, 2022a). This included the time to bond with other students in the learning space. In addition, relationships nurtured in the leadership learning community can help students develop social and human capital to succeed as leadership actors (Guthrie & Jenkins, 2018). According to the revised social change model, a fellowship community, where familial capital and kinship develop, is valuable in teaching students how to create collective change (Harper & Kezar, 2021).

As socially just leadership educators, creating a learning space that encourages good humor and friendly exchanges can help *camaraderie* arise. This can be as simple as, but not limited to, allowing students breathing time to organically connect between discussions, creating a holding environment, or facilitating activities where students can share their life stories and have time to chat after. It can also entail integrating fun, engaging games and learning simulations into the curriculum (Guthrie & Jenkins, 2018).

Growth Mindset

Self-improvement is a core element of leadership learning. All participants shared how elements of a *growth mindset* approach was a component of their leadership development (Maia, 2022a). This value echoes Dweck's (2008) work on growth mindset: integrating feedback, practice, and grit into the learning experience. Students learned to embrace mistakes and that leadership development is a lifelong journey. Culturally relevant leadership educators model *growth mindset*. Examples can include sharing stories about their own development through failures. They can also impart to the learning community the definition of *growth mindset* and examples of culturally relevant leaders who persevered in the face of adversity.

Reflection

Critical reflection is a core component of socially just leadership learning (Owen, 2014), leadership metacognition (Guthrie & Jenkins, 2018), and a powerful pedagogical tool (Volpe White & Guthrie, 2015). During the study, all participants reflected on their leadership learning experiences and shared how they made meaning from such experiences (Maia, 2022a). These findings align with extant research on the benefits of frequent reflection, increasing students' capacity and efficacy to lead (Ashford & DeRue, 2012).

Socially just leadership educators create intentional space for meaningful reflection (Volpe White & Guthrie, 2015). For example, creating learning experiences that include opportunities for active observation and contemplation; creative thought to evolve; journaling or written deliberation; expression through virtual formats; and dialogue with peers

(Volpe White et al., 2019). By intentionally developing CRLL experiences inclusive of *reflection*, encouraging *growth mindset*, cultivating *camaraderie*, and fostering a *brave space*, educators are setting the stage for students to develop as social justice leadership actors. These four fundamental values should be integrated into leadership experiences.

Experience Attributes

Educators creating CRLL experiences consider incorporating at least one *experience attribute* in the FCRLD. These *experience attributes* facilitate culturally relevant leadership identity, capacity, and efficacy development. They also attend to the elements of the leadership learning framework: knowledge, development, training, observation, engagement, and meta-cognition (Guthrie & Jenkins, 2018). Students personally and collectively shared how meaningful CRLL experiences (1) empowered them, (2) promoted opportunities for enacting change, (3) collectively connected them with others, (4) allowed them to practice appreciating differences in others, 4) taught them to embrace the complexity within leadership, and (5) celebrated counternarratives on leading (Maia, 2022a).

Empowers Individuals

According to the participants, the most powerful leadership learning experiences empowered them as individuals and as group members (Maia, 2022a). Such experiences enabled students of traditionally underserved identities to build cultural, social, and human capital; understand the value of a variety of individual strengths (including non-dominant ways of leading); support recognition of students' accomplishments; increase students' self-confidence; and advance students' communication skills. These values align with Harper and Kezar's (2021) revised version of the social change model—specifically reinforcing the group values of acknowledging power and oppression (to understand and eradicate power imbalances) and creating support networks.

Promotes Enacting Change

Consistent with *growth mindset*, effective CRLL experiences provide students with opportunities to practice leadership skills in group settings. These instances promoted both individual confidence and collective agency, as described by Chunoo and French (2021). These learning experiences are also experiential in nature. When they are deliberately designed for students to apply their knowledge, skills, and abilities, they retain maximum impact (Guthrie & Jenkins, 2018). For example, service-learning can be a powerful pedagogical approach to socially just leadership education (Volpe White, 2018). Participants shared how their semester-long advocacy project in the local community provided the opportunity to further enhance their leadership skills (Maia, 2022a). They also disclosed how they practiced enacting leadership during a two-hour session at the university challenge course.

Collectively Connects

In addition to building camaraderie in a brave space, *connecting with peers* to create change increased participants' leadership identity, capacity, and efficacy (Maia, 2022a). Teambuilding is foundational to leadership learning (Guthrie & Jenkins, 2018) and liberatory leadership practice (Owen, 2014). Such experiences helped participants build collective efficacy—an essential factor in addressing systemic injustice (Guthrie et al., 2021). Even short-term leadership group activities can aid in this development. Activities can include involved simulations, such as Star Power (Prince et al., 2015) or a problem-based project; group activities like the marshmallow challenge or egg drop; or even move-involved community service projects addressing a local problem.

Appreciates Differences in Others

A core component of the CRLL includes regarding all students as assets in the learning experience (Bertrand Jones et al., 2016). This approach showed up in the participants' narratives and influenced their identity development (Maia, 2022a). They learned how everyone can contribute to the leadership process with their own set of strengths.

Social justice leadership educators facilitate experiences to expand students' social skills and appreciation for different ways of leading. There should be a focus on activities addressing students' identities and inter-sectionality (Guthrie & Chunoo, 2021). Such learning experiences can include a model of the multiple dimensions of identity activity with a pair-and-share discussion or using inventories such as Gallup's CliftonStrengths or Myers-Briggs Type Indicator in a group setting through a critical lens (Barnes et al., 2018; Maia, 2021; Myers, 1962; Rath, 2007). Moreover, *appreciating differences in others* also requires students to acknowledge the complexity innate in leadership.

Embraces Complexity

In the study, all participants discussed the challenge of understanding the complexity inherent in leadership (Maia, 2022a). They asked themselves questions such as, "What is good versus bad leadership?" and faced challenges when defining the concept based on individual skills and different situations. In fact, "individuals may define this complex process differently based on personal identities, experiences, traits, behaviors, or worldviews" (Guthrie & Jenkins, 2018, p. 4). After all, leadership is socially constructed and intricate (Dugan, 2017; Guthrie et al., 2013).

As a socially just leadership educator, it can be beneficial to share examples of leaders and leadership that differ from mainstream depictions. This can entail engaging students in experiential activities containing a critical *reflection* component (e.g., an ethics barometer, four corners activity, and/or case studies containing different styles of leading). Social justice leadership learning experiences that deepen one's understanding also include the sharing of non-traditional ways of leading.

Celebrates Counternarratives on Leading

CRLL experiences are incomplete without examples of, and stories from, minoritized groups (Mahoney, 2017). Surfacing counternarratives can be validating and empowering, especially for traditionally underrepresented students (Ardoin & Guthrie, 2021). In addition to the activities mentioned in *embraces complexity*, educators can provide the *brave space* for students to share their own experiences such as using Life Maps or *testimonios* (Maia, 2022a; Torres, 2019). Story sharing allows students to critically examine the group value of power and oppression acknowledgement and expand students' understanding of systemic inequities (Harper & Kezar, 2021).

FUTURE DIRECTIONS AND IMPLICATIONS

Maia's (2022a) study explored the leadership identity, capacity, and efficiency development of college students from their unique perspectives. This was an in-depth qualitative study with nine participants. Further empirical research could explore students' experience of the elements in the FCRLD, such as the *fundamental values* or the *experience attributes*, from multiple perspectives and in a larger, quantitative scale. Students with specific intersections of identities may also benefit and/or experience the FCRLD elements differently.

Additionally, there is also a need to study the educators' experience when building leadership learning FCRLD content. This includes more studies on leadership educator preparedness—especially when learning to facilitate such complex, sensitive, socially just content. It is easy to say that a *brave space* is imperative to CRLL, but it is difficult to put into practice when students enter the learning space with differing levels of privilege.

Finally, I believe the FCRLD and its applications can be implemented in other student affairs, academic affairs, and interdisciplinary contexts; or even to students beyond the traditionally aged college demographic (i.e., K–12 system, senior citizens, middle-aged adults). Future research in these areas could help further socially just leadership education outside of the realms of the university setting, teaching more individuals to enact change.

REFERENCES

Arao, B., & Clemens, K. (2013). From safe spaces to brave spaces: A new way to frame dialogue around diversity and social justice. In L. M. Landreman (Ed.), *The art of effective facilitation: Reflections from social justice educators* (pp. 135–150). Stylus.

Ardoin, S., & Guthrie, K. L. (2021). Who we are impacts how we lead: Social class influence on leader identity, capacity, and efficacy. *New Directions for Student Leadership, 2021*, 13–21. https://doi.org/10.1002/yd.20416

Ashford, S. J., & DeRue, D. S. (2012). Developing as a leader: The power of mindful engagement. *Organizational Dynamics, 41*(2), 146–154. https://doi.org/10.1016/j.orgdyn.2012.01.008

Barnes, A. C., Olson, T. H., & Reynolds, D. J. (2018). Teaching power as an inconvenient but imperative dimension of critical leadership development. In J. P. Dugan (Ed.), *Integrating critical perspectives into leadership development* (New Directions for Student Leadership, No. 159, pp. 77–90). https://doi.org/10.1002/yd.20299

Beatty, C. C., & Guthrie, K. L. (2021). Operationalizing culturally relevant leadership learning. Information Age Publishing.

Beatty, C. C., Irwin, L., Owen, J. E., Tapia-Fuselier, N., Guthrie, K. L., Cohen-Derr, E., Hassell-Goodman, S., Rocco, M. L., & Yamanaka, A. (2020). A call for centering social identities: Priority 1 of the National Leadership Education Research Agenda 2020–2025. *Journal of Leadership Studies, 14*(3), 39–44. https://doi.org/10.1002/jls.21719

Bertrand Jones, T., Guthrie, K. L., & Osteen, L. (2016). Critical domains of culturally relevant leadership learning: A call to transform leadership programs. In K. L. Guthrie, T. Bertrand Jones, & L. Osteen (Eds.), *Developing culturally relevant leadership learning.* (New Directions for Student Leadership, No. 152, pp. 9–21). Jossey-Bass. https://doi.org/10.1002/yd.20205

Brazill, S. C. (2020). Pedagogical strategies for teaching a multicultural education course: From safe space to brave space for a community of learners. *Educational Research: Theory and Practice, 31*(2), 56–71.

Chunoo, V. S., & Callahan, K. (2017). Pedagogy in action: Teaching culturally relevant leadership. *Journal of Leadership Studies*, *11*(3), 42–47. https://doi.org/10.1002/jls.21544

Chunoo, V. S., & French, G. (2021). Socially just leadership education in action: Applying the culturally relevant leadership learning model. In K. L. Guthrie & V. S. Chunoo (Eds.), *Shifting the mindset: Socially just leadership education* (pp. 207–219). Information Age Publishing.

Chunoo, V. S., Tevis, T., Guthrie, K. L., Norman, S., & Corces-Zimmerman, C. (2020). Evolution and revolution: Social justice and critical theory in leadership education research: Priority 2 of the National Leadership Education Research Agenda 2020–2025. *Journal of Leadership Studies*, *14*(3), 45–49. https://doi.org/10.1002/jls.21713

Dweck, C. S. (2008). *Mindset: The new psychology of success.* Ballantine Books.

Dugan, J. P. (2017). *Leadership theory: Cultivating critical perspectives.* John Wiley & Sons.

Guthrie, K. L., Beatty, C. C., & Wiborg, E. R. (2021). *Engaging in the leadership process: Identity, capacity, and efficacy for college students.* Information Age Publishing.

Guthrie, K. L., Jones, T. B., Osteen, L., & Hu, S. (2013). *Cultivating leader identity and capacity in students from diverse backgrounds: ASHE higher education report, 39: 4.* John Wiley & Sons.

Guthrie, K. L., & Chunoo, V. S. (Eds.). (2018). *Changing the narrative: Socially just leadership education.* Information Age Publishing.

Guthrie, K. L., & Chunoo, V. S. (Eds.). (2021). *Shifting the mindset: Socially just leadership education.* Information Age Publishing.

Guthrie, K. L., & Jenkins, D. M. (2018). *The role of leadership educators: Transforming learning.* Information Age Publishing.

Harper, J., & Kezar, A. (2021). Leadership development for racially minoritized students: An expansion of the social change model of leadership. *Journal of Leadership Education*, *20*(3), 156–169. https://doi.org/10.12806/V20/I3/T2

Hurtado, S., Milem, J., Clayton-Pedersen, A., & Allen, W. (1999). *Enacting diverse learning environments: Improving the climate for racial/ethnic diversity in higher education.* ERIC Clearinghouse on Higher Education. https://eric.ed.gov/?id=ED430514

Komives, S. R., & Sowcik, M. (2020). The status and scope of leadership education in higher education. In M. Sowcik, & S. R. Komives (Eds.), *How academic disciplines approach leadership development* (New Directions for Student Leadership, No. 165, pp. 23–36). https://doi.org/10.1002/yd.20366

Ladson-Billings, G. (1995). Toward a theory of culturally relevant pedagogy. *American Educational Research Journal*, *32*(3), 465–491. https://doi.org/10.3102/00028312032003465

Maia, A. C. (2021). Co-curricular leadership tools: The use of inventories outside of the college classroom. *New Directions for Student Leadership*, *2021*, 77–85. https://doi.org/10.1002/yd.20444

Maia, A. C. (2022a). *Educating culturally relevant leaders: Experiences in leadership identity, capacity, and efficacy development in college students* [Doctoral dissertation, University of South Florida]. https://digitalcommons.usf.edu/etd/9792

Maia, A. C. (2022b). (Un)modeling the way: Reflecting on the complexity of the leadership educator identity for culturally relevant facilitation. *Journal of Leadership Studies*, *16*(3), 28–32. https://doi.org/10.1002/jls.21824

Milem, J. F., Chang, M. J., & Antonio, A. L. (2005). *Making diversity work on campus: A research-based perspective*. Association American Colleges and Universities.

Mitchell, T. D., Museus, S. D., Puente, M., & Ting, M. P. (2023). Reframing leadership for a more just society. *New Directions for Student Leadership*, 2023, 11–22. https://doi.org/10.1002/yd.20537

Mahoney, A. D. (2017). Being at the heart of the matter: Culturally relevant leadership learning, emotions, and storytelling. *Journal of Leadership Studies*, *11*(3), 55–60.

Myers, I. B. (1962). *The Myers-Briggs type indicator: Manual*. Consulting Psychologists Press. https://doi.org/10.1037/14404-000

Osteen, L., Guthrie, K. L., & Bertrand Jones, T. (2016). Leading to transgress: Critical considerations for transforming leadership learning. In K. L. Guthrie, T. Bertrand Jones, & L. Osteen (Eds.), *Developing culturally relevant leadership learning*. (New Directions for Student Leadership, No. 152, pp. 95–106). https://doi.org/10.1002/yd.20212

Owen. J. (2016). Fostering critical reflection: Moving from a service to social justice paradigm. In W. Wagner, & J. M. Pigza, (Eds)., *Leadership development through service-learning* (New Directions for Student Leadership, No. 150, pp. 37–48). Jossey-Bass. https://www.doi.org/10.1002/yd.20169

Prince, B. F., Kozimor-King, M. L., & Steele, J. (2015). An old tool reexamined: Using the Star Power Simulation to teach social inequality. *Teaching Sociology*, *43*(4), 301–309. https://doi.org/10.1177/0092055X15598205

Rath, T. (2007). *StrengthsFinder 2.0*, Gallup Press.

Torres, M. (2019). *Ella creyó que podía, así que lo hizo exploring latina leader identity development through testimonio* [Doctoral dissertation, Florida State University]. ProQuest Dissertations.

Volpe White, J. M. (2018). Service-learning as a pedagogy for socially just leadership education. In K. L. Guthrie & V. S. Chunoo (Eds.), *Changing the narrative: Socially just leadership education* (pp. 291–306). Information Age Publishing.

Volpe White, J. M., & Guthrie, K. L. (2015). Creating a meaningful learning environment: Reflection in leadership education. *Journal of Leadership Education*, *15*(1), 60–75. https://doi.org/1012806/V15/I1/R5

Volpe White, J. M., Guthrie, K. L., & Torres, M. (2019). *Thinking to transform: Reflection in leadership learning*. Information Age Publishing.

CHAPTER 6

TROUBLING BOUNDARIES TO INTEGRATE SOCIAL JUSTICE IN LEADERSHIP EDUCATION PRACTICE

Lauren N. Irwin

Increasingly, higher education institutions offer plans, goals, and initiatives to further diversity, equity, inclusion, and social justice (DEISJ). These efforts have also gained momentum in leadership education spaces—recognizing how leadership education theory and practice have neglected critical considerations of identity and power for too long (e.g., Dugan, 2017; Dugan & Leonette, 2021; Guthrie & Chunoo, 2018). However, DEISJ commitments often allude to action without requiring meaningful change (Ahmed, 2012; Squire et al., 2019).

The growth in critical, socially-just, culturally-relevant, and liberatory leadership education scholarship (e.g., Beatty et al., 2021; Chunoo et al., 2019; Guthrie et al., 2013; Guthrie & Chunoo, 2018; Mahoney, 2016; Pendakur & Furr, 2016) urges leadership educators to integrate explorations of and content about oppressive systems, social identities, and social change. Such approaches necessitate pedagogical and theoretical changes, as normative leadership tools and theories often discuss difference in power-evasive and shallow ways (Irwin & Posselt, 2022; Museus et al., 2017). Despite the rise of scholarship and content about socially-just approaches to leadership education, scholarship demonstrates that dominant norms—which largely neglect power and social justice—persist in practice (Irwin,

Committing to Action: Socially Just Leadership Educations, pp. 63–74
Copyright © 2025 by Information Age Publishing
www.infoagepub.com
All rights of reproduction in any form reserved.

2021). Some leadership educators face personal and organizational resistance to socially-just approaches to leadership education (Duran et al., 2022), while others feel unsure about how to translate critical tools into practice (Irwin, 2021). These shortcomings, coupled with the overwhelming demographic Whiteness of leadership educators (Jenkins & Owen, 2016), illustrate a likely gulf between present leadership education efforts and those needed to foster inclusive leadership education environments for marginalized students and ensure that colleges are graduating leaders who are equipped to lead positive social change and contribute to healthy and diverse democracies.

BOUNDARY TRANSGRESSION AND MAINTENANCE

One possible explanation for the challenges leadership educators face in implementing socially-just approaches in practice is that existing individual and organizational beliefs about leadership and social justice bifurcate rather than integrate these concepts. Leadership educators' work is complex and multifaceted—bridging pedagogical, theoretical, and procedural knowledge to bear on educational environments. Further, many leadership educators have substantial agency in determining the content and process of leadership education efforts (Guthrie & Jenkins, 2018). Thus, it is important to consider how leadership educators maintain or transgress socially constructed boundaries between leadership and DEISJ.

Higher education scholars have leveraged social and cultural perspectives on boundaries to investigate barriers to equity in contexts like physics graduate education (Posselt et al., 2017). People regularly create boundaries to classify people, things, and experiences—categories are essential for making sense of the world. However, these distinctions are consequential and powerfully influence what and how things are seen as similar or distinct. Often, these symbolic distinctions are not value-neutral but laden with cultural valuations of worth, status, and power (Lamont & Molnár, 2002). Agreed-upon symbolic boundaries—like conceptualizations of intelligence, sociability, and leadership—pattern social interaction in consequential ways. Understanding organizational actors' shared symbolic boundaries can illuminate norms, which might be challenged or strengthened in pursuit of inclusion (Lamont & Molnár, 2002; Posselt et al., 2017). As such, this chapter draws on data from a critical comparative qualitative case study of racialization and Whiteness in leadership education programs (LEPs) to examine how two campus contexts and the leadership programs within them illustrate the relationship between symbolic boundaries and socially-just approaches to leadership education.

CONTEXT AND DATA SOURCES

The examples featured in this chapter are drawn from a larger critical comparative case study (Pasque et al., 2017; Stake, 2005) of racialization and Whiteness in student leadership education efforts across three diverse campus contexts (see: Irwin, 2023). By bounding institutions as cases, I analyzed how institutional contexts shaped leadership efforts broadly, with attention to racialization and Whiteness. I selected institutions with missions committed to facilitating holistic student development, including preparing students as citizens and leaders. Further, I chose institutions that (1) espoused a commitment to DEISJ and (2) had a co-curricular LEP that was at least 5 years old. Further, I focused on co-curricular or hybrid LEPs, as they are generally designed to serve all students rather than students in specific academic disciplines. I also sought variation in institutional type (e.g., Minority-Serving Institutions [MSIs], Carnegie classification), geographic location, and approaches to LEP practice (e.g., centering of social justice). Since these criteria alone would apply to many institutions, I used multiple strategies to select cases that are explained in detail in the full study description (Irwin, 2023). For this chapter, I draw on data from two of the three campuses—both large public universities with extremely high research activity. Though both campuses had long-standing LEPs, their differing contexts, goals, and approaches shaped how social justice was integrated.

Data consist of 36 university and program documents and websites; 40 interviews with staff, senior administrators, and students; and observations of 10 staff meetings and leadership workshops and activities. In examining these data sources and considering how leadership educators and LEPs replicated and/or resisted Whiteness in practice, I noticed two LEPs communicated starkly different beliefs about the relationship between leadership and DEISJ (Irwin, 2023). These boundaries—or lack thereof—shaped how DEISJ (did not) inform practice. Before detailing how these boundaries manifested, I describe each campus and LEP context.

Eastern Public University

Eastern Public University (EPU) is a large, public, historically and predominantly White, four-year research institution in the United States' east coast. The Division of Student Affairs houses EPU's longstanding and nationally recognized LEP program. The LEP uses leadership models that center power alongside traditional models. EPU's LEP staff is all White, which led one staff member to share, "We are a lily-White staff, and we worry about why we can't retain our Students of Color. Well, are we saying leaders have to be White?" LEP staff value research-informed leadership praxis, which has caused challenges in recruiting candidates for open roles who "fit" their office's values. EPU's LEP also charges students to participate. LEP offers scholarships and fundraising opportunities to students to offset program costs, and is cultivating donor relationships to expand these resources.

Western Public University

Western Public University (WPU) is a large, non-selective, public, urban, four-year historically White institution in the western United States that recently gained R1 status. WPU is designated as a Hispanic-Serving Institution (HSI) and Asian American Native American and Pacific Islander-Serving Institution (AANAPISI). Unfortunately, WPU has experienced a near-constant state of turnover and organizational change in recent years. WPU's LEP is housed in the Division of Student Affairs and encompasses service-learning, scholarship programs, basic needs resources, voter engagement, and leadership education. WPU's LEP staff are the most diverse of the three campuses—in terms of academic backgrounds and racial, gender, and sexuality identities. A focus on social justice unites all LEP programs. All LEP programs are free. However, LEP is "severely understaffed" with multiple vacancies and temporary staff. Further, WPU's LEP increasingly relies on grant funding to sustain its services—especially basic needs and student support services. While several grants have been funded, LEP staff seek donations and partnerships to fund services once the grant funding ends.

ILLUSTRATING BOUNDARIES IN LEADERSHIP EDUCATION PRACTICE

Preserving Boundaries at EPU

EPU's LEP website referenced multiple leadership models that undergird their programs, including the social change model of leadership development (Komives & Wagner, 2016) and the social action, leadership, and transformation model (SALT; Museus et al., 2017)—which explicitly centers power and minoritized communities in the leadership process. EPU's LEP website also indicates that diversity, equity, and inclusion are a core program competencies. However, connections to DEISJ and the SALT model are not mentioned elsewhere.

Across interviews, LEP staff communicated a consistent message: leadership and DEISJ are distinct concepts and competencies. Dana, a White woman and LEP staff member, explained, "We are a leadership program that has social justice included. I will say it is not our number one focus... We have social justice implications in the work that we're doing, but I don't necessarily teach about it." Michael, a White man and LEP staff member shared similar sentiments:

> Social justice needs to be a part of [leadership education], but it doesn't need to be the whole of our program ... I don't want to have to only be a social justice leadership program. In my view, it's a violin in the orchestra that has a solo and needs to have a solo and it's a beautiful solo, but the violin is not the entire orchestra.

Further, Mindy, a White woman, and the newest LEP staff member, attributed her rigid distinction between DEISJ and leadership to leadership's supposed neutrality:

> I think social justice, community engagement, leadership, it all goes together. But using words like social justice would inevitably pigeonhole yourself into a DEI [program].... [And it] inherently alienates folks who vehemently know they don't want to be a part of social justice. They don't want to be part of DEI efforts. Leadership is not liberal. It's not conservative. It's not political. Leadership is leadership.

Although many EPU LEP staff sought to express their appreciation for DEISJ as one aspect of leadership, their fervent focus on distinguishing between leadership and DEISJ translated to leadership offerings that generally neglected DEISJ content in favor of elevating traditional leadership notions. Next, I share several examples to illustrate how these boundaries endured.

Maintaining Boundaries in Practice

Staff's ardent boundaries between leadership and DEISJ powerfully shaped LEP's content and approach. EPU's LEP offered a single DEISJ workshop as one of many options in their introductory program—making DEISJ an optional "checkbox." In advanced LEP components, where DEISJ was supposedly integrated throughout, staff like Dana admitted they "don't necessarily teach [DEISJ]." Dana shared more about the limitations of their checkbox approach, "There is a diversity and inclusion workshop requirement, so [students] do have to attend at least one. We always encourage them to attend more." Michael confirmed this reality, "[DEISJ is a] checkbox.... We partner with [diversity office] to provide workshops, but we also have a myriad of other topics that can count for that. Our students aren't getting a comprehensive view of identity, intersecting identities, privilege and oppression." Staff recognized that a checkbox approach resulted in programming that largely marginalized DEISJ content.

Ironically, Jim, a White man and senior EPU administrator, believed DEISJ was interwoven much more intentionally than LEP staff did, sharing: "[Social justice] is interwoven throughout the [program]....They're constantly revisiting it through their conversations, through the reflection, through the core values of the program." June, a Black queer man who worked in the campus diversity office, was a newer LEP partner who was now frequently tapped to facilitate LEP's DEISJ workshop. June shared, "I keep asking [Dana] if there is a way that we can make these [DESIJ] workshops required and consistent ... I would like to see [DEISJ] be required for any program leadership program." Despite broader messaging that purported to value DEISJ, those responsible for facilitating this content recognized how little DEISJ was considered or integrated across LEP programs.

Further, staff recognized that their all-White office sent a problematic message about diversity. During data collection, EPU's LEP was hiring a new staff member and expressed a desire to hire a person of color. However, they struggled to identify and recruit candidates with the leadership expertise they felt was necessary. Ultimately, they hired another White woman—Mindy. I interviewed Mindy a month after she started and asked about her leadership background. She shared, "To be perfectly honest, the most amount of leadership readings I have done have been from Brené Brown ... I obviously know Tuckman and understand the leadership challenge and all those basics. But yeah, I'm not well versed in [leadership theory]." EPU LEP staff constructed a narrative that their office remained White because they focused on hiring candidates with deep theoretical leadership expertise but ultimately hired somebody who was both White and lacked expertise. LEP staff's enduring boundaries, which emphasized the distinction between leadership and DEISJ, justified efforts that neglected DEISJ in hiring and leadership practice.

Weakening Boundaries at WPU

In contrast, WPU's LEP website consistently referenced social justice and systemic change, noting that their programs' primary goal was to help students "influence systems while pursuing social justice." Several concepts undergirded the unit's work, including identity development, systems literacy, and criticality. These concepts were regularly referenced by staff. Further, WPU's HSI and AANAPISI status meant the LEP served more racially minoritized students than EPU's, and WPU's LEP included a wider array of functional areas, including service programs, basic needs services, and other supports for minoritized students. Although many LEP staff agreed there was "more work to be done" to support minoritized students, staff often went beyond institutional approaches that focused only on racial diversity by integrating social justice, systems, and leadership.

WPU students challenged LEP staff to think differently about DEISJ and leadership. Adam, a White man and LEP staff member, explained:

> We couldn't just slap a leadership workshop on a poster and expect students to show up. There were very real barriers there and different lived experiences. We've been shifting so that our portfolio of very explicit leadership development initiatives has morphed into a primary focus around community challenges, community capacity building, and community engagement. It's a fundamental reorientation in terms of how we're thinking about meaningful leadership development.

As a result, LEP's initiatives evolved. In discussing these changes, I asked Adam how he reconciled LEP's approach alongside perspectives that distinguish between leadership and DEISJ. He replied:

> I would call that hogwash…. If I were to apply a more compartmentalized lens on the operations of our office and a traditional understanding of what leadership development looks like, we would have very few offerings, and not a lot of programming would fall under that traditional [leadership] label. But I think we do a hell of a lot.

In addition to contributing to meaningful leadership development, Ash, a Latina staff member, reflected on how LEP's evolution made them different from many other WPU units that focused simply on diversity. Ash explained:

> We have social justice and racial equity built into [our values].… Then we realized we need to be more intentional. What is our programming doing? How are we building identity? How are we making sure racial and social justice are coming into it? Those core threads kind of lead a lot of the programming.

However, Daniel, a Latino LEP staff member, felt it was important to emphasize the distinction between service and social justice, explaining, "We like to differentiate between service and social justice. Service is like a band-aid. Social justice would be actually addressing it in the long run." Esperanza, a Latina LEP staff member, shared how this approach manifested in her work:

I want my students to be fully aware that the disparities [community] organizations are addressing are being caused by systemic inequities. And systems of privilege and oppression that continue to exist and how to interrupt that. [We] try to go into anti-racism, but of course, do it in a way that's for first-year scholars. And then after that, we go into the leadership aspect and service in terms of really introducing [students] to a couple of models so that social change doesn't seem so overwhelming. Using the social change wheel, servant leadership, just so [students] are aware that they're all leaders in their own way, but there's different ways to lead.

To support these aims, Esperanza and other LEP staff talked at length about using theories and perspectives, like Community Cultural Wealth and intersectionality, in their programming. Sarah, a White woman and LEP staff member, explained that these critical perspectives help her teach students "critical thinking" while balancing "self-work" and "systems" work.

DESIJ as a Boundary Spanning Competence

Unlike EPU, many WPU LEP staff members were hired because of their DEISJ knowledge, commitments, and experiences. Further, several staff members mentioned engaging in ongoing learning as a team. Wes, a White nonbinary staff member, described LEP's approach:

[During meetings] we all take turns [doing] an activity, having a conversation, or reading an article. More often than not, it's social justice aligned, and that's where anti-racism comes in. I think part of that is our [office leaders] really taking the lead to make sure that that's an ongoing value. But I think we're all committed to this work.

Wes also explained that many LEP staff members held minoritized identities, which increased their personal investment in DEISJ work. Ash, a Latina LEP staff member, also emphasized staff members' DEISJ commitments:

[LEP staff are] making sure social justice and equity are always at the top of [our work]. And making sure that our programming is doing the best for our student population and that we're really bringing these topics. Because we might not see that on campus in other offices because they feel it's not their job.

WPU LEP's staff were more diverse than EPU's—in terms of professional training and racial, gender, and sexuality identities. WPU LEP staff were also more likely to center DEISJ in discussions of leadership. Further, they regularly erased distinctions between leadership and social justice competencies and leadership, service, and social justice programming. WPU's student and LEP staff diversity may contribute to their efforts to erase boundaries between leadership and DEISJ. Regardless, WPU's LEP offerings more thoroughly integrated DEISJ.

RECOMMENDATIONS

Findings illustrated how individual and organizational boundaries related to leadership and DEISJ shaped practice. From these findings, I offer several recommendations. First, LEPs and leadership educator hiring committees should critically examine how they construct job postings and evaluate candidate qualifications. By recognizing that leadership theories and perspectives can be learned—a key value that informs the leadership education field (Owen, 2011)—committees can prioritize interviewing candidates with demonstrated DEISJ experience who express enthusiasm for leadership. To support these efforts, search committees should include key translators, like campus partners invested in DEISJ work, who can help identify or bridge connections between leadership and DEISJ. Additionally, staff should consider what transferable skills and knowledge are necessary for immediate success in the role (e.g., facilitation experience, supervision experience, event planning), identify what skills or knowledge might be presently lacking in their office, and discuss existing conceptualizations of leaders and leadership. These conversations will help illuminate LEP needs and likely expand shared understandings of merit and fit for open LEP roles.

Second, by questioning long-held assumptions about what constitutes leadership, LEPs can expand the repertoire of tools they leverage and share with students. LEPs might consider using Yosso's (2005) community cultural wealth model paired with Harper and Kezar's (2021) leadership model for racially minoritized students to invite a wider array of lived experiences and conceptions of leadership. In support of these efforts, LEPs can invite campus and community collaborators as equal partners in erasing distinctions between leadership and DEISJ. This erasure would likely result in blurred boundaries between social justice, leadership, advocacy, organizing, service, and community engagement efforts, much like at WPU. LEPs might then attract a wider array of interested students while organically infusing DEISJ across programmatic offerings.

Finally, given the increased hostility toward higher education DEISJ initiatives (e.g., The Chronicle of Higher Education, 2023), LEPs that integrate DEISJ can function as important spaces for shielding campus DEISJ efforts from scrutiny. Since leadership is a polysemous term that rarely centers on social justice (e.g., Irwin et al., 2023), leadership offices may be less likely to appear on the radar of external stakeholders who critique DEISJ efforts. Thus, if staff are committed to revising symbolic boundaries that distinguish leadership and DEISJ, they may effectively find ways to ensure DEISJ work can continue, despite increased external scrutiny. To foster equity and inclusion, LEPs and leadership educators must erase artificial boundaries between DEISJ and leadership.

REFERENCES

Ahmed, S. (2012). *On being included: Racism and diversity in institutional life.* Duke University Press.

Beatty, C. C., Manning-Ouellette, A., & Wiborg, E. R. (2021). Addressing White fragility in leadership education. In K. L. Guthrie & V. S. Chunoo (Eds.), *Shifting the mindset: Socially just leadership education* (pp. 257–270). Information Age Publishing.

Chunoo, V. S., Beatty, C. C., & Gruver, M. D. (2019). Leadership educator as social justice educator. In K. L. Priest, & D. M. Jenkins (Eds.), *Becoming and being a leadership educator* (New Directions for Student Leadership, No. 164, pp. 87–103). https://doi.org/10.1002/yd.20360

Dugan, J. P. (2017). *Leadership theory: Cultivating critical perspectives.* John Wiley & Sons.

Dugan, J. P., & Leonette, H. (2021). The complicit omission: Leadership development's radical silence on equity. *Journal of College Student Development, 62*(3), 379–382. https://doi.org/10.1353/csd.2021.0030

Duran, A., Bitton, A. L., & Barnes, A. C. (2022). Mobilizing critical perspectives on leadership: Narratives of early-career professionals' self-efficacy in translating leadership theory to practice. *College Student Affairs Journal, 40*(2), 33–46. https://doi.org/10.1353/csj.2022.0013

Guthrie, K. L., Bertrand Jones, T., Osteen, L., & Hu, S. (2013). *Cultivating leader identity and capacity in students from diverse backgrounds.* ASHE Higher Education Report, 39(4). John Wiley & Sons.

Guthrie, K. L., & Chunoo, V. S. (Eds.). (2018). *Changing the narrative: Socially just leadership education.* Information Age Publishing.

Guthrie, K. L., & Jenkins, D. M. (2018). *The role of leadership educators: Transforming learning.* Information Age Publishing.

Harper, J., & Kezar, A. (2021). Leadership development for racially minoritized students: An expansion of the social change model of leadership. *Journal of Leadership Education, 20*(3), 156–166. https://doi.org/10.12806/v20/i3/t2

Irwin, L. N. (2023). *Racialization and Whiteness in college student leadership education efforts.* [Doctoral dissertation, University of Iowa].

Irwin, L. N. (2021). Student affairs leadership educators' negotiations of racialized legitimacy. *Journal of Leadership Education, 20*(4), 132–151. https://doi.org/10.12806/v20/i4/r10

Irwin, L. N., & Posselt, J. R. (2022). A critical discourse analysis of mainstream college student leadership models. *Journal of Leadership Education, 21*(4), 76–97. https://doi.org/10.12806/v21/i4/r1

Irwin, L. N., Reynolds., D. J., Bitton, A. L., Hassell-Goodman, S., Teig, T., & Tapia-Fuselier, N. (2023). Insights from a critical qualitative inquiry in leadership scholarship. In S. R. Komives & J. E. Owen (Eds.), *A research agenda for learning and developing leadership in higher education* (pp. 253–270). Edward Elgar.

Jenkins, D. M., & Owen, J. E. (2016). Who teaches leadership? A comparative analysis of faculty and student affairs leadership educators and implications for leadership learning. *Journal of Leadership Education, 15*(2), 98–113. https://doi.org/10.12806/v15/i2/r1

Komives, S. R., & Wagner, W. E. (2016). *Leadership for a better world: Understanding the social change model of leadership development.* John Wiley & Sons.

Lamont, M., & Molnár, V. (2002). The study of boundaries in the social sciences. *Annual Review of Sociology, 28,* 167–195.

Mahoney, A. D. (2016). Culturally responsive integrative learning environments: A critical displacement approach. In K. Guthrie, T. Bertrand Jones, & L. Osteen (Eds.), *Developing culturally relevant leadership learning* (New Directions for Student Leadership, No. 152, pp. 47–59). https://doi.org/10.1002/yd.20208

Museus, S., Lee, N., Calhoun, K., Sánchez-Parkinson, L., & Ting, M. (2017). The social action, leadership, and transformation (SALT) model. *National Center for Institutional Diversity and National Institute for Transformation and Equity.* https://lsa.umich. edu/content/dam/ncid-assets/nciddocuments/Museus% 20et% 20al, 20.

Owen, J. E. (2011). Considerations of student learning in leadership. In S. R. Komives, J. P. Dugan, J. E. Owen, C. Slack, W. Wagner, & Associates (Eds.), *The handbook for student leadership development* (2nd ed., pp. 85–108). Jossey-Bass.

Pasque, P. A., Khader, L. M., & Still, C. (2017). Critical case study as an imperative for organizational activism and institutional change: Critical methodologies in higher education organization research. In P. A. Pasque & V. M. Lechuga (Eds.), *Qualitative inquiry in higher education organization and policy research* (pp. 75–92). Routledge.

Pendakur, V., & Furr, S. C. (2016). Critical leadership pedagogy: Engaging power, identity, and culture in leadership education for college students of color. In K. L. Guthrie, & L. Osteen (Eds.), *Reclaiming higher education's purpose in leadership development* (New Directions for Higher Education, No. 174, pp. 45–55). https://doi.org/10.1002/he.20188

Posselt, J., Reyes, K. A., Slay, K. A., Kamimura, A., & Porter, K. A. (2017). Equity efforts as boundary work: How symbolic and social boundaries shape access and inclusion in graduate education. *Teachers College Record, 119,* 1–38. https://doi.org/10.1177/016146811711901003

Squire, D., Nicolazzo, Z., & Perez, R. J. (2019). Institutional response as non-performative: What university communications (don't) say about movements toward justice. *The Review of Higher Education, 42*(5), 109–122. https://doi.org/10.1353/rhe.2019.0047_

Stake, R. E. (2005). Qualitative case studies. In N. K. Denzin & Y. S. Lincoln (Eds.), *Handbook of Qualitative Research* (pp. 443–462). SAGE.

The Chronicle of Higher Education. (2023, July 14). *DEI legislation tracker.* https://www.chronicle.com/article/here-are-the-states-where-lawmakers-are-seeking-to-ban-colleges-dei-efforts

Yosso, T. J. (2005). Whose culture has capital? A critical race theory discussion of community cultural wealth. *Race, ethnicity, and education, 8*(1), 69–91.

CHAPTER 7

WHAT CAN WE KNOW AND HOW DO WE FIND IT?

A Guide to Systematic Inquiry in Leadership Education

Vivechkanand S. Chunoo

In the 1986 video game *The Legend of Zelda*, the hero Link is offered his first weapon with the warning, "It's dangerous to go alone. Take this!" (Nintendo, 1986). The same could said to those of us seeking to engage (or forced into engaging with) systematic inquiry in leadership education. By *systematic inquiry*, I am referring to leadership education research, assessment, and/or evaluation projects. To help others not "go alone" on what could be an otherwise dangerous journey ahead unarmed, the following chapter highlights key issues in leadership education inquiry, offers an example of a completed project, and attempts to motivate others to develop their own initiatives. While an exhaustive review of research methods and/or program evaluation and assessment is beyond the scope of a single chapter, the ideas showcased here should be ample to get any nascent inquiry moving in the right direction. Additionally, it may help course correct those endeavors which might have come a bit unmoored. Take this with you as you embark on deeply examining how social justice and leadership education can be rigorously and simultaneously pursued in your own work.

Committing to Action: Socially Just Leadership Educations, pp. 75–91
Copyright © 2025 by Information Age Publishing
www.infoagepub.com

WHAT IS LEADERSHIP EDUCATION INQUIRY?

To best understand the broad landscape of research, assessment, and evaluation in leadership education, we first need to unpack the general philosophies of leadership inquiry, as well as examine the assumptions about knowledge underlying these philosophies. Next, it would be to our benefit to consider issues of rigor and relevance when conducting systematic inquiries while acknowledging the challenges inherent to studying leadership. Finally, as you consider your own projects, we are forced to make decisions about what to focus on and why.

Fundamental Concepts in Inquiry

Beginning the processes of research, assessment, and evaluation often includes a disambiguation of terms. For our purposes, *research* refers to the application of specific data collection methods and analytic procedures to produce results and findings to better understand the natural or social world (Creswell, 2014). *Assessment* is the gathering of information that may be used to make future decisions (Rossman & Wilson, 1895). Subsequently, *evaluation* is the decision-making process applied to assessment data (Lincoln & Guba, 1986). While there is often a dividing line among forms of systematic inquiry (research on one side; assessment and evaluation on the other), all forms are important to the continual evolution of our craft. Often the choice of which strategies best fit any given situation depends on how we intend on using the information obtained; evaluation and assessment are generally leveraged for change proximal to the investigator whereas research is usually meant to inform a more distal audience, or the community of scholars at large (Sechrest & Sidana, 1985). Throughout this chapter, the term *systemic inquiry* will be used to refer to research, assessment, and evaluation collectively without distinction among them, although important differences do exist.

Underlying any great systemic inquiry project is some form of organization represented by one or more theories. Theories are typically either implicit (informal) or explicit (formal). *Implicit, also referred to as informal or working, theory* is generally a loosely aggregated set of beliefs or assumptions we carry with us through our work. (Green et al., 1989). They are usually founded on personal beliefs and/or individual experiences. *Explicit theories*, by comparison, are often well-organized sets of philosophies, constructs, or ideas which coherently allow us to describe, explain, and/or predict natural or social phenomena, and have a specific name or title. (English & Anderson, 1995). While formal theories usually lend themselves to empirical testing, thereby making them great candidates for systemic inquiry projects, informal theories can also serve this purpose.

In making decisions about the nature of your inquiry project, and the theories that might form its foundations, it may be helpful to establish the purpose behind your project. In other words, what do you hope to accomplish by embarking on this journey? Some of us hope to change the entire field of leadership education toward specific outcomes or processes. Others among us are trying to demonstrate our programs, classes, and other initiatives deserve another round of funding. There may be a few who are trying to construct a thesis or dissertation to obtain an advanced degree. Regardless of your motivation, clarity around what you intend to discover, what you hope to find, and what you are fearful of learning absolutely serves as guiding lights through these processes.

Moving beyond purpose, carefully crafted questions are the engine of systematic inquiry. Unfortunately, good inquiry questions are seldom created overnight. The process of crafting such questions follows an iterative cycle—drafting language, refining based on purpose, and attempting to match methods to intended outcomes (Johnson et al., 2007). This can be challenging to accomplish alone; therefore, enlist others to help! Assistance can come from supervisors or mentors, co-workers and colleagues, even your students and/or prospective participants. When seeking feedback from others, you may feel as though you must represent everyone's feedback in your final project. However, this is your inquiry, not theirs. Seek just enough feedback to make your ideas better without relinquishing ownership of the entire enterprise.

Identity and Ethical Matters in Leadership Inquiry

The personal, professional, and social identities of investigators influence the "how" and "why" of their inquiry projects. This is no less true in leadership education research, assessment, and evaluation given the relative newness of the field (as compared to other social sciences), and the diversity of scholars from both identity and academic perspectives. The common refrain of "all research is me-search" could reasonably be accompanied by "all evaluation is me-valuation" and "all assessment is I-sessment." Whether you are embarking on your first project, or are an already accomplished investigator, regular and rigorous reflection on the impact of our identities on our work can only improve our positionality and our relationship with our projects.

Another subtle shaper of our work is our orientation around ethics and morals. While an exhaustive discussion of both (or either) is beyond the scope of this chapter, I encourage readers to consider ethics as the study of how to decide what is "Right" and "Wrong," while morals are the applications of those decision-making paradigms (i.e., *doing* what is right; *avoiding* what is wrong). Both ethics and morals enjoy long and storied histories, and include perspectives such as utilitarianism, libertarianism, justice-as-fairness, and various categorical imperatives, to name a few. It is less important for an investigator to pick a *specific* moral perspective or ethical code in systematic inquiry, however; it is of great importance to consistently *apply* the one selected. Many, if not most share emphasis in varying degrees on minimizing harm, protecting individual autonomy, and upholding personal and collective protections. Each of these reflects a core ethical priority in leadership education inquiry.

When conducting research, especially the type that might involve review by a human subject protections committee, high standards for the treatment of participants must be met. However, there is very little reason why these standards could not be applied in assessment/evaluation projects as well. The three highest standards for the ethical treatment of participants include: (1) respect for persons and their autonomy; (2) the reasonable expectation of beneficence of the project and its goals; and (3) fair treatment (also referred to as justice in some contexts). These principles manifest in implements such as informed consent, truthfulness by the investigator, the ability to withdraw from an inquiry project without negative consequences, reasonable protections from foreseeable dangers, and privacy safeguards. While these standards and practices govern most research projects, any systematic inquiry in leadership education is strengthened by adhering to them.

What Might Already Be Known?: Conducting Literature Reviews

Literature reviews in systematic inquiry represent a unique paradox. On one hand, it is incredibly helpful to know what our field has already discovered about itself; however, if an abundance of scholarly and empirical writing already exists on your topic, it becomes more difficult to differentiate your project from what might already be known! Somewhere between a plethora of sources and a dearth of references is exactly what we are looking for. While it can be difficult to situate a project in precisely the middle of these two extremes, literature reviews in research, assessment, and evaluation projects illustrate the value of our inquiries, provide a theoretical (and empirical) basis for our work, assist in refining our methods, and often serve as framing tools for our data, information, conclusions, and implications. Thankfully, there are more tools and resources than ever to make composing literature reviews as streamlined as possible.

A variety of sources can be used to compile a literature review. Scholarly and empirical research articles form the heart of many reviews, especially among thesis and dissertation writers. Alongside these, books and book chapters are also helpful, especially in relationship to theoretical underpinnings and conceptual frameworks. However, technical reports and manuals, conference presentations, practice articles, and research-in-brief citations are often overlooked, especially in assessment and evaluation projects. Even personal communications, such as meeting notes, emails, and public lectures, can inform our ideas and help shape our projects. Nearly any source of knowledge can find its way into our thinking and planning, and to the extent they find their way into our writing and presenting, should be attributed as appropriate.

Regardless of the nature of our sources, they can be instrumental in shaping both the content and the process of the literature review itself. Every new piece of knowledge we encounter can change our thinking about the nature of our problem, the way we conceptualize the members of our population, or perspectives through which we see either (or both). One hazard in reviewing literature is confronting our own confirmation biases; we are more likely to include information we already agree with, and less likely to incorporate data that refutes our thinking. The very contradictions we uncover in our search for what is already known can make for some of the most compelling sections should we be willing and able to embrace the dissonance it creates for us. In turn, reflecting for our audience the best of what is already known—not just what we agree with, adds to our credibility and the integrity of our inquiry.

Our sources provide more than information and data, however. Great literature reviews, like the ones you will no doubt encounter, tell great stories. Not very many of us may have been English majors, but any of us can recognize a powerful narrative when we read one. Building such narratives into our own writing and presenting helps bring what could otherwise be a dry and boring list of facts to life. As you compile a list of sources for any project, I recommend having a separate repository of well-written studies (regardless of topic) to read and reread for inspiration on crafting your own narratives. Not many scholars review literature for fun, but those who do are well-served by it.

One of the biggest challenges of reviewing sources for inquiry projects is staying organized. A variety of strategies and tools exists, and the selection of the right one for you can be a daunting task. While you may choose to organize your sources by-hand (e.g., printing, annotating, and maintaining physical copies), the advent of technological organization tools can be more efficient under the right circumstances. Citation/reference management software has become an entire cottage industry to support academic and scholarly endeavors, and there are no shortages of options in this space.

Some scholars even use qualitative data analysis programs to sort and organize their sources. Regardless of your choice, I suggest making one early in your project and sticking to it consistently.

Quantitative Approaches to Inquiry

Many inquiry questions require the analysis of data and information as expressed in numbers to obtain answers. Such *quantitative designs*, in addition to a research question, rely on various forms of *hypotheses* (or educated guesses on what may or may not be found among those data), and a series of *independent and dependent variables*. When one group in a sample remains 'untouched' or unaltered by the investigator, it can be used as a *control group*; comparing a control group to one or more experimental groups is one hallmark of a true *experimental design* study. However, randomly assigning population and/or sample members to control and/or experimental groups may not always be feasible (or ethical), and therefore, many systematic inquiries into leadership education rely on near experimental or *quasi-experimental* designs. While many projects are interested in producing evidence of *causal* relationships (e.g., the effect of our program, workshop, event, etc. is meaningful and positive change), most are only able to generate proof of *correlational* (i.e., when X changes, Y also changes in a predictable manner) *relationships*. Regardless of your specific choices, the highest quality quantitative inquiries align inquiry questions with hypotheses, the selection of sample members, the variables chosen, the analytic procedures applied, the conclusions drawn from those analyses, and the explanations of the implications of those conclusions.

Returning to the topic of "the variables chosen" for a moment, every quantitative investigator must decide how they are going to measure their markers of interest. The best measurement instruments are those that have demonstrated a high capacity for *reliability* (consistent results over long periods of retesting) and *validity* (the tool measures what it intends to). Before embarking on your inquiry project, you may have noticed in your literature review how the same (or similar) measurement instruments have been repeatedly used. That is a fairly clear sign it, or they, might have utility in your project. Alternatively, you may not see a clear use pattern among others' projects, meaning you may need to create your own. While home-grown instruments can be adapted for use in your local context, additional statistical testing (like the type described in the example study below) may be needed to determine how reliable and valid it is. These issues of psycho-metric soundness are particularly salient when working with *self-report data*, as peoples' perceptions of themselves, their opinions, and their actions (among other aspects) are subject to well-documented forms of bias (for more information, see: Donaldson & Grant-Vallone, 2002). Unfortunately, it is often these necessarily flawed accounts that we are most interested in, which requires us to acknowledge and address the limitations of our measurement instruments in quantitative systematic inquiries.

Attendant to data collection choices, data analysis decisions must also be made. Depending on the metrics of interest, most projects will require us to report the total number of people in our sample, a *frequency analysis* of how many of those people aggregate into meaningful categories (e.g., numbers of people by race/ethnicity, sex/gender, year in school, years of experience, GPA, etc.), as well as the range of the outcome(s) of interest and any important measures of central tendency, such as arithmetic averages (*means*), midpoints (*medians*), and/or the most frequently offered answers (*modes*). Such *descriptive statistics* can help us communicate the nature of our results to an audience who is not as familiar with the data, inquiry questions, or participants as we are. However, most projects are interested in answering questions beyond mere demographics, ranges, and averages; thus, *inferential statistical analyses* are often also required.

The specific inferential analyses applied should be selected to both answer the inquiry question(s) and match the type of data collected. Some of your options include tests to compare individual members to the group within which they belong (*z-test*), comparisons of whole samples to a zero measurement (*one-sample t-test*), comparisons of a whole group to another completely different group with no overlapping members (*independent samples t-test*); comparisons of a whole group to another somewhat similar group with potentially overlapping members, such as in a pre-/post- design (*dependent samples t-test*), comparisons of central tendency across more than two groups (*analysis of variance or ANOVA*), systematic relationships between continuous variable (*correlation*), and causal relationships among continuous variables (*linear modeling*). While more inferential statistical tests exist beyond this list, the examples above are useful starting points to plan your inquiry and will likely reflect the efforts used in other studies, technical reports, and/or conference presentations from your grounding literature.

Qualitative Approaches to Inquiry

Despite their utility, not all inquiries are best addressed using quantitative approaches. Some require the analysis of data and information as expressed in forms other than numbers to obtain answers. Just like their numerically-driven brethren, such *qualitative approaches* to inquiry adhere to specific standards of quality, reflect their own unique structures and designs, and come with distinct limitations.

Rosch et al. (2023) helpfully provided a list of *eight standards of quality* in qualitative inquiry. Table 7.1 highlights their list as well as some key indicators by which each standard may be satisfied.

Table 7.1

Eight Standards of Quality in Qualitative Inquiry

#	Description of Standard:	Key Indicator(s):
1	The inquiry components are aligned	Inquiry questions follow naturally from problem statements and/or theoretical/conceptual frameworks.
2	The inquiry topic is significant	The project centers issues that are specific, measurable, attainable, and relevant to the population studied, or lead to significant change.
3	The inquiry assumptions are clear	The investigator(s) have made plain their values and beliefs related to the project as well as describe any shortcomings of their chosen approach.
4	The methods are appropriately implemented	The investigators have followed one or more traditions in systematic inquiry as closely as reasonable to other, similar projects. In the (rare) cases of newer methods, the exact procedure followed is described in ways others can mimic in the future.
5	The data collection procedures are appropriate	Investigators pursue as rigorous a data collection protocol as possible; rich, deep, or thick data is collected by following the stated data collection plan.
6	The data analysis procedures are appropriate	Data is thoroughly examined using analytic approaches matched to both the inquiry questions and the shape/form of the information collected. Transparent steps are taken to improve investigator trustworthiness and credibility (Miles et al., 2018).
7	The findings contribute new and significant knowledge	Conclusions and statements of impact add to extant body of knowledge already possessed on the topic and/or shift how other, future inquiries (and/or practice; and/or policy; etc.) take shape.
8	The project is conducted ethically	Ethical guidelines for inquiry are followed in every step. Investigators may seek internal and/or external review of their efforts to ensure ethical integrity. In the case of research specifically, projects are reviewed by the appropriate governing body prior to investigation.

Note. Adapted from Rosch et al. (2023).

While these standards may seem a high bar to clear, especially when considered together, these metrics become easier to attain with additional experience, exposure to others' systematic inquiries, and additional education/professional development experiences. The benefit of adhering to these standards are inquiry projects worth the time, energy, and other resources they consume in their production.

The structure and design of qualitative approaches to inquiry can vary greatly and each represents unique applicability to various projects. While an exhaustive review of qualitative methodologies is beyond the scope of this chapter, options include case studies, narrative inquiries, phenomenologies, ethnographies, ground theory studies, action and/or engaged research, and arts-derived inquiries. Often (although not always) the simplest decision to make when it comes to qualitative methods might be the one between talking directly to people, observing social occurrences, and/or analyzing physical objects. Sometimes these decisions are made for us by what is feasible; however, our goal should always be to strive for the most rigorous implementation of our inquiry as possible. Making methodological decisions early, and revisiting them often in our projects, contributes greatly to overall project success.

Making the methodological decision detailed above (talking to people, observing occurrences, and/or reviewing objects) can lead to specific methods consequences. For example, choosing to talk to people may result in conducting interviews and/or focus groups. Observing occurrences could lead to the creation of field notes and/or audio/video recordings. Analyzing text, objects, and/or audio/visual information can produce rich and detailed descriptions. Regardless of the form your data and information take, multiple rounds of sense-making and categorizing can occur; some of which may require the use of qualitative data analysis software. New and different qualitative data software are routinely developed, each with a rich feature set, and differential reporting capabilities. Whether you choose a high- or low- tech solution to data collection and analysis, the reporting we seek to produce from those tools strives to balance depth and breadth of what we have found, with little (although some) attention paid to applicability across contexts.

Combined and Critical Approaches to Inquiry

Approaches to systematic inquiry that combine the above, or *mixed methods inquiry*, involves integrating both qualitative and quantitative methods into a single project (Johnson & Onwuegbuzie, 2004). While daunting, such a combined approach may be necessary when certain conditions exist, including but not limited to, qualitatively explaining quantitative results and/or quantifying qualitative findings. Balancing both quantitative and qualitative approaches can be challenging; therefore, we must be careful to not violate the assumptions of either in the pursuit of both. Important questions of which inquiry tradition (qualitative or quantitative) should come first and/or which should have the greater emphasis when both cannot be focused equally are always present in mixed methods projects. While great gains can be achieved from combining inquiry traditions, doubling the methodology usually results in at least three times the labor, so caution is advised in such undertakings.

Critical leadership education investigators question what we think we already know about the teaching and learning of leadership (Collins et al., 2006). They challenge previous knowledge on the basis of those project being conducted under social circumstances dissimilar to those of the modern day and seek to create new knowledge more reflective of current conditions. Doing so often requires rethinking historical inquiry paradigms, the development of new measurement and analysis tools, and/ or using previously established methodologies and methods in new ways. However, critical leadership education scholarship is still subject to high standards of rigor and ethics. The benefits of engaging in such a manner include increased potential for social justice in teaching, learning, and leadership education practice.

Regardless of the inquiry tradition(s) chosen, it is important to understand *why* those choices are made. Those who do this work regularly tend to develop *personal traditions of inquiry*, reflective of our beliefs, values, attitudes, biases, and experiences (among other influences) on leadership education and its attendant scholarship. However, just because these approaches become familiar and comfortable does not mean they will always yield the answers we seek! Veteran and novice investigators alike bear the responsibility to ensure their projects remain well-suited to the intended task, maintain theoretical relevance, and are crafted to reflect the most current information available. To illustrate this, in the next section, an original study is offered as an example of systematic inquiry in leadership education.

EXAMPLE STUDY:
CULTURAL RESPONSIVENESS IN LEADERSHIP EDUCATION

Between 2016 and 2018, I engaged in mixed methods dissertation study attempting to examine the role, if any should exist, of cultural responsiveness in a particular undergraduate certificate in leadership studies, with special focus on the experiences of diverse college students (Chunoo, 2018). This example is just one of many ways to investigate what we as leadership educators tending toward social justice do and how we do it.

One of the most significant benefits of engaging a mixed methods inquiry is that the results and findings highlight both qualitative and quantitative ways of knowing. However, the most significant drawback is the volume of resources such an investigation consumes; including, but not limited to, researcher time and investigator expertise in melding approaches not necessarily designed to complement one another. Additionally, while not all research involves assessment and/or evaluation, and not all assessment/evaluation projects require research, both are needed to move the needle on socially just leadership education. Finally, not all systematic inquiry projects require the development of new protocols and/or instruments, but this one did; it serves as both encouragement and warning.

Study Introduction, Significance, and Research Questions

This dissertation study centered *cultural responsiveness*, defined as, "using the cultural knowledge, prior experiences, frames of reference, and performance styles of ethnically diverse students to make learning ... more relevant and effective for them" (Gay, 2000, p. 29). The goal of this inquiry was to more thoroughly understand and describe diversity, equity, inclusion, cultural relevance, and cultural responsiveness expressed by leadership educators, and experienced by their students, within a particular undergraduate leadership certificate program. The results and findings obtained here were intended to improve leadership teaching experiences for faculty, and leadership learning opportunities for students by reinforcing the social justice orientations that already existed, drawing attention areas for improvement, and platforming student voices that might otherwise go un- or underrepresented (see Figure 7.1).

An original theoretical framework (see Figure 7.1) grounded this project, drawing from tenets of leadership education (Day, 2000), cultural capital (Coleman, 1988), and culturally responsive pedagogy (Gay, 2000). Described briefly, *leadership education* is preparation to lead in a non-specific role, task, or position (Day, 2000); *cultural capital* consists of the social assets someone possesses that collectively advances their social mobility (Coleman, 1988), and *culturally responsive pedagogy* is represented by teaching and learning strategies that attend to both educator and student social identities, lived histories, and ethnic upbringings (Gay, 2000). Three specific research questions guided this study: (1) What elements of teaching do leadership educators identify as culturally responsive in their instruction?; (2) Which classroom experiences, if any, do leadership students describe as reflecting their diverse backgrounds?; and, (3) Where are the areas of convergence and divergence in the responses to the previous two questions?

Figure 7.1

Cultural Capital, Culturally Responsive Pedagogy, and Leadership Education

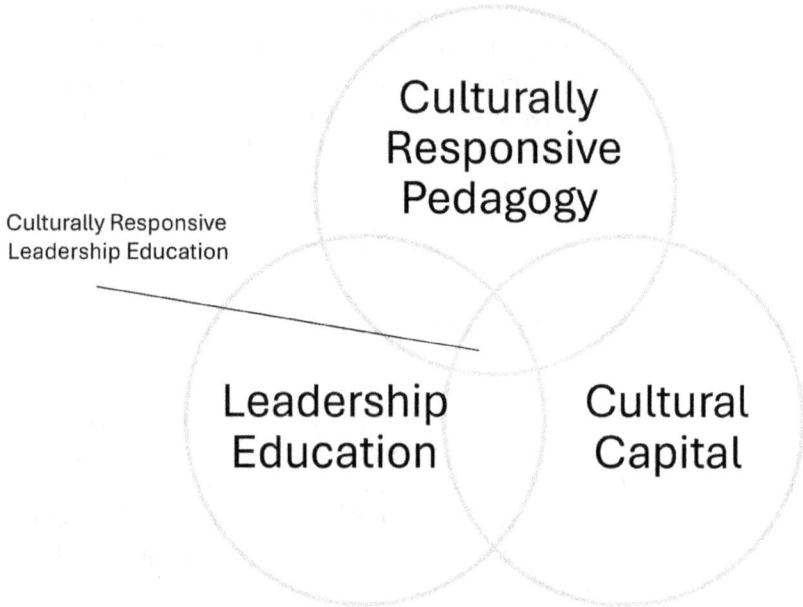

Culturally Responsive
Leadership Education

Culturally
Responsive
Pedagogy

Leadership
Education

Cultural
Capital

Source. Chunoo (2018). Reprinted with permission.

Study Methodology and Methods

An exploratory sequential mixed methods design (Creswell & Plano Clark, 2011) was used to pursue the previously described research questions. This methodology is so named because it employed both qualitative and quantitative methods, in that specific order. To address the first research question, semi-structured in-depth interviews were conducted with leadership educators from the focal certificate program. To respond to the second research question, a survey instrument consisting of closed-ended Likert-type questions was derived from educator responses in the first data collection phase and administered to their students (as the second phase of data collection). Given the novel nature of this outcome measure, survey responses we subject to psychometric testing, the results of which are reported below. Additional causal statistical analyses were performed to answer the third and final research question.

While combining qualitative and quantitative methods would seem to compensate for shortcomings or either approach, this strategy comes with unique limitations. Self-selection biases in both the educator and student samples can impact which data is obtained. Self-report information, whether obtained in an interview or on a survey can also skew results. Both stages of data collection required the creation of novel instruments; while the reliability and validity of the student survey can be demonstrated, credibility and trustworthiness of the interview protocol cannot be demonstrated in the same way. Finally, all studies regardless of nature must contend with missing data and/or otherwise unusable cases. While this investigation omitted cases with missing data wholesale, there may have been fundamental differences among those who persisted in the final analytic sample as compared to those who did not, potentially influencing the interpretations and conclusions. Nonetheless, responsible and rigorous steps were taken to mitigate the impact of these limiting factors.

Study Findings and Results

This inquiry's findings and results were aggregated into categories of leadership educators' characteristics, identities, philosophies, and histories; culturally relevant classroom management and approaches to pedagogy; and leadership students' characteristics and perceptions of cultural responsiveness. Of the 17 members of the educator sample, 71% identified as a woman, 53% identified as racially White, 76% reported a master's degree as their highest academic credential obtained, 88% held degrees in higher education/student affairs, and 40% had 5 years of teaching experience or more. Additionally, 58% had participated leadership education as an undergraduate, 53% had participated in leadership education as a graduate master's student, and 64% had participated in leadership education as doctoral graduate students.

Instructors interviewed also reported *retaining an identity as a leadership educator*, which differentially consisted of advocate, mentor, learner, and expert. They also reported different motivations for pursuing careers as leadership instructors, which ranged from life-long intentions for this occupational field to fulfilling shorter-term commitments tied to their larger employment role at the institution. Furthermore, the leadership educators studied represented a wide array of preparations to teach; some hailed from families where one or more parent was teacher (although not necessarily of leadership), some were prepared for their roles by formal training and development programs, while others described little to no teaching preparation at all. Philosophies of education also varied wildly between educators, including but not limited to leadership education as, "participatory, authentic, process-oriented, empathetic, context-driven, and evolutionary over time" (Chunoo, 2018).

A wide array of classroom management strategies were uncovered through instructor interviews, including classroom climate and course syllabi; course texts, readings, and other resources; course activities, discussion, and guest speakers; individual assignments and group projects; and grading policies and learning outcomes. Additionally, educators described their strategic deployment of pedagogical approaches, such as applied and experiential learning, activism and advocacy as pedagogy, and the way leadership learning language was adopted and adapted to fit student culture. Each of the classroom management strategies and pedagogical approaches were used to compile a 60-item Likert-style survey administered to the student sample as described below.

Among the 61-member student sample, 70% identified as a woman, 54% identified as racially White, 36% identified as Christian, 49% identified as second-year undergraduates, and all were enrolled in at least one leadership studies course, with the highest concentration (24%) attending a peer leadership class at the time of investigation. Student responses on the survey instrument were used to obtain test statistics for both validity and reliability. Principal component analysis (a test of statistical validity) yielded results indicating the survey instrument was, within a reasonable confidence interval, measuring one and only one construct; henceforth, referred to as *perceptions of cultural responsiveness*, or PCR.

Results from a statistical measure of reliability ($\alpha=.96$) indicated the instrument demonstrated consistent response patterns across participants. Students responded "Strongly Agree," or its equivalent, on 50 of the 60 items making it the modal answer across the entire survey. In the aggregate, total survey scores ranged from 149 to 292 (out of a possible 300), with an average of 256 and a standard deviation of 28. Analyses of student scores by various social factors (sex, race, year-in-school, etc.) failed to produce evidence of significant differences among members of these groups. Linear modeling techniques were employed to determine which, if any, independent variables significantly predicted changes in PCR scores. Enrollment in certain leadership courses—*Leadership in Groups and Communities* (+44.8), *Latinx Leadership* (+35.31), and *Peer Leadership* (+35.34), were all found to predict statistically significant PCR score gains at conventional confidence thresholds. Overall, the linear model used accounted for nearly 33% of the variance in PCR total scores.

Study Conclusions, Discussion, and Implications

Several important conclusions were derived from the proceeding analysis, with significant implications for culturally responsive leadership education. First, leadership educators in the sample identified a wide range of strategies infusing culturality into their teaching praxis. Nearly every aspect of teaching was named as an opportunity for cultural responsiveness should a leadership educator be ready, willing, and able to engage it as such. While important differences in *which strategies* were applied, in *what courses*, and in *what manner*, it became clearly apparent no educator or course studied was completely bereft of cultural responsiveness. In fact, many offered meaningful suggestions for future practice. Perhaps after seeing the findings presented here, those in the sample themselves (and beyond) will consider expanding their teaching approaches to incorporate their colleagues' good examples.

Second, students, by virtue of their near-universal strong agreement on the perceptions of cultural responsiveness survey items, appeared to feel attended to culturally in their leadership coursework. The inability of statistical measures to detect any significant differences in average perceptions cultural responsiveness scores by demographic groups can mean the attention paid to their social factors occurs evenly and without substantial discrimination. Noting how some scores on the instrument were improved in certain coursework, however; seemed to indicate a special benefit to leadership courses rooted in personal and/or identity development among students. Future inquiry is needed to determine which elements of these course have the greatest impact in this area, and whether those elements can be appropriately recreated in other courses to subsequently raise average perceptions of cultural responsiveness among all students.

Finally, both leadership educators and leadership students seem to agree cultural responsiveness is occurring in their classes. Moreover, the evidence produced here adds confidence to the notion that educators' and students' reasons for these perceptions also matched. Little to no proof exists insofar as this study is concerned of educators and students being focused on different course elements when informally developing their own senses of diversity, equity, and inclusion in their shared courses. This alignment speaks to the strong emphasis on curricular structure and design in the focal leadership studies certificate, as well as the efficiency and effectiveness of the educators transmitting those elements through their teaching. It should also be noted that students, by virtue of self-selecting into these courses and this certificate, may do so because of expectations of cultural responsiveness (perhaps passed down and across by their peers) and therefore, were more likely to report finding it due to their expectation bias.

COMMITTING TO SYSTEMATIC INQUIRY FOR LEADERSHIP EDUCATION

Every inquiry project needs a plan. The intent of this chapter was to provide the tools by which such a plan could be developed and implemented.

Theoretical orientations, inquiry questions, methodology and methods, data collection and analysis, conclusion drawing and sensemaking all have a role to play in systematic inquiry. The example study was offered to illustrate the steps in following an inquiry plan while simultaneously acknowledging how no plan is perfect. Hopefully, these ideas help differentiate between the map and the terrain in systematic leadership inquiry.

You may have noticed the example study was rooted in cultural relevance and not specifically social justice, despite its inclusion in a text on socially just leadership education. This is reflective of both the content and process of my own development as a scholar and leadership educator. My path to socially just leadership education started with cultural responsiveness (as noted above), moved thorough cultural relevance (see, Bertrand Jones et al., 2016), and presently resides in socially just leadership education. As we continue to (re)commit to social justice in leadership education, I encourage you to consider which ideas do and do not belong to such a concept for you, and perhaps more importantly, why they fit.

Starting with our why (Sinek, 2011) reveals more of what we can know about socially just leadership learning, while simultaneously teaching us how best to pursue our deepest goals and outcomes. This kind of reflexivity moves both us and our projects forward. The more deeply and frequently we communicate what we care about in the leadership learning enterprise, the more robust of a reputation we develop for ourselves, and the richer a community of like-minded others aggregate around us. The more we learn about how to foster socially just leadership learning, our thinking, acting, and searching becomes more nuanced and better able to serve more and different learners. Armed with your curiosities, and armored by your colleagues, may you never have to go alone on the journey to address your most important queries.

REFERENCES

Bertrand Jones, T., Guthrie, K. L., & Osteen, L. (2016). Critical domains of culturally relevant leadership learning: A call to transform leadership programs. In K. L. Guthrie, T. Bertrand Jones, & L. Osteen (Eds.), *Developing cultural relevant leadership learning*. (New Directions for Student Leadership, No. 153, pp. 9–21). Jossey-Bass.

Chunoo, V. S. (2018). *Examining the role of cultural responsiveness in leadership education among diverse college students*. (Publication No. 10745869) [Doctoral dissertation, Florida State University]. ProQuest Dissertations & Theses Global.

Coleman, J. S. (1988). Social capital in the creation of human capital. *American Journal of Sociology, 94*, S95–S120.

Collins, K. M. T., Onwuegbuzie, A. J., & Sutton, I. L. (2006). A model incorporating the rationale and purpose for conducting mixed methods research in special education and beyond. *Learning Disabilities: A Contemporary Journal, 4*(1), 67–100.

Creswell, J. W. (2014). *Research design: Qualitative, quantitative, and mixed methods approaches* (4th ed.). SAGE.

Creswell, J. W., & Plano Clark, V. L. (2011). *Designing and conducting missed methods research* (2nd ed.) SAGE.

Day, D. V. (2000). Leadership development: A review in context. *The Leadership Quarterly, 11*(4), 581–613.

Donaldson, S. I., & Grant-Vallone, E. J. (2002). Understanding self-report bias in organizational behavior research. *Journal of Business and Psychology, 17*(2), 245–260.

English, F. W., & Anderson, G. L. (2005). *The sage handbook of educational leadership: Advances in theory, research, and practice*. SAGE.

Gay, G. (2000). *Culturally responsive teaching: Theory, research, and practice*. Teachers College Press.

Greene, J. C., Caracelli, V. J., & Graham, W. F. (1989). Toward a conceptual framework for mixed-method evaluation designs. *Educational Evaluation and Policy Analysis, 11*(3), 255–274.

Johnson, R. B., & Onwuegbuzie, A. J. (2004). Mixed methods research: A research paradigm whose time has come. *Educational Researcher, 33*(7), 14–26.

Johnson, R. B., Onwuegbuzie, A. J., & Turner, L. A. (2007). Toward a definition of mixed methods research. *Journal of Mixed Methods Research, 1*(2), 112–133.

Lincoln, Y. S., & Guba, E. G. (1986). But is it rigorous? Trustworthiness and authenticity in naturalistic evaluation. *New Directions for Program Evaluation, 30*, 73–84.

Miles, M. B., Huberman, A. M., & Saldana, J. (2018). *Qualitative data analysis: A methods sourcebook* (4th ed.). SAGE.

Nintendo. (1986). *The Legend of Zelda*. [Video Game].

Rossman, G. B., & Wilson, B. L. (1985). Numbers and words: Combining quantitative and qualitative methods in a single large-scale evaluation study. *Evaluation Review, 9*(5), 627–643.

Rosch, D. M., Kniffen, L. E., & Guthrie, K. L. (2023). *Introduction to research in leadership*. Information Age Publishing.

Sechrest, L., & Sidana, S. (1995). Quantitative and qualitative methods: Is there an alternative? *Evaluation and Program Planning, 18*(1), 77–87.

Sinek, S. (2011). *Start with why: How great leaders inspire everyone to take action*. Portfolio/Penguin.

PART II

SOCIAL IDENTITY AND SOCIALLY JUST LEADERSHIP EDUCATION

CHAPTER 8

DE LA PLAYA A LAS PALMAS

From the Beach to the Palm Trees
Caribbean-American Student
Leadership Development

Derrick Raphael Pacheco

"Todo aquel que piense que esto nunca va a cambiar.

Tiene que saber que no es así

Que al mal tiempo, buena cara, y todo cambia"

—La Vida es un Carnaval, Celia Cruz (1998)*

The demographics of students, faculty, and staff continually shift and change, requiring the field of higher education to adapt or face irrelevance. As we continuously explore socially just leadership, it is of utmost importance for leadership educators across contexts to find inclusive strategies for use with those who hold minoritized identities, such as Caribbean and Caribbean Americans. The purpose of this chapter is to engage in a conversation about the inclusion of Caribbean and Caribbean American experiences into leadership education by modifying our curricular and co-curricular environments. The goal of this chapter is to advance the field of leadership education to emphasize social justice and inclusion while helping center all voices in leadership programs; not just those that

Committing to Action: Socially Just Leadership Educations, pp. 95–107
Copyright © 2025 by Information Age Publishing
www.infoagepub.com

have historically been upheld by scholarship in the field. For context, the words Caribbean and Caribbean American will be used interchangeably to indicate the experiences of both groups and their relation to leadership education and the American higher education system.

Over time, leadership educators have learned, through the process of researching and empowering others, that it is necessary to share diverse lived experiences as they relate to cultural heritage. In spaces where leadership educators create curricular and co-curricular opportunities for students, many Caribbeans get grouped under Black/African American and/or Hispanic/Latiné identity clusters, which in some cases are not accurate descriptors of those engaging in these opportunities. To disrupt and prevent this kind of misidentification, we need to create theoretical models that allow these individuals to be accounted for and represented in both leadership education and higher education (Lozano, 2015).

We face a fundamental mandate to create leadership learning opportunities specifically tailored to the unique needs of individuals who identify as Black (Meriweather, 2018; Spencer Jr., 2018) as well as Latiné (Guardia & Salinas, 2018; Torres, 2018). These calls also beg the question—is there also not a need to create leadership development programs for those who identify as Caribbean? Most research conducted on the lived experiences of Latiné individuals in the American higher education system, for example, comes from the western part of the United States and disproportionately showcases the experiences of Central and Southern Americans; specifically, those with Mexican and Mexican American heritages (Felix-Ortiz et al., 1994; Sanchez, 2013; Torres et al., 2019). Although this body of literature is crucial to our understanding of the leadership development among these individuals, we need to be more inclusive of those who come from different backgrounds and lived experiences, such as those who have heritage in the Caribbean and other parts of the world.

QUIÈN SOY? QUIENES SOMOS?
WHO AM I? WHO ARE WE?

In addition to the dearth of Caribbean representation in leadership learning, this void persists in research and scholarship. Due to the aggregation of Caribbean-identifying individuals within the aforementioned cultural groups, the experiences of those in the Caribbean get generalized with those from other cultural identity groups. The term *Latiné* is often used to explain the experience of individuals who have heritage in Latin America as a way to dismantle the inherent gendering of the Spanish language, while also being favored among those who claim affinity to this group and have strong connections to their ethnic heritage (Salinas, 2020). As the use of the term Latiné continues to grow, it was selected for use in this chapter to center lived experiences of those who created the term as they strived toward gender-inclusive language from native Spanish speakers (El Centro, n.d.). It is also important to acknowledge that not every country in the Caribbean is predominately Spanish-speaking; hence why I take a more specified lens on certain islands over others in this piece; due to the shared understanding of language as a means of culture. In no way does this indicate the superiority of experiences in the region based on shared language, as that would inherently steer away from developing a socially just orientation.

Due to my lived experiences, I have come to understand the different components of my identity in many ways. Specifically, I differentiate my identity as a first-generation Cuban American and how this perspective influences the views I have about my Caribbean and Latiné identities as intersecting and individual identities. Because of this, and the recognition of identity groups as not monolithic, my approach to this chapter will necessarily not fully encompass all Caribbean people; it would be irresponsible to generalize across the lived experiences of such a diverse set of individuals. In contrast, this chapter engages the reader toward thinking and acting on behalf of individuals who are connected to Latiné, Hispanic, and Caribbean identities, specifically those from Cuba, the Dominican Republic, and Puerto Rico. Although there are many ways to engage with the extant literature to highlight these experiences individually, I choose to highlight intersectional identities within the human experience.

DE QUE ESTAMOS HABLANDO?
WHAT ARE WE TALKING ABOUT?

Across leadership education, and specifically at postsecondary educational institutions, leadership learning initiatives exist to support the experiences of all students. However, some offerings are specifically crafted toward the unique needs of those who hold minoritized social identities and are structured from a culturally-based perspective. Within these leadership development programs, we can see how various identity groups are regarded in curriculum and how they aid students in developing resilience around singular social identities. Although these programs provide demonstrable support to individuals from minoritized social groups, the ability to relate to leadership processes through diverse and intersecting social identities is one of the reasons that make these programs effective (Brooms, 2019). Although there have been efforts to diversify collegiate leadership development programs, some are nonetheless regarded as exclusionary.

In specific, among those who identify at the intersection of various social identities, such as those who identify as Caribbean and Black or Caribbean and Latiné. Rarely do large-scale leadership development programs center intersectional identities; often due to a lack of facilitator training resources, programmatic funding, and robust outreach efforts.

To better understand how socially just leadership educators support students with intersecting identities in their leadership development, we need to better represent their lived experiences. Leadership development is holistic human development. As demonstrated throughout the canon of leadership education (to the degree one exists), there is a need to study the lived experiences of individuals and how they engage with leadership. Although including a diverse set of ethnic and racial groups in research samples have increased over time, little has been done to create models and theoretical frameworks representative of Caribbeans. As we continue moving toward equity through socially just leadership education, there is a need for leadership programs to ensure the representation of all people.

Contextualizing the Conversation

In this chapter, when Caribbeans and Caribbean Americans are mentioned, I am explicitly referring to those who are currently situated in or emigrated from a Caribbean Island (Caribbean) to the United States or those who are first-generation American with heritage from a Caribbean Island (Caribbean American). The independent countries found in the Caribbean are: Antigua and Barbuda, the Bahamas, Barbados, Cuba, Dominica, the Dominican Republic, Grenada, Haiti, Jamaica, St. Kitts and Nevis, St. Lucia, St. Vincent and the Grenadines, and Trinidad and Tobago (Shvili, 2021). In addition to these independent nations, many other territories belonging to larger nations, such as the U.S. Virgin Islands and the Cayman Islands, to name a few. Although not always recognized as independent nations, these islands share many of the same cultural practices as their independent counterparts. In addition to these countries and territories, Puerto Rico must also be acknowledged explicitly, although being a U.S. territory, for the intersectional contributions this island has had on immigration and culture around the world.

Historical Foundations

Throughout history, individuals from around the world have immigrated to other nations for various reasons. Some of these reasons may be to seek a better life filled with promises, both kept and unkept, or to seek refuge.

Regardless of the reasoning, immigration patterns affect the national identity of a country. The concept of nationalism in the United States has inherently been in "alignment with the exclusion of non-White individuals" (Hernandez, 2018, p. 28). This can be found at all levels of our U.S. governmental system. The first large wave of immigration from the Caribbean to the United States occurred during the times of slavery; although the slave trade caused forced migration to the United States from all parts of the world, the number of forced migrants from all parts of the trade to the Caribbean, and then into the United States, is immeasurable. The Migration Policy Center reported the first large-scale voluntary migration to the United States from the Caribbean occurred in the mid-1940s from Cuba where people sought to escape political tensions on the island (Zong & Batalova, 2019), which later led to the peak of the Cuban Revolution and the overthrowing of the Cuban government.

The American higher education system was heavily impacted by the effects of integrating Caribbeans. In the early 1900s, the Cuban Educational Association was created to give students from Cuba the ability to study in the American higher education system as long as they returned to the island upon degree completion (MacDonald, 2004). The mixed-race identity many Caribbeans held posed an issue for higher education institutions, especially during racial segregation. Many individuals who received scholarships and opportunities to study in the United States were seen as White or White-passing (MacDonald, 2004). As described by MacDonald (2004), Puerto Rican students who were allowed to study in the United States often attended Historically Black Colleges and Universities (HBCUs), and by 1905, almost 500 Puerto Rican students were attending various postsecondary educational institutions.

Current-Day Influences of Caribbeans in the United States

An important aspect of leadership education is being able to contextualize experiences. According to the Pew Research Center, six million people—2% of all U.S. adults and 12% of Latiné adults identify as Afro Latiné (Gonzalez-Barrera, 2022). Of these six million people, 23% of them identified as having Puerto Rican heritage, 18% identified as having heritage from the Dominican Republic, and 7% identified as having Cuban heritage (Gonzalez-Barrera, 2022). In addition, there are clear indicators that many Caribbean individuals who fall within Hispanic/Latiné and Black/African American identity groups struggle to experience a sense of belonging. One in seven Afro Latiné people do not claim Hispanic or Latiné heritage; they instead identify as solely Black (Gonzalez-Barrera, 2022). Although identity is both personal and social, it is curious why these individuals may feel connected to certain identity groups over others. Based on the aforementioned demographics, there is a clear need to enhance leadership growth among those who are Caribbean, not only at higher education institutions, but in all areas of their development.

During the 2020 Fall Semester, the National Center for Education Statistics (NCES) reported roughly 22% of students attending degree-granting postsecondary institutions in the United States identified as Hispanic, and 13% identified as Black (National Center for Educational Statistics, 2022). These statistics reinforce the need to raise the prominence of the experiences of these individuals in our decision-making as higher education professionals. Higher education institutions serve as a testing ground for the dual socialization process to occur among those who come from different cultural atmospheres. Dual socialization occurs when an individual who belongs to both a majority and minority culture creates their own understanding of inter-group customs, values, and beliefs (Rendon et al., 2011). As highlighted by the work of Anzaldua (1996), especially in her piece, *To live in the borderlands means you...*, it is important to remember how living in the social borderlands of varying identity groups does not make one person more of one identity over another. It makes each individual person a unique mix of multiple identity groups whose saliency becomes more prevalent based on context and situation. Socially just leadership educators need to focus on these concepts to be inclusive of the lived experiences of their students.

COMO SEGUIMOS ADELANTE?
HOW DO WE MOVE FORWARD?

The field of leadership education has developed throughout time in ways that have allowed us to center diversity in the human experience. While embracing this diversity, the goal of leadership education has gone through many transformations: from initial theories and models that showcase leadership as a skill or trait that we are born with, to more recent theories focused on cultural relevance and social justice. To continue engaging in this process, it is our responsibility as leadership educators to center the experiences of one another in ways that strive toward equity, fairness, and social justice. As we aim to center lived experiences of Caribbeans in the field of leadership education, centering social justice and cultural relevance are important concepts that need to be implemented in our praxis.

Social justice is a term that is always evolving. As leadership educators, it is our responsibility to likewise continually grow and change. As defined by the John Lewis Institute for Social Justice at Central Connecticut State University (n.d.), social justice is, "a communal effort dedicated to creating and sustaining a fair and equal society in which each person and all groups are valued and affirmed" (para. 1). Engaging with the lived experiences of all people, especially those who have been underrepresented, offers us ways to center social justice in our praxis. As a field, leadership educators cannot dismiss culturally relevant pedagogy as we engage with socially just leadership. As coined by Gloria Ladson-Billings (1995), culturally relevant pedagogy centers the human experiences as they relate to the academic success, critical consciousness, and cultural competence of all individuals involved in educational processes.

Culturally Relevant Leadership Learning Model

Socially just leadership educators are called to craft and maintain spaces where we act in both socially just and culturally relevant ways. To answer this call and be inclusive of communities and identity groups that are underrepresented in leadership education, approaches like the culturally relevant leadership learning model (CRLL; Bertrand Jones et al., 2016) were created, which highlights the need for the inclusion of other non-dominant norms and expectations. CRLL allows us to critically examine how individuals engage with leadership processes. This model helps us make meaning of our leader identity, capacity, and efficacy while acknowledging five environmental factors that shape our understanding of leadership (Bertrand Jones et al., 2016). These five environmental factors: history and legacy of inclusion and exclusion, compositional diversity, behavioral dimension, organizational/structural dimension, and psychological dimension all play a crucial role in the leader and leadership development of people from all backgrounds; especially among those who hold minoritized social identities (Bertrand Jones et al., 2016; Beatty & Guthrie, 2021). Socially just leadership educators strive to develop culturally relevant citizens of the world; those who are equipped to better engage with the diversity found within the human experience. Implementing the culturally relevant leadership learning model to amplify the lived experiences of Caribbean people requires engaging in the complexities that come with "living in the hyphen," or the borderlands, of various identity groups, that are uniquely different.

Committing to Socially Just Leadership Education

Including Caribbean experiences in the future canon of leadership education requires understanding how we can implement the culturally relevant leadership learning model in our work. This starts by first understanding the history of inclusion and exclusion by asking ourselves why members of these groups have been excluded from our narratives in the first place. In addition to this interrogation, socially just leadership educators also conceptualize how differences in compositional diversity have played a role in the global contextualization of this group. Once this foundation has been established, it is important to engage with individuals who hold this identity to gain a better understanding of the remaining dimensions of the culturally relevant leadership learning model and their needs within a leadership development program. It is important to note, the implementation of such theories and models in our programs requires an analysis of institutional context and the resources allocated to the offices and departments supporting such programs. Different institution types have different needs for their students and resources allocated to them, for example, supporting students who come from Caribbean descent may be more prevalent at Hispanic Serving Institutions (HSIs) and Historically Black Colleges and Universities (HBCUs) than at Historically/Predominantly White Institutions (H/PWIs), but nonetheless, this support should be found across all institution types for all students.

Y AHORA QUE? NOW WHAT?: RECOMMENDATIONS FOR THE FUTURE

We commit to action by shifting our field toward justice. This requires transitioning our focus from unilateral approaches to identity-based leadership development programs and establishing intersectional approaches using culturally relevant and socially just leadership practices. By using preferred language, effective program evaluation, and critical reflection, socially just leadership educators discover ways to create space for those with minoritized intersecting identities. As these concepts are explored, at the end of each of the following sections, critical questions are provided to aid in the interrogation of our practices.

Language

Language is a key indicator of culture and should be utilized in ways that approach and appreciate groups and communities from an asset-based and preferred-use approach. We know language "is the way by which people communicate with one another, build relationships, and create a sense of community" (Holmes, 2015, para. 1). One of the most important tools leadership educators have in their praxis is validation, especially when engaging with identity-based language and the variations of one's language, such as accents and dialects. For many Caribbean individuals, the concepts behind language are heavily influenced by colonization and in resistance to adaptation and assimilation toward dominant norms. Throughout history, many Caribbean individuals have been critiqued for their speaking speeds, or that their language is considered "broken" when our socially constructed notion of language cannot be broken. As leadership educators, it is our responsibility to educate others about proper terminology and concepts, as well as unlearning certain phrases and terms. Related reflection questions include:

- Are the learning outcomes for leadership development programs inclusive of those who hold different identities than those in the majority?
- How can we make sure to highlight the experiences of those who hold minoritized identities in our leadership development programs and frameworks?
- How can we center our language in programming to highlight identity groups from an asset-based approach than a deficit-based approach?

Program Assessment and Evaluation

One of the most important ways to assure our leadership development programs are meeting our intended outcomes is by engaging in program assessment and evaluation. In these processes, program personnel should engage in socially just formative evaluation and assessment. As defined by Fitzpatrick et al. (2010), the goal of a formative program evaluation should be to provide feedback that improves the quality of the program on a frequent basis, not solely at timed intervals. To better offer diverse perspectives, it is important that we engage with these evaluations with a diverse set of individuals, especially with those who hold a diversity of thought, experience, and exposure to the subject matter. This last point is especially important to ensure leadership development programs are reaching participants in spaces where they are within their journey. Those in power should reflect on the importance of the organizational/ structural dimension of CRLL in specific, and the ways programs have remained stagnant with the experiences of evaluators. Related reflection questions include:

- Who is doing the program evaluations? How are they centering equity in their practices?

- Are systems of oppression being addressed in program evaluation, especially those that may relate to Caribbean individuals such as, for example, immigratory constraints?
- What are some structural barriers that limit the participation of Caribbeans in leadership development programs? How can these barriers be overcome?

Critical Reflection

Reflection is one of the most important aspects of human experiences, especially as it relates to the understanding of us, others, and the world (Volpe White et al., 2019). As leadership educators engage in reflective practices, socially just leadership educators shift their mindset from simple remembering to one trained on critical reflection. To enhance our leadership development programs, especially as we consider incorporating the lived experiences of others, it is important to also reflect on the culturally relevant leadership learning model and what it asks us as leadership educators to consider. As defined by Volpe White et al. (2019), it is our goal to not only reflect on our experiences and how they relate to us as individuals and communities we represent but also to critically examine the how and why. As we center critical reflection in leadership education, we are asked to question assumptions, consider sociopolitical factors, integrate social theory, and act toward justice (Volpe White et al., 2019) to better understand situations and experiences. Owen (2016) gave us additional tools, allowing leadership educators to move between different levels of reflection and into realms of critical discourse where one can focus on committing to action. Related reflection questions include:

- When reflecting, are SMART (specific, measurable, achievable, relevant, and time-bound) goals created as part of this critical reflection? Who is creating these smart goals?
- When thinking about critical reflection, are materials available in formats to fit the needs of those with different learning styles and who speak a different language?
- How can group reflection be changed into critical group reflection?

YA LLEGAMOS? ARE WE THERE YET?: CONCLUSION

The goal of this chapter was to present valuable perspectives on the incorporation of Caribbean narratives, experiences, and literature in leadership development programs. As socially just leadership educators, it is our responsibility to interrogate models and frameworks as we strive toward inclusion in all fields of study, specifically in higher education and leadership education (Beatty & Guthrie, 2021). My lived experiences as a first-generation Cuban-American have inspired me to develop, engage with, and study the Caribbean identity, its diaspora, and in specific, how we, as higher education professionals and leadership educators, engage with stakeholders in ways that bring this, and all identity groups, to the forefront. Although I acknowledge the saliency that this identity group holds for me, it should be the responsibility and duty of leadership educators to ensure all people are validated in our work.

All those that think that this will never change

Has to know that this is not how it is

That to the bad times, good face, all can change

*Translated from above

REFERENCES

Anzaldua, G. (1996). To live in the Borderlands means you. *Frontiers, 17*(3), 4–5. https://www.proquest.com/scholarly-journals/live-borderlands-means-you/docview/232315403/se-2

Beatty, C. C., & Guthrie, K. L. (2021). *Operationalizing culturally relevant leadership learning*. Information Age Publishing.

Bertrand Jones, T., Guthrie, K. L., & Osteen, L. (2016). Critical domains of culturally relevant leadership learning: A call to transform leadership programs. In K. L. Guthrie, T. Bertrand Jones, & L. Osteen (Eds.), *Developing culturally relevant leadership learning*. (New Directions for Student Leadership, No. 152, pp. 9–21). Jossey-Bass. https://doi.org/10.1002/yd.20205

Brooms, D. R. (2019). Not in this alone: Black men's bonding, learning, and sense of belonging in Black male initiative programs. *The Urban Review, 51*. 748–767. https://doi.org/10.1007/s11256-019-00506-5

Cruz, C. (1998). *La vida es un carnaval* [Song]. Isidrio Infante.

El Centro. (n.d.). Why Latinx/e?. *Colorado State University*, Retrieved on September 29, 2022, from https://elcentro.colostate.edu/about/why-latinx/

Felix-Ortiz, M., Newcomb, M. D., & Myers, H. (1994). A multidimensional measure of cultural identity for Latino and Latina adolescents. *Hispanic Journal of Behavioral Sciences, 16*(2), 99–115. https://doi.org/10.1177/07399863940162001

Fitzpatrick, J. L., Sanders, J. R., & Worthen, B. R. (2011). *Program evaluation: Alternative approaches and practical guidelines* (4th ed.). Pearson.

Gonzalez-Barrera, A. (2022, May 2). *About 6 million U.S. adults identify as Afro-Latino.* Pew Research Center. https://www.pewresearch.org/fact-tank/2022/05/02/about-6-million-u-s-adults-identify-as-afro-latino/

Guardia, J. R., & Salinas Jr., C. (2018). Latino male leadership: A social justice approach. In K. L. Guthrie & V. S. Chunoo (Eds.), *Changing the narrative: Socially just leadership education* (pp. 145–158). Information Age Publishing.

Hernandez, M. A. (2018). More than just words: Transforming leadership education towards liberty and justice of all. In K. L. Guthrie & V. S. Chunoo (Eds.), *Changing the narrative: Socially just leadership education* (pp. 27–40). Information Age Publishing.

Holmes, K. (2015). *Language: The essence of culture.* Greenheart International. https://greenheart.org/blog/greenheart-international/language-the-essence-of-culture/

John Lewis Institute for Social Justice. (n.d.). *Our definition of social justice.* Central Connecticut State University. Retrieved October 28, 2022, from https://www.ccsu.edu/johnlewisinstitute/terminology.html

Ladson-Billings, G. (1995). But that's just good teaching! The case for culturally relevant pedagogy. *Theory into Practice, 34*(3), 159–165. https://doi.org/10.1080/00405849509543675

Lozano, A. (2015). Re-imagining Latina/o student success at historically White institutions. In A. Lozano (Ed.), *Latino/a college student leadership: Emerging theory, promising practice* (pp. 3–28). Lexington Books.

MacDonald, V. M. (Ed.). (2004). *Latino education in the United States: A narrated history from 1513–2000.* Palgrave Macmillan.

Meriweather, L. R. (2018). Getting in formation to lead: Black female student leadership development. In K. L. Guthrie & V. S. Chunoo (Eds.), *Changing the narrative: Socially just leadership education* (pp. 93–108). Information Age Publishing.

National Center for Education Statistics. (2022). Characteristics of Postsecondary Students. *Condition of Education.* U.S. Department of Education, Institute of Education Sciences. Retrieved September 22, 2022, from https://nces.ed.gov/programs/coe/indicator/csb.

Owen. J. (2016). Fostering critical reflection: Moving from a service to social justice paradigm. In W. Wagner, & J. M. Pigza, (Eds)., *Leadership development through service-learning* (New Directions for Student Leadership, No. 150, pp. 37–48). Jossey-Bass. https://www.doi.org/10.1002/yd.20169

Rendon, L. I., Jalomo, R. E., & Nora, A. (2011). Theoretical considerations in the study of minority student retention in higher education. In S. R. Harper & J. L. Jackson (Eds.), *Introduction to American higher education.* Routledge.

Salinas, C. (2020). The complexity of the "x" in Latinx: How Latinx/a/o students relate to, identify with, and understand the term Latinx. *Journal of Hispanic Higher Education, 19*(2), 149–168. https://doi.org/10.1177/1538192719900382

Sanchez, D. (2013). Racial identity attitudes and ego identity statuses in Dominican and Puerto Rican college students. *Journal of College Student Development, 54*(5), 497–510. https://doi.org/10.1353/csd.2013.0077

Shvili, J. (2021, March 23). Caribbean countries. *WorldAtlas.* Retrieved October 1, 2022, from https://www.worldatlas.com/articles/caribbean-countries.html

Spencer Jr., D. (2018). The world is yours: Cultivating Black male leadership learning. In K. L. Guthrie & V. S. Chunoo (Eds.), *Changing the narrative: Socially just leadership education* (pp. 109–126). Information Age Publishing.

Torres, M. (2018). Pa'lante siempre pa'lante: Latina leader identity development In K. L. Guthrie & V. S. Chunoo (Eds.), *Changing the narrative: Socially just leadership education* (pp. 127–146). Information Age Publishing.

Torres, V., Hernandez, E., & Martinez, S. (2019). *Understanding the Latinx experience: Developmental and contextual influences.* Stylus.

Volpe White, J. M., Guthrie, K. L., & Torres, M. (2019). *Thinking to transform: Reflection in leadership learning.* Information Age Publishing.

Zong, J., & Batalova, J. (2019, February 13). Caribbean immigrants in the United States. *The Online Journal of the Migration Policy Institute.* https://www.migrationpolicy.org/article/caribbean-immigrants-united-states-2017

CHAPTER 9

IT'S FOR EVERY "BODY"

How Body Image
Influences Leaders and Leadership

Challen Wellington

Imagine a dancer from the southern United States desires to dance professionally in California. She picks up her life and moves out west to further her education as a dance major. In her community of origin, she was always considered very fit and muscular, but immediately in a different context, she was suddenly considered "fat." Her peers ate minimal amounts of food to avoid weight gain, and on average, people in her new location just had smaller bodies. The body she had been comfortable in mere weeks ago suddenly was unacceptable, and she was othered. This experience influenced how she got involved on campus and her desire to pursue other goals where her body might be more accepted. Though this is not everyone's story, it is helpful to understand a true story of how body image influences leadership development.

INTRODUCTION

Historically, leadership was conceptualized using industrial definitions rooted in positions of power (Rost, 1997). Leadership as leader-centric roles reinforced a static view of tall, athletic White men as depicted in the great man theory of leadership (Carlyle et al., 1893). However, from

Committing to Action: Socially Just Leadership Educations, pp. 109–119
Copyright © 2025 by Information Age Publishing
www.infoagepub.com

a post-industrial perspective, leaders and leadership are not bound by these standards (Rost, 1997). In accepting leadership not as role-bound or leader-centered, and understanding it as socially constructed, we recognize how leadership can be learned and leaders are made; not born (Dugan, 2017; Beatty & Guthrie, 2021). Since leaders can be crafted through growth in leadership knowledge, skill, and abilities, anyone can learn, anyone can be a leader.

Owen (2020) posed the question of how structural oppression, privilege, and gender influences a person's view of leadership and affirmed all of these factors as pivotal in shaping our views on leadership. Considering these premises, I am adding to this list of factors how perceptions of our own, and others', capacities to lead based on how we physically show up in spaces. To do this, I interrogate how body image and sexism intersect with leadership education in postsecondary educational settings. I will use the social change model of leadership development (Higher Education Research Institute, 1996) and invoke the feminist literature of Julie Owen (2020), Roxane Gay (2014), and bell hooks (2000) to overlay the concepts of sizeism and leadership in the academy. Furthermore, it is necessary to note that just as leadership is socially constructed, which bodies are deemed healthy, attractive, and worthy of representation is also based on socially constructed narratives of size. This chapter will address body image from the feminine lens; however, the context is widely applicable.

One of the earliest messages women receive about their self-worth is tied to vanity and whether they are deemed pretty, beautiful, or cute. This messaging is seemingly harmless; however, it begins a story women tell themselves for the rest of their lives and perpetuate for other women: our primary value is derived from how we look. Opposingly, little boys (and the men they become) are told to grow up big and strong because their value is awarded by the capacity for protection (Harris, 2010). In even these two early and seemingly small messages, the capacity for leadership is being built already because being protective and/or tough is a story often told about good leaders, while aesthetic beauty is frequently regarded as superficial. These messages tend to continue on through socialization related to physical size and body stature (Harro, 1986). Women often deal with societal pressures as stated by bell hooks's (2000) description of the "Feminist struggle to end eating disorders [which] has been an ongoing battle because of our nation's obsession with judging females of all ages on the basis of *how we look* was never completely eliminated" (p. 33, emphasis added). This societal pressure, which sits at the intersection of body image and sexism, contributes to women's capacity for leadership and the efficacy for seeing oneself in such a manner (Dugan, 2017).

Women of various body shapes experience the world, and the messages they receive based on their identities, in direct opposition to the taken-for-granted assumptions about what makes a good leader. In addition to the messages surrounding leader gender and race, weight is an additional factor contributing to how we see ourselves as leaders and how others perceive our capabilities for leadership. To make progress against these socializing forces, Gay (2014) recommended, "Feminism will better succeed with collective effort, but feminist success can also rise out of personal conduct" (p. 10). Thus, as we continue to construct leadership for ourselves and others, socially just leadership educators resolve to include bodies that exist outside the mainstream view of leadership.

INTERSECTIONALITY AND BODY IMAGERY

Intersections of race, ethnicity, class, gender, and sexual orientation are often at the forefront of progressive educational leadership models because these social identities affect and are affected by both interpersonal and structural systems (Owen, 2020). Additionally, they impact how we view our own leadership capacity and reciprocally impact our own efficacy. Less attention is generally given to how body image interacts with our perceptions of others' capacities as well as our own. Furthermore, body size and type have additional complexities when considered alongside with the aforementioned social identities. Based on the social change model of leadership development, *consciousness of self* is one of the most vital areas for creating social change (Dugan, 2017).

The activities we typically see for communing with ourselves include understanding our personal perspectives in the world, and it is also necessary to consider how our physical presence shows up in spaces. Rucker and Cash (1992) uncovered empirical evidence that in a Black and White racial binary, Black women tended to have fewer negative feelings towards their bodies, sizes, and weight changes, but the viewpoints of both groups of women positively correlated negative body image with developing eating disorders. The researchers also described how perceptions of one's own body, and others' body, are predicated on media representation; thin White women who are often overrepresented is likely contributing to White women participants' body self-image (Rucker & Cash, 1992). Though this study was conducted before the advent of social media, it nonetheless demonstrated how prized imagery of beauty impacted college women (Vandenbosch et al., 2022).

These important findings about women's experiences are applicable to leadership in general, and socially just leadership education specifically. When we accept social identities as completely intertwined in perspectives of leadership, we cannot ignore how body image contributes to (and detracts from) confidence based on our bodies appear (Beatty & Guthrie,

2021). Moreover, these effects intersect; for example, consider how a stately Black man is perceived differently than a voluptuous Latina. Society socializes us toward connotations for how we "should" view both of those individuals, yet we have to work to change the ways in which we perceive each of them as leaders.

BODY IMAGE EXPECTATIONS OF LEADERS

We begin receiving messages about how our bodies are supposed to look around the same age we develop memory capabilities. We hear things like, "oh look how big you've gotten," or "drink your milk so you can grow big and strong." While these statements seem harmless, they frame our bodies' growth and development as if it was up for debate with everyday people. For women in the U.S., these messages reinforce Western beauty standards and the expectations of how gender should be performed. Similarly, to how we discuss gender and race as part of leader identity development, socially just leadership educators challenge assumptions about body size and image of leaders.

Another theme surrounding bodies and what it means to "appropriately" show up in a space is how to dress one's body and the influence clothing and culture has on efficacy for leadership. Killen's (n.d.) study on women's body image and leadership found employers ambiguously described appropriate dress and how a, "woman's confidence is often inextricably bound up in her body" (para. 3). Consequently, confidence and self-esteem are most certainly contributing factors for someone's efficacy and motivation to see themselves as leaders and to act on these thoughts. Recommendations derived from this study included how leadership models and training must acknowledge and confront the "pressure of women's bodies to conform to narrow oppressive standards of femininity" (Killen, n.d., p. 4). While this has direct implications for women, it is applicable to people of all gender identifications because wherever there are oppressive standards of femininity, comparable masculinity standards can create toxic and harmful environments for anyone who does not fall into the typical gender binary. As hooks (2000) stated:

> Cultures of domination attack self-esteem, replacing it with a notion that we derive our sense of being from dominion over another. Patriarchal masculinity teaches men that their sense of self and identity, their reason for being, resides in their capacity to dominate others. (p. 70)

These sentiments illustrate how socially constructed views of leadership are not inclusive of the way women are expected to be, and furthermore, does not leave room for differences within any gender expression.

Remembering the interwoven nature of these influences on leadership, socially just leadership educators interrogate how sizeism intersects with other social identities. Many leadership theories and models indicate saliency with social identities produces better leaders because they are leaning into their own talents instead of trying to fill a preestablished mold. To these ends, Haslam et al. (2022) proposed identity leadership and leadership identity were intertwined because of the nature of social demographic categories, stating, "the leader's identity as *both* leader *and* group member allows them to mobilize the resources of both personal and social identity" (p. 10). However, to get to this point of motivation and engagement, socially just leadership educators begin by developing leaders across all social categories to develop a leader's self-image. Simultaneously, the work must begin to dismantle the systemic nature of oppressive body size metrics.

HISTORY OF BODIES AND BODY SIZE

Body Image as Oppression

When I consider the history of body size, I often refer to times when White women worked inside the home and maintaining a thin figure was part of the homemaker physique. However, this form of idealized body image predates the prized graphic view of the 1940s American woman. Strings's (2019) *Fearing the Black Body: The Racial Origins of Fatphobia,* described how being "fleshier" and having a thicker body that was well proportioned, was prized in the eyes of society during the Renaissance period from the 14th to 17th century (p. 16). It is important to note how this societal view is heavily influenced by men-centered sexism and the preferences for aesthetically pleasing wives. However, as time progressed, and the transatlantic slave trade grew during the early 19th century, the idea of a plump woman was in juxtaposition with the ideal woman because of the types of bodies the enslaved Africans had, as their bodies were commodified for labor (Strings, 2019). Nonetheless, in both instances, women's bodies were under the regulation of men's needs and desires for either wealth, legacy, and/or pleasure. The divide that has been left because of the racism and sexism of three centuries ago has had lasting effects. The components aesthetics and prescribed health outcomes based on body size are a direct result of how sexism bleeds into the workplace and, in this case, higher education.

Much of our reactions to people's bodies stem from societal norms that are often internalized by many through socialization. As described earlier, our thoughts about our identities contribute to our capacity and efficacy to position ourselves as leaders. Tiggeman and Lynch (2001) assessed women's perceptions of their bodies across the lifespan by using the Body Esteem Scale, which included participants' thoughts around self-objectification, habitual body monitoring, body shame, appearance anxiety, disordered eating, dietary restraint, and self-esteem. They found body dissatisfaction did not decrease with age; however, as women aged, they began placing less importance on the image of their bodies (Tiggeman & Lynch, 2001). This information is useful while working in the realm of higher education, where the focus on the traditional college-aged student usually sees a time in students' lives where they are independently managing their food and bodies for the first time.

Additionally, they are surrounded by peers who can influence their own bodily perceptions and their thoughts on others. As indicated by both Tiggeman and Lynch (2001), and Strings (2019), people's bodies come attached with preconceived notions about their capacities and are entangled with one's own view of their bodies based on the norms experienced in society. Considering the information, it seems just as easy to move away from the broken view that size does not equal health. Furthermore, someone's personal medical information should not be widely assessed (D. Wellington, personal communication, October 13, 2022). Unfortunately, that is not our reality. Though often subconsciously, our bodies are viewed as pieces of a puzzle in a greater capitalist picture and when the body is a commodified object required for labor, people in positions of power and authority tend to cast judgements on "right" and "wrong" based on the economic bottom line (Sharp, 2000). Thus, the idea that size and health are not mutually exclusive goes against the grain that the way we show up in spaces can be neutral and we should be judged on our skills and not appearance. Regrettably, reality exists differently until the process of change begins and people are held to the existing standards.

INFLUENCES ON EDUCATION

Almost certainly, the experiences students and employees have on campus should not be predicated on how their bodies look and fit into spaces. Yet often student organizations' shirt orders do not extend beyond an extra large, or disordered eating signs are missed because someone sees size before behavior. There are numerous occasions when higher education needs to be aware of the ways it can better serve people of different sizes. Of course, the ultimate goal is leadership development, but if a factor of someone's identity is not properly considered, we are falling short of meeting the mark of being inclusive of people's various intersectional identities (Crenshaw, 1988).

Moreover, someone's body is an identity marker that is always visible no matter what the circumstances, and it can influence their experiences and choices on campus and life. Stoll (2019) described fatphobia as a social justice issue, offering discrimination based on size contributes to the larger narrative of how oppression impacts the lived experiences of individuals. Furthermore, pathologizing of size, and its roots in anti-Black practices, the oppression is so enmeshed into how we think about people's skills because we see their visible identities before recognizing their cognitive skills (Stoll, 2019; Strings, 2019). These notions are problematic in leadership education because, unlike other forms of systemic oppression, which are frequently studied to produce culturally responsive leadership models, sizeism is still newly studied in the realm of sociology and education (Stoll, 2019).

Hence, it is imperative for socially just leadership educators to be cognizant of how skills for leadership are idealized and taught. Scholars have devised methods to teach body image skills and offer transferable tools that can be used in higher education settings (Bergen & Mollen, 2019). Bergen and Mollen (2019) encouraged educators to view size as another system of oppression when discussing how the intersection of experiences can compound oppression, avoid language that others' people in bigger bodies, present examples of positive leadership through people of multiple sizes, and encourage bodily acceptance within spaces (Crenshaw, 1988). These tools can be useful to socially just leadership educators in developing leadership learning by helping students develop the capacity and efficacy to see themselves as leaders as a result of their identities being affirmed.

The information presented from the psychological perspective is further affirming for the five environmental dimensions the culturally relevant leadership learning model focuses on including: historical legacy of inclusion/exclusion, compositional diversity, psychological climate, behavioral climate, and organizational/structural aspects of campus climate (Bertrand Jones et al., 2016). These factors are all existent in the ways society has developed a narrative about size and should therefore be used to inform the ways educators develop student leaders. Socially just leadership educators focus on change from a systemic level and how it must include "constituents of the system and the system and the environment" (Guthrie et al., 2017, para. 6). In acknowledging how it takes a dualistic approach of minding both the systemic and individual levels within an issue, sizeism in leadership education first assesses how postsecondary education perpetuates the harm to understand how to dismantle the structures. However, disassembling in twofold, because of how pervasive oppression is, educators must also reflect on how they personally contribute to the weathered landscape of sizeism.

In addition to how size is both perceived and experienced, socially just leadership educators remember how multiple and intersecting social identities impact someone's experiences. As mentioned by Jones and Bitton (2021), the way we provide support for students has to acknowledge students' identities and how some come with power and others come with oppression. Subsequently, these practices will further result in a more holistic leadership development model of education.

INTERSECTIONAL FEMINISM AND LEADERSHIP

Feminism has evolved to be taboo in many places outside of diverse spaces in the academy; however, it seems the benefits of feminism for men should be more widely discussed (hooks, 2000). When analyzing how a structural component of society supports men over people of other genders, including those with no gender identification, it is harder to interrogate how men are harmed by the very system that gives them power. Sexism produces environments where men are rewarded for being strong, dominant, commanding, and outspoken. Less clear is what happens when those attributes are not present within a self-identified man. Many such men are then perceived to be weak and incapable of leadership. Examining historical leadership models shows a framework of patriarchal characteristics that were unavailable to people who were "othered." As feminist models of leadership surfaced, they reflected women's ways of leading. Fleming et al. (2014) discussed how we typically see masculinity show up through aggression, power, and dominance, and unfortunately, the lack of vulnerability negatively impacts the experiences of everyone around them. These traits, produced from hypermasculinity, and lack of awareness, influence how students and professionals experience their leadership development. Furthermore, when leadership is perceived through the *male gaze*, it contributes to the landscape that people's size and bodies are up for conversation and debate (Sampson, 2015). Therefore, the necessity of intersectional feminist pedagogy is woefully apparent.

These factors bleed into how we perceive capability based on stature in other ways; whether that be a short man, a tall woman, or someone whose expression of gender does not conform to the ubiquitous binary. Due to the socially constructed nature of leadership, identity, and their intersections, the time is ripe to reimagine body image and how it influences leaders and leadership development education.

Applying anti-racist feminism to body size considerations, the information yields useful tools for socially just leadership (Gay, 2014; hooks,

2000). Just as intersectional leadership must be explicitly anti-racist, dismantling fatphobia in leadership must also be intentional. Peters and Nash (2021) claimed, "Intersectional leadership is explicitly anti-sexist, disrupting hetero-normative male-centric hegemonic practices, protections, and privileges" (para. 43). This may be as deep as requiring healthcare partnerships to remove Body Mass Index (frequently referred to as BMI) as a metric of evaluating appropriate care, or as surface as offering opportunities to request ergonomic chairs that support bigger bodies in better ways. Nonetheless, both encompass changing the narrative of conversation to de-pathologize people's appearance based on their size. By changing daily practices and including sizeism in identity conversations brings for interrogating body image into socially just leadership education.

CONCLUSION

I have offered a brief review of body image and sizeism in the higher education setting. Specifically looking at the ways in which fatphobia can fall under a system of structural oppression and thus needs to be advocated for in identity-based leadership education and models. Furthermore, tying the origins to patriarchal viewpoints of bodies only holds value when they are appealing to men. The social change model and feminist theories indicate the most appropriate ways to approach change in this realm is to acknowledge intersections and how sizeism is based on heteronormative points of view. Moving past acknowledgement, educators can begin to unlearn sizeist and sexist assumptions about their bodies and the bodies of others. Many movements such as body positivity and body neutrality exist to help disrupt sizeist thinking and encourage people to look at health as a marker of internal needs and not outward appearance.

Though much of the work surrounding sizeism in leadership education is relatively new, here are a few reflective questions educators show consider around this topic:

1. How does leadership development include body size as a socially constructed identity?
2. How has higher education historically privileged smaller bodies over bigger bodies? How does this privilege differ by perceived gender identity?
3. How do we scaffold the steps to unlearn someone's appearance based on former inaccurate health metrics?
4. How do students of varying body size identities explore their efficacy and motivation to engage in leadership?

These questions are designed to provide context to some student, faculty, and staff experiences, and to foster reflection on how these things show up for them personally. The future of socially just leadership education includes body image and size considerations because these factors impact emerging leader college students who often experience substantial changes in themselves during, and beyond, their college experiences.

REFERENCES

Beatty, C. C., & Guthrie, K. L. (2021). *Operationalizing culturally relevant leadership learning*. Information Age Publishing.

Bergen, M., & Mollen, D. (2019). Teaching sizeism: Integrating size into multicultural education and clinical training. *Women & Therapy, 42*(1–2), 164–180. https://doi.org/10.1080/02703149.2018.1524065

Bertrand Jones, T., Guthrie, K. L., & Osteen, L. (2016). Critical domains of culturally relevant leadership learning: A call to transform leadership programs. In K. L. Guthrie, T. Bertrand Jones, & L. Osteen (Eds.), *Developing culturally relevant leadership learning*. (New Directions for Student Leadership, No. 152, pp. 9–21). Jossey-Bass. https://doi.org/10.1002/yd.20205

Carlyle, T., Linson, C. K., & Gunn, A. (1893). On heroes, hero-worship and the heroic in history. [New York, Frederick A. Stokes company] [Pdf] Retrieved from the Library of Congress, https://www.loc.gov/item/25002119/.

Crenshaw, K. W. (1988). Race, reform, and retrenchment: Transformation and legitimation in antidiscrimination law. *Harvard Law Review, 101*(7), 1331. https://doi.org/10.2307/1341398

Dugan, J. P. (2017). *Leadership theory: Cultivating critical perspectives*. Jossey-Bass.

Fleming, P. J., Lee, J. G. L., & Dworkin, S. L. (2014). "Real men don't": Constructions of masculinity and inadvertent harm in public health interventions. *American Journal of Public Health, 104*(6), 1029–1035. https://doi.org/10.2105/AJPH.2013.301820

Gay, R. (2014). *Bad feminist: Essays*. Harper Perennial.

Guthrie, K. L., Bertrand Jones, T., & Osteen, L. (2017). The teaching, learning, and being of leadership: Exploring context and practice of the culturally relevant leadership learning model. *Journal of Leadership Studies, 11*(3), 61–67. https://doi.org/10.1002/jls.21547

Harris III, F. (2010). College men's meanings of masculinities and contextual influences: Toward a conceptual model. *Journal of College Student Development, 51*(3), 297–318. https://www.proquest.com/scholarly-journals/college-mens-meanings-masculinities-contextual/docview/366345406/se-2

Harro, B. (1986). *The cycle of socialization*. Sticks & stones: Understanding implicit bias, microaggressions, & stereotypes. https://www.nea.org/sites/default/files/2021-02/Cycle%20of%20Socialization%20HARRO.pdf

Haslam, S. A., Gaffney, A. M., Hogg, M. A., Rast III, D. E., & Steffens, N. K. (2022). Reconciling identity leadership and leader identity: A dual-identity framework. *The Leadership Quarterly, 33*(4), 1–15. https://doi.org/10.1016/j.leaqua.2022.101620

Higher Education Research Institute (1996). *A social change model of leadership development: Guidebook version III*. National Clearinghouse for Leadership Programs.

hooks, b. (2000). *Feminism is for everybody: Passionate politics*. South End Press.

Jones, S., & Bitton, A. (2021). Applying the lens of intersectionality to leadership learning. In K. L. Guthrie & V. S. Chunoo (Ed.). *Shifting the mindset: Socially just leadership education*, (pp. 163-174). Information Age Publishing.

Killen, G. (n.d.). Young women, body image, and leadership. https://www.academia.edu/19204723/Young_Women_Body_Image_and_Leadership

Owen, J. (2020). *We are the leaders we've been waiting for: Women and leadership development in college*. Stylus.

Peters, A. L., & Nash, A. M. (2021). I'm every woman: Advancing the intersectional leadership of Black women school leaders as anti-racist praxis. *Journal of School Leadership, 31*(1–2), 7–28. https://doi.org/10.1177/1052684621992759

Rost, J. C. (1997). Moving from individual to relationship: A postindustrial paradigm of leadership. *Journal of Leadership Studies, 4*(4), 3–16. https://doi.org/10.1177/107179199700400402

Rucker, C. E., III, & Cash, T. F. (1992). Body images, body-size perceptions, and eating behaviors among African-American and White college women. *The International Journal of Eating Disorders, 12*(3), 291–299.

Sampson, R. (2015 October 27). *Film theory 101-Laura Mulvey: The male gaze theory*. Film Theory. https://www.filminquiry.com/film-theory-basics-laura-mulvey-male-gaze-theory/

Sharp, L. A. (2000). The commodification of the body and its parts. *Annual Review of Anthropology, 29*(2000), 287–328. http://www.jstor.org/stable/223423

Stoll, L. C. (2019). Fat is a social justice issue, too. *Humanity & Society, 43*(4), 421–441. https://doi.org/10.1177/0160597619832051

Strings, S. (2019). *Fearing the black body: The racial origins of fat phobia*. New York University Press.

Tiggemann, M., & Lynch, J. E. (2001). Body image across the life span in adult women: The role of self-objectification. *Developmental Psychology, 37*(2), 243–253. https://doi.org/10.1037/0012-1649.37.2.243

Vandenbosch, L., Fardouly, J., & Tiggemann, M. (2022). Social media and body image: Recent trends and future directions. *Current Opinion in Psychology, 45*, 1–6. https://doi.org/10.1016/j.copsyc.2021.12.002

CHAPTER 10

AYA ANA THYA

Desi Leadership Here and There

Ravi Bhatt

Identity serves as the core of several theories and models within and surrounding leadership literature. Approaches, such as the trait approach to leadership, and theories, such as the path-goal theory, conceptualize themselves around the identity of the leaders and followers within continual leadership interaction and exchange (Northouse, 2019). Relating to leadership literature is important and should be approachable and attainable. However, extant leadership literature has underserved people of color and minoritized identities in treating their leadership experiences and conceptualizations as unique experiences rather than as foundations for authentic leadership understandings and theories (Ospina & Foldy, 2009).

Desi students make up a significant portion of the higher education population in the United States. In 2016, 74% of Asian Indian individuals in the United States held a bachelor's, master's, or terminal degree (National Center for Education Statistics, 2019). Soon after, in 2022, the U.S. Embassy of India boasted the 200,000 Desi students that elected to pursue higher education in the United States (U.S. Embassy, 2022). Desi students are embraced as a part of the economic systems of higher education institutions, and space is granted to authors of color so long as the stories are about their lived trauma (Tager & Shariyf, 2022). In focusing on Desi American leadership, this chapter will begin the process of filling a gap in the literature by critically analyzing Desi culture and identity

Committing to Action: Socially Just Leadership Educations, pp. 121–132
Copyright © 2025 by Information Age Publishing
www.infoagepub.com
121

development. This text will engage in meaningful dialogue uplifting and supporting additional Desi voices within literature and practice.

LĒKHAKANÜ STHITI-AUTHOR'S POSITIONALITY
(TRANSLATED FROM GUJARATI)

Before addressing Desi American Leadership, allow me a moment to introduce myself and how I came into this work. I am a first-generation doctoral student within my immediate family as well as a proud Desi American. As a Desi American, an individual who identifies as being from the Indian subcontinent (Chan, 2017), I have had the gift of exploring a unique and powerful relationship between American and Desi culture. This, as relevant to many individuals with minoritized identities, highlighted the need to conceptualize my role within several spaces and inadvertently fall into categories when experiencing these different spaces.

I was born in India and have spent over 20 years in the United States where I attended private schools through 12th grade. Throughout those formative years, I also enjoyed my identity as the "youngest" in the room as I am often the youngest cousin, uncle, nephew, and so on. Additionally, I am an only child to two born-and-raised Indian parents, but have considered cousins, extended family, and family friends as part of the immediate family and graciously serve in the titles they bestow on me. As this deep routed sense of familial bonds reflects the family-focal point of Indian culture (Chadda & Deb, 2013), it shapes Desi American leadership in a continually reflective way. As with any individual and culture, this is my experience and I acknowledge holding identities alike and different from my fellow Desi family, friends, peers, and colleagues, and as such cannot grasp all elements of the leader identity as it relates to Desi Americans. With that context, I invite you along on this journey of exploration.

DESI SANSRUKTI- DESI CULTURE
(TRANSLATED FROM GUJARATI)

Before exploring Desi American leadership, it is pivotal to further conceptualize what Desi American culture encapsulates. In understanding this culture from a physical and personal context, the elements that play into the Desi American leader and their leadership in higher education become plainly apparent. These elements include family first, identity development, and intersecting identities, among others described in more detail in the following sections.

Parivaar Pahele—Family First (Translated From Hindi)

In 2019, there were an estimated 198 million cattle, of which 5 million were stray in India (Sahu et al., 2021). This is a very believable statistic for anyone who has been to India and, like me, has walked side by side with a cow marked with a *Tilak* on their foreheads; a religious marking given by Hindu individuals. This is the culture I experienced as a Desi American visiting India, and in that physical context, I felt extremely comfortable living out that part of my identity. I felt this comfort as that culture of respect for our surroundings, our faith, and our connection to people travel back to the United States with me. This culture of respect supersedes any other cultural expectations and is especially upheld within the family.

Hilton et al. (2001) spoke to the socialization of household practices, familial pressure, and perceptions that would come from Desi individuals steering away from deeply rooted norms and values. Such norms include a culture of respect bounded by age; as an individual holds a title that indicates authority, "Kaki (*aunt*)," "Dada (*grandfather*)," "Mumi (*mom*)," and/ or is older than other members of the family, there is an expectation that they receive respect and are, often, seen as the leader within that space. As reflective of position power, wherein the individual derives power from their rank within the space (Northouse, 2019), this can often influence the youngest's members' ability in the space to recognize or present themselves as a leader. Though the experiences of the older members of the family are extremely valid and important, this element may remove the ability of younger members of the family to apply their leadership ability within the space. Respect is of utmost importance within the family, and though positional leadership may be witnessed within it, each person's unique identity is often admired and celebrated as identity development occurs.

Ōḷakha Vikāsa—Identity Development (Translated From Marathi)

With negative experiences and trauma constantly circulating, Asian Americans are forced to develop their identity with a foundation of resilience (Kim, 2001). In 2019, there were greater than 4,600,000 Indians in the United States, yet Desi hate continues to run rampant (Budiman, 2021). As internal and social pressure continues to bind Desi Americans to pick a side, Desi or American, racism and prejudice threaten to pick the side for us. Context matters deeply when developing our identities as Desi Americans, and often, the acceptance and cultivation of one's identity as a Desi American happens when socialization and acceptance by and with other Desi American and non-Desi American peers occur (Chan, 2017).

Through forced assimilation into higher educational spaces and internalized pressure to remain resilient and strong, Asian Americans continually face racism along their developmental journey (Museus & Park, 2015; Lu & Wong, 2013). One such catastrophic example of racism Asian Americans face is the model minority myth. The model minority myth, a misguided understanding of Asian Americans in the United States that praises the academic, social, and political success of this community, has led immense colorism among communities of color (Park, 2008). This pressure, racism, and colorism does not evaporate in college, rather the understanding of the ramifications of the model minority myth is often emphasized.

Developing one's identity as an Asian American often occurs in college which represents the macrocosmic society. As an Asian American, I may hope to understand who I am related to my Desi identity, as well as other minoritized identities I hold, such as my Hindu identity, through participation in social groups, open space for dialogue and discourse in courses, and other social access points (Chan, 2017). As a Desi American, I have only had the opportunity to think about my leadership and leader identity in times that I do so intentionally and in my recent graduate programs. Otherwise, I have to balance the spaces where I can authentically be myself or switch to a version of the person expected. It is important to note that this internalized, institutionalized, and socialized pressure differs for each Desi American given their context which only further recognizes need for additional voices within literature. Having these spaces in college certainly helped with the authentic presentation of oneself, and one's authentic leadership but begs the question: *Is college too late?*

Antarvibhaajak Pahachaan—Intersecting Identities (Translated From Hindi)

As I am developing my own identity within socially-constructed contexts, I may also be recognizing my identity concerning the world around me intersecting with several other identities. The reconceptualized model of multiple dimensions of identity (RMMDI) demonstrates how context, along with making meaning of personal experiences, influences our path toward self-authorship (Jones & Abes, 2013). Positive and negative interactions invite meaning-making that determines how Desi Americans conceptualize their intersecting identities and lived experiences.

One such intersecting identity Desi Americans may grapple with is social class as it has incredibly historic and recognizable ramifications for Desis, especially in India. Though now illegal, India had historically implemented a caste system, which, with a religious foundation, highlighted four main classes wherein families grew up with practically no chances for upward mobility (BBC, 2019). The ramifications of a national caste system continue to impact present-day India, it is not, as Berreman (1960) alludes to, entirely dissimilar to the United States class system wherein minoritized populations often have to work comparatively harder to gain less than much their White counterparts. Ardoin and Martinez (2019) stated, "Because we all learn messages related to social class from the get-go, such a narrative is both internal and external" (p. 164). Internalized perceptions associated with social class may determine the desire to pursue higher education, a specific academic field, and their pedagogy of leadership.

The identity as a scholar also comes into play often when considering the Desi identity. The model minority myth, wherein Asian Americans are expected to be elite academics due to their academic histories (Chow, 2017), comes with the intention of not praising Asian Americans, but rather berating and dehumanizing Black people. In using Asian Americans' academic performances, White people create a narrative that Black people may not be well-educated and are thereby dismissed from the opportunity. This proves to be inaccurate and racist but not without challenging the minoritized identities included within that. As Desi Americans navigate spaces with individuals who hold different identities, they, for protection or connection, may practice code-switching while steering through the routes of racism caused by the model-minority myth (Gardner-Chloros, 2009).

The opportunity to present one's Desi identity in the Mandir, or Temple, amongst other Desis will look different than when a group of Desis are attending a concert on campus. Thus, socialization processes influence identity development and greatly impacts the leader identity in that often in spaces where there is less emphasis on age-based/positional leadership, Desi Americans can truly hone in on their leader identity and develop it.

Ucca Śikṣaṇa Dēśī Nētṛtva—Higher Education Desi Leadership (Translated From Gujaratri)

In 2018, 59% of students enrolled in higher education in the United States were Asian-identifying students; more than any other identity (National Center for Education Statistics, n.d.). From these statistics, we are aware that this is representative of all Asian-identifying students beyond just Desi American students and that Desi American leaders have, and continue to, navigate through United States institutions. These demographics change, yet leadership pedagogy continues to move at a slow pace emphasizing the gap that is supporting these students. Indian students, teachers, and researchers experienced immense levels of stress and depression during the COVID-19 pandemic (Rehman et al., 2021) and are likely still recovering from these mental health issues. Supporting the new fast paced waves of entering students requires reflective literature, representation, and motivation throughout leadership learning.

Ucca Śikṣaṇātīla Anubhava—Experiences in Higher Education (Translated From Marathi)

Stereotypes, preconceived notions, inaccessibility, and inattention impede opportunities to serve as a leader in several spaces in higher education. There is a balance between the pressure to succeed throughout one's collegiate experience and serving as a leader in the process. In a narrative about the opportunity to serve as leaders, Villavicencio (2021) commented:

> There is an enduring perception that Asians lack the "chutzpa" to be strong leaders. Oftentimes, they are perceived to be the opposite; they are too quiet, too nice, and unable to make tough decisions. Most participants strongly contradicted this notion. (p. 99)

This perception comes from a racist ideology that Asian Americans, including Desi Americans, are there simply to learn and not to serve or participate in the institutional study, as evidenced by the model minority myth. Desi American students are more than willing and capable to lead in spaces as their leader identity continues to develop as well. Villavicencio (2021) also highlighted how Desi Americans need to continuously push themselves to serve as leaders and apply pressure on themselves to not quit or give up, and even over-prepare, to stray away from the myth that Desi American students are not able to lead within higher education. Not only might Desi Americans be expected to succeed by the familial pressures of immediate and extended family, but they are now also expected to succeed by peers as a mechanism to break and prove stereotypes wrong. Stereotype threat, or the pressure to not prove stereotypes right (Center for Teaching and Learning, n.d.); additional immense pressure to be a conducive leader, matched only by the rigor of any higher education space, continuously self-perpetuates.

During my undergraduate experience, I was employed by my institution's Department of Residential Life. With my incredibly strong peer connections, the immense amount of passion I had for my work and my students, and the support and love from the internal and executive teams, I was able to continuously move into new positions throughout the Department. Though I have those incredible experiences, I will never forget when I took on the role of Lead Resident Assistant, one of my peer's congratulated me and said, "You can stop showing off now," within the same breath. This experience was astonishing to me as I did not know what to feel; on one hand, I achieved a position for which I worked and on the other, his comment would have me believe that I took the position from someone else. This is not unlike Desi American experiences; a give-and-take that gets exhausting.

Desi Americans, and Desis, are leaders and can serve as incredible leaders in their academic, personal, professional, and social lives. With the amount of balance, pressure, and identities that Desi Americans navigate, they continuously prove this identity, whether through will or social expectation. The onus falls on all of us to create conducive spaces for Desi American students to succeed and in taking this onus, we are able to dismantle a structure of racism that has guided Desi American experiences thus far.

YAHAAN SE KAANHA JAAYENGE? WHERE DO WE GO FROM HERE? (TRANSLATED FROM HINDI)

As we navigate the several nuances that exist within Desi leadership, Figure 10.1 highlights what Desi American students are navigating at once, while conglomerating the outside factors that are impacting their experience. Figure 10.1 should be read as a Venn diagram where each space will look different for every individual, the relationship with the other factors and with the person themselves, and the amount of space each factor encapsulates varies from person to person. This will be the framework as we dive into how best to support Desi American students within your spaces.

Dēśī Avājō Ut'thāo—Uplift Desi Voices (Translated From Gujarati)

Desi voices surround us all. Desi American students, friends, colleagues, peers, and neighbors, each have stories to tell. These stories embrace their identities, and histories wherein their identities have been challenged. These tales are important for us to conceptualize as they embrace the ability to better support Desi Americans. Not only are Desi Americans humans with lived experiences, they, too, are leaders who have expertise on driving positive, sustainable, and and who are pro social change. The way my parents can set up, prepare, participate in, and facilitate our household events is leadership if I have ever seen it. Their story matters as a leader just as much as mine and my White peers' do. In incorporating Desi Americans into storytelling and leadership learning spaces, you are able to recognize in action what the interactions of Figure 10.1 become and how they play a role in several contexts. Including Desi Americans in leadership means giving space to learn from a leader as leaders.

Figure 10.1

Desi American Student Responsibilities at Any Time

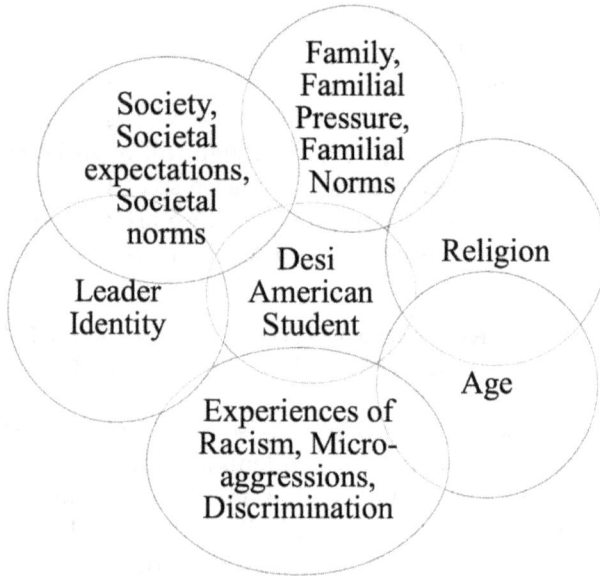

Family,
Familial
Pressure,
Familial
Norms

Society,
Societal
expectations,
Societal
norms

Religion

Desi
American
Student

Leader
Identity

Age

Experiences of
Racism, Micro-
aggressions,
Discrimination

Dēsī Jāgā—Desi Spaces (Translated From Marathi)

As Desi Americans navigate their leader identity, they may not see Desi literature often. The literature even in this chapter spans from either very long ago to more recent depending on the content. This is because there is a large gap in Desi American literature, perpetuated by the foundational combination of several Asian identities. This gap is also reflected in leadership where very little literature exists about Desi Americans and their development of the leader identity. As a friend to a Desi American, take time to reflect on how Desi American leaders, and their leadership, can be represented within work that you may write or do through intentional collaboration to help disseminate the experiences of this identity into the world.

Javābadārī anē Sansādhanō—Responsibility and Resources (Translated From Gujarati)

Table 10.1 may be helpful in supporting Desi American student leaders. This is not an exhaustive list but can certainly ensure to your Desi American student leaders that their experiences are being heard and supported in some capacity.

Table 10.1

Resources for Educators

Awareness of Desi-Holidays & Celebrations	As a result of the deep-routed traditions and history Desi Americans often are engulfed in, Desi students may feel under supported or unseen during major Indian holidays. One attainable and quick way to help Desi students feel seen is by wishing them a "Happy Diwali" or "Happy Holi" when those Holidays come around. Being aware of the Holiday and of any associated celebration of the Holiday on or near your campus is a compelling way to support your students. If your Desi-students are Hindu, search up a nearby Mandir if they are Muslim, a Mosque. Having this awareness is incredibly meaningful and can help build and cultivate trust amongst your Desi-students. The following resource is helpful in providing dates of Hindu Holidays. https://www.hinduamerican.org/hindu-holidays-guide
Your Office and/or Classroom	Culturally relevant leadership learning (CRLL) suggests utilizing a critical lens when considering student demographic makeup, encourages diversified literature in classrooms, and signals a need for social justice within leadership (Guthrie et al., 2016). Desi students need for you to do just the same as you cultivate your classroom and professional experiences. Consider the following question when reflecting on your engagement with Desi-students: Have I read literature from a Desi author today that has provided me insight useful for my course or practice? Incorporating Desi literature can indeed be challenging as the availability of it within literature is unfortunately limited. Regardless, intentional incorporation of authors who are Desi, as well as authors that represent individuals within your communities can open up and cultivate not only your students' perspectives but your own.
Engage and Refer	As leadership educators, professors, practitioners, and more, we have the capacity make meaningful change in the lives of students. As we build trust and relationships with students, it is also not uncommon for students to express their distresses with us. Desi American students who come to you are coming to you with the knowledge that there is a safe space between you and them. They are coming to you knowing that you are aware of the holidays that are important to them as well as are intentional in learning about contemporary events related to Desi Americans. Further, Desi students are coming to you with the weight of all of the responsibilities in Figure 10.1. Your support is commendable and indeed appreciated and you should be aware of the high rates or mental illness matched with the low rates of attained mental health support in Desi students (Zhou, 2020). Engage in dialogue and support and motivate your Desi students to continue leading as this often means so much for them. You also have the ability to break the deep routed stigma against mental health within Desi communities (Zhou, 2020) by encouraging and embracing mental health services and having open conversations about those services to your comfort level. Most institutions have affiliated mental health services, but addition non-institutional mental health services are available in several states and countries.

Embracing difficult conversations, engaging in meaningful ways, and being aware of the elements of Desi communities can go a long way for Desi students and can empower them to continue sharing and expressing their heritage and identity.

Ham Ise Ek Saath Kar Sakate Hain—We Can Do This Together (Translated From Hindi)

Collaborating, empowering, supporting, and engaging Desi Americans is a responsibility of all of us. Desi Americans have such impactful leadership capacity and efficacy and are constantly exhibiting it in the several spaces we find ourselves. Our lived experiences with the elements of Figure 10.1, as well as with the many more elements that are not shown, cultivate our leader identities. In collaboration with Desi Americans, we are able to conceptualize the reality of Desi American leadership, and in centering this identity that has long been overlooked, we can continue to cultivate our own identities as leaders. Collaboration means commitment, though, and I hope that this has empowered you to cultivate these experiences.

NISKARSA—CONCLUSION (TRANSLATED FROM GUJARATI)

Desi American leadership is a powerful phenomenon that has so much more to offer but has yet to be studied in depth. Through our lived experiences, families, religions, languages, relationships, and so much more, we build our leader identity. This leader identity fluctuates and is malleable by nature. In building literature surrounding this identity, we risk dismantling a silencing system with admiration for an identity. There is so much exciting work to be done with Desi American leadership and I am so grateful to have been part of this journey with you.

REFERENCES

Ardoin, S., & Martinez, B. (2019). *Straddling class in the academy: 26 stories of students, administrators, and faculty from poor and working-class backgrounds and their compelling lessons for higher education policy and practice*. Stylus.

Berreman, G. (1960). Caste in India and the United States. *The American Journal of Sociology*, 66(2), 120–127. https://doi.org/10.1086/222839

British Broadcasting Company [BBC]. (2019, June 19). *What is India's caste system?* BBC News. https://www.bbc.com/news/world-asia-india-35650616

Budiman, A. (2021, April 29) *Indians in the U.S. fact sheet.* Pew Research Center's Social & Demographic Trends Project. https://www.pewresearch.org/social-trends/fact-sheet/asian-americans-indians-in-the-u-s/

Center for Teaching and Learning. (n.d.). *Stereotype threat.* University of Colorado, Boulder. https://www.colorado.edu/center/teaching-learning/inclusivity/stereotype-threat#:~:text=Stereotype%20threat%20refers%20to%20the,reduce%20academic%20focus%20and%20performance

Chadda, R. K., & Deb, K. S. (2013). Indian family systems, collectivistic society and psychotherapy. *Indian Journal of Psychiatry, 55*(2), 299–309. https://doi.org/10.4103/0019-5545.105555

Chan, J. (2017). Complexities of racial identity development for Asian Pacific Islander Desi American (APIDA) college students. In D. C. Maramba & C. M. Kodama (Eds.), *Bridging research and practice to support Asian American students* (160th ed.). Jossey-Bass. https://doi.org/10.1002/Ss.20240

Chow, K. (2017, April 19). *'Model Minority' myth again used as a racial wedge between Asians and Blacks.* NPR. https://www.npr.org/sections/codeswitch/2017/04/19/524571669/model-minority-myth-again-used-as-a-racial-wedge-between-asians-and-blacks

Gardner-Chloros, P. (2009). *Code-switching.* Cambridge University Press.

Guthrie, K. L., Bertrand Jones, T., & Osteen, L. (Eds.). (2016). Developing culturally relevant leadership learning. *New Directions for Student Leadership, 152.* Jossey-Bass.

Hilton, B. A., Grewal, S., Popatia, N., Bottorff, J. L., Johnson, J. L., Clarke, H., Venables, L. J., Bilkhu, S., Sumel, P. (2001). The Desi ways: Traditional health practices of South Asian women in Canada. *Health Care for Women International, 22*(6), 553–567. https://doi.org/10.1080/07399330127195

Jones, S., & Abes, E. S. (2013). *Identity development of college students advancing frameworks for multiple dimensions of identity* (1st ed.). Jossey-Bass.

Kim, J. (2001). Asian American identity development theory. In C. L. Wijeyesinghe, & B. W. Jackson, III (Eds.), *New perspectives on racial identity development: Integrating emerging frameworks* (2nd ed., pp. 138–160). New York University Press.

Lu, A., & Wong, Y. J. (2013). Stressful experiences of masculinity among U.S.-born and immigrant Asian American men. *Gender & Society, 27*(3), 345–371. https://doi.org/10.1177/0891243213479446

Museus, S. S., & Park, J. J. (2015). The continuing significance of racism in the lives of Asian American college students. *Journal of College Student Development, 56*(6), 551–569. https://doi.org/10.1353/csd.2015.0059

National Center for Education Statistics. (2019, February). *Indicator 27 snapshot: Attainment of a bachelor's or higher degree for racial/ethnic subgroups.* National Center for Education Statistics, Institute of Education Science. https://nces.ed.gov/programs/raceindicators/indicator_rfas.asp

National Center for Education Statistics. (n.d.). *Condition of education.* National Center for Education Statistics, Institute of Education Science. https://nces.ed.gov/programs/coe/

Northouse, P. G. (2019). *Leadership: theory and practice* (8th ed.) SAGE.

Ospina, S., & Foldy, E. (2009, December). A critical review of race and ethnicity in the leadership literature: Surfacing context, power and the collective dimensions of leadership. *ScienceDirect, 20*(6), 876–896. https://www.sciencedirect.com/science/article/abs/pii/S1048984309001751#preview-section-introduction

Park, L. S. (2008). Continuing significance of the model minority myth: The second generation. In A. Aguirre, Jr., & S. Lio (Eds.), *Social justice: A journal of crime, conflict & world opatrder* (Vol 35, 2). http://www.jstor.org/stable/29768492

Rehman, U., Shahnawaz, M. G., Khan, N. H., Kharshiing, K. D., Khursheed, M., Gupta, K., Kashyap, D., & Uniyal, R. (2021). Depression, anxiety and stress among Indians in times of Covid-19 lockdown. *Community Mental Health Journal, 57*(1), 42–48. https://doi.org/10.1007/s10597-020-00664-x

Sahu, B. K., Parganiha, A., & Pati, A. K. (2021). A population estimation study reveals a staggeringly high number Oof cattle on the streets of urban Raipur in India. *PloS One, 16*(1), 1–16. https://doi.org/10.1371/Journal.Pone.0234594

Tager, J., & Shariyf, C. R. (2022, October 17). *Reading between the lines: Race, equity, and book publishing.* Pen America. https://pen.org/report/race-equity-and-book-publishing/

U.S. Embassy India [@USAndIndia]. (2022, November 14). *Excited to share that almost 200,000 Indian students chose the United States as their higher education destination in the 2021–22 academic year* [Image attached] [Tweet]. Twitter. https://tinyurl.com/2s4xw2vu

Villavicencio, C. (2021). *The Asian American and Pacific Islander higher education leadership experience in California's four-year universities: A phenomenological study* (Publication No. 28495633). [Doctoral dissertation, University of Wyoming]. ProQuest Dissertations Publishing. https://www.proquest.com/dissertations-theses/asian-american-pacific-islander-higher-education/docview/2566065634/se-2

Zhou, J. (2020). *Breaking the silence: Mental health and treatment utilization among Asian Pacific Islander Desi American college and university students* (Publication No. 28240334) [Doctoral dissertation, University of Michigan]. ProQuest Dissertations Publishing. https://www.proquest.com/dissertations-theses/breaking-silence-mental-health-treatment/docview/2516285800/se-2

CHAPTER 11

CHALLENGES AND OPPORTUNITIES

Key Lessons in Using CRLL Environmental Dimensions to Research Queer Student Leadership

Adam Kuhn

The room felt stuffy. Not in a bad way, but in an encouraging way; in a way that the air felt like it was filled with stories. On a warm Toronto day, in a boardroom at the ArQuives (Canada's LGBTQ+ Archives), I sat with piles of folders in front of me spread across the table, each from a different university in Canada. I picked up the folder of the university I attended as an undergraduate student, opened it wide, and carefully started reviewing the treasures it held inside. The folder contained many different archival items including clippings from the campus newspapers about hate crimes, posters from the 1970s that were promoting a newly formed student group for gays and lesbians, educational pamphlets, club constitutions, flyers promoting parties and dances, copies of opinion pieces about how the campus was getting too gay, and more. As I sat there holding and taking in these items, delicately putting one down before carefully picking up the next, I saw glimpses of how my leadership learning experiences at that institution were contoured by the histories of queer inclusion and exclusion on campus.

Committing to Action: Socially Just Leadership Educations, pp. 133–140

When I began researching the leadership experiences of queer university students, I was really focused on their present and contemporary contexts, and it was not until I came across the CRLL that I had even thought to consider the sociohistorical contexts of leadership learning. The rich history I held in my hands—the evidence of years of on-campus oppression, the ephemera generated by years of queer activism—summoned a new level of consideration for the research project that had brought me to the ArQuives in the first place.

INTRODUCTION

Many leadership educators and scholars are interested in understanding how students learn and grow as leaders, and there appears to be increasing attention being paid to how students from equity-denied communities navigate their leadership learning experiences. Consensus around the best ways to study leadership development does not exist, and while there may be many models and frameworks to draw from, few of these approaches examine leadership learning from a social justice lens.

The culturally relevant leadership learning (CRLL) model (Bertrand Jones et al., 2016) is a powerful social justice-oriented tool for analyzing how individuals from any identity engage in leadership processes by developing their leadership capacity, leadership identity, and sense of leadership efficacy (Beatty & Guthrie, 2021). The five environmental dimensions (compositional diversity, behavioural, psychological, historical legacy of inclusion/exclusion, and organizational/structural) and the domains of identity, efficacy, and capacity, are profoundly useful for designing leadership development programming, reviewing leadership development curricula, and evaluating leadership education initiatives.

In addition to designing and evaluating leadership education programming, the CRLL can also be put to use in the process of conducting research, "rooted in addressing dominant ideologies of leadership education" (Beatty & Guthrie, 2021, p. 181). In particular, the environmental dimensions outline a comprehensive and robust accounting for the contexts in which leadership learning experiences take place, which can help shape a research project's literature review, research questions, and methods. While all dimensions of the CRLL are valuable, the environmental dimensions are particularly helpful as they "drive educators to reflect on the impact diverse students' lived experiences within climates at a program and organizational level have" (Beatty & Guthrie, 2021, p. 23). In my efforts to study the leadership experiences of queer undergraduate students, I have found the CRLL to be a generative model to draw from in designing the research study. The emphasis on lived experiences and campus climates is optimal for considering the total environment that animates the experiences of queer leadership learners. This chapter, using one CRLL environmental dimension as an example, will highlight the generative possibilities of using the CRLL to study the leadership experiences of queer students, and offer three key lessons that I have learned through my experience.

THE IMPORTANCE OF LANGUAGE

In any text describing student identities and communities, it is helpful to first clarify language and terminology. Through this chapter, the term *queer* will refer to sexual and gender identities existing outside dominant standards (Woodford et al., 2015). The term queer has been, and still is, used as a slur used to insult, degrade, and dehumanize non-heterosexuals and non-cisgender individuals, or broadly to imply that being anything other than cisgender and/or heterosexual is wrong or bad. My use of this term is part of the lineage of activists and scholars who have worked to reclaim the word and reframe it as a liberatory expression to describe those who challenge societies' sense of what is or is not acceptable.

In deploying the term queer, it is critical to acknowledge the plurality within and among queer communities. There is no universal queer experience, and it is important to avoid conflating gender identities and sexual identities. However, unifying terms like "queer community" and LGBTQ2S+ can be used in strategically impactful ways, drawing connections among those who experience oppression because of their sexual and gender identities. The limits of such terms, however, are reached when it is presumed the individuals within these groups exist with any type of homogeneity.

The language of queerness offers some interesting possibilities when we attach it to the language of leadership. Queer Canadian health advocate Zena Sharman (2019) suggested to queer leadership is "to resist assimilation and reproducing the status quo in favour of building something more nurturing and liberatory" (para. 17). In this regard, queer leadership can hold a similar stance to queer theory, which aims to resist traditional hegemonic norms, and to offer transformational ways of understanding society and culture. Perhaps queering leadership means to question, avoid, resist, and dismantle traditional ways of thinking about leadership. Queering leadership could involve a re-imagining of how groups work, how communities are governed, and how social change takes place.

There have been queer leaders in the world for generations, and Ware suggested "maybe Queering leadership is tracing to a different set of ancestors" (Shah, 2021, 00:28:29). Here Ware suggested there are ancestors such as American activist and drag queen Marsha P. Johnson, and others, who have been instrumental in collective action that has resulted in social change for queer communities. Ware offered that drawing connections to these queer leader ancestors may illuminate some new possibilities for the modern discussion regarding queer leadership. This invitation to turn to our ancestors and reflecting on our queer histories is an exciting idea that will be explored more broadly in the following section.

HISTORICAL LEGACY OF INCLUSION AND EXCLUSION

Within the CRLL, the historical legacy of inclusion/exclusion is an environmental dimension that "highlights systemic advantages and disadvantages in leadership learning" (Chunoo & French, 2021, p. 208). Student leadership experiences are not always created in a culturally responsive fashion, drawing on ideas and worldviews that are built on exclusionary traditions. Some leadership curricula are developed *ahistorically*, which is to say that they are developed without an understanding of "what remnants of those exclusionary traditions exist today" (Pierre & Okstad, 2021, p. 55). Without an understanding of sociohistoric contexts, leadership educators exclude diverse students, reproduce harm, and promote colonial and Eurocentric leadership concepts that endorse a limited and exclusive understanding of leadership. This principle applies to leadership researchers, as they must also attend to the historical contexts of the phenomenon they are investigating.

Beatty and Guthrie (2021) asked leadership researchers to consider how histories and contexts can "be explored and connected to the theoretical and conceptual framework guiding the research" (p. 179). In preparing to conduct a research project on the leadership experiences of queer undergraduate students, the CRLL model has been an effective tool for the conceptual framework and research design. Through the process of working with the CRLL on a research project, I have learned three key lessons: Queer campus histories can be difficult to trace, exploring diverse sources and texts can be invaluable, and that histories are multi-layered.

Key Lesson: Queer Campus Histories Can Be Difficult to Trace

Researching queer campus histories is challenging because institutions of higher learning tend to be more interested in documenting and sharing their histories of inclusion than their histories of exclusion. As a result, queer student experiences of oppression and resistance are often excluded or straight-washed from dominant institutional narratives. While queer people have always existed, our histories and stories are not often acknowledged as acceptable therefore, invalidating our stories. As Collins (2021) stated "history does not remember what it does not value" (para. 17) and so, because of this persistent devaluing of queer experiences, researching the historical legacy of inclusion/exclusion of queer students and queer student leaders on Canadian campuses is a challenging task.

Key Lesson: Exploring Diverse Sources and Texts Can Be Invaluable

Knowing how challenging it is to explore queer histories, researchers may need to explore texts and sources that are outside the typically permitted origins. Squire (2020) asked "does knowledge only come from books and journal articles, or can knowledge also come from lyrics, poetry, blog posts, Twitter, and other more accessible sources that resonate and speak to the experience of a wider swath of people?" (p. 193). As a queer researcher researching queer leadership experiences, it is important to consider the literature available through traditional academic resources and to also seek out and acknowledge the just-as-valid queer stories from places that the traditional academy would not usually deem scholarly. Munoz (1996), highlighted the ephemeral nature of queer stories and experiences and noted:

> Instead of being clearly available as visible evidence, queerness has instead existed as innuendo, gossip, fleeting moments, and performances that are meant to be interacted with by those within its epistemological sphere—while evaporating at the touch of those who would eliminate queer possibility. (p. 6)

Munoz argued there is a dominant institutional regime in place that gatekeeps what is or is not considered rigorous. Cruising through various sources, ephemera, and stories is a necessary, vital, and rigorous approach for anyone looking to explore the histories, presents, and futures of individuals and communities that have been historically and systematically excluded.

In leveraging the CRLL model to research the historical inclusion/exclusion of queer students on Canadian campuses, I have turned to sources which might be considered alternative compared to so-called traditional academic texts. Sources such as grey literature, archival documents, campus ephemera, student campaigns, memos, posters, flyers, social media, student journalism, blogs, institutional websites, among others, have been useful in exploring the complicated histories of colleges and universities.

Visiting campus and community archives has proven to be a generative research tactic; connecting with rich sources of insights on the events surrounding the historical legacy of inclusion and exclusion for queer students in higher education. For example, copies of constitutions from early homophile associations and gay liberation groups (early iterations of present-day queer student groups) highlighted the early goals and structures of queer campus organizing. Posters promoting protests revealed a great deal about campus politics, while flyers advertising dances and parties demonstrated tactics queer students used to create spaces for queer joy and queer worldmaking. These artifacts showcase the stories of inclusion and exclusion on campuses while also hinting at the type of community leadership, advocacy, and organizing demanded of queer students to survive in heteronormative and cis-normative institutions.

Key Lesson: Histories Are Multilayered

The CRLL model helps leadership educators understand how, if they wish to create impactful and culturally relevant leadership learning experiences, they must contend with the sociohistorical context that informs their present circumstances. The same goes for researchers with a goal of exploring the leadership experiences of students. This means scholars and practitioners alike must reflect on the historical legacy of inclusion/exclusion on multiple levels, including program/service histories, departmental, campus histories, and also regional, provincial, national, and global histories.

At the program level, one could investigate the curriculum and the worldviews and perspectives that are included and excluded. At the departmental level, one could explore the unit's history of hiring and promotion of staff and faculty, and what identities and experiences are included/excluded. At the campus level, one could look into the policies in place for students and how governance processes allow (or do not allow) for social change. Looking at broader regional, provincial, national, and global histories can offer legislative and political lenses which are sometimes lacking in the analysis of leadership learning.

It can also be interesting to layer the historical legacy of inclusion/exclusion onto the CRLL's other four environmental dimensions. Layering the historical legacy of inclusion and exclusion onto compositional diversity and the organizational and structural dimension, for example, could yield some interesting insights. In my research, I came across an example of an institution that appeared to attract more and more queer students once their campus launched some queer affirming policies and programs. The composition of the queer community on campus seems to be influenced by the institution's organizational structures, thus influencing their history of inclusion and exclusion. This exemplifies how these three dimensions interact in leadership learning for queer students. Viewing the environmental dimensions as a Venn diagram has been a useful tactic for exploring the multi-dimensionality of student experiences.

CONCLUSION

Formal and structured leadership learning has not always been a process available to all students on our campuses. Leadership is often so narrowly defined that students from marginalized populations are not welcomed to the process, nor are they able to "read work written by or about their perspectives in the leadership canon" (Spencer, 2021, p. 192). For many queer students, their leadership development has come from activism and the labour of creating programs and services for other queer students to fill institutional gaps. Appreciating this historical context can lead to the following questions: What are the responsibilities for leadership educators and scholars today? How can leadership educators and researchers recognize the often exclusive and oppressive climates experienced by queer students, and work to create thoughtful learning environments and experiences?

One of the ways the CRLL model attempts to contend with this is by including the historical legacy of inclusion/exclusion as one of its five domains. The CRLL centres contextual dimensions which can allow leadership educators and researchers to "take responsibility for disrupting dominant narratives of leadership, and legitimizing who is framed as a leader on campus, in the community, in our nation, and globally" (Beatty & Guthrie, 2021, p. 204). The CRLL model is a useful framework for conducting research on the leadership experiences of students who have not always been seen as part of the traditional prototype of what is considered a leader. In particular, the five environmental dimensions offer a set of contextual domains to consider when examining research questions that focus on the leadership experiences of queer students. The five environmental dimensions intersect and interact in ways that generate insights into the spaces and places that queer students experience leadership learning.

This chapter focused on examining queer leadership experiences using one environmental dimension, however the CRLL could be similarly useful in exploring the experiences of other groups that have experienced historical and systematic exclusion and oppression. In researching the leadership experiences of queer students who "need to survive in a heteronormative and gendered world that can be harmful to their well being" (Taylor, 2020, p. 76), models like CRLL and its five environmental dimensions provide a comprehensive structure to review their campus contexts. Through the examination of one of the environmental dimensions, it is possible to conduct research that may contribute, even in small ways, to more socially just and liberatory leadership learning experiences for queer students.

REFERENCES

Beatty, C. C., & Guthrie, K. L. (2021). *Operationalizing culturally relevant leadership learning*. Information Age Publishing.

Bertrand Jones, T., Guthrie, K. L., & Osteen, L. (2016). Critical domains of culturally relevant leadership learning: A call to transform leadership programs. *New Directions for Student Leadership, 2016*(152), 9–21. https://doi.org/10.1002/yd.20205

Chunoo, V. S., & French, G. E. (2021). Socially just leadership education in action: Applying the culturally relevant leadership learning model. In K. L. Guthrie & V. S. Chunoo, (Eds.), *Shifting the mindset: Socially just leadership education* (pp. 207–219). Information Age Publishing.

Collins, C. (2021, March 21). Queer people have always existed- teach like it. *Learning for Justice*. https://www.learningforjustice.org/magazine/queer-people-have-always-existed-teach-like-it

Muñoz, J. E. (1996). Ephemera as evidence: Introductory notes to queer acts. *Women & Performance: A Journal of Feminist Theory, 8*(2), 5–16. https://doi.org/10.1080/07407709608571228

Pierre, D. E., & Okstad, J. J. (2021). Developing lesbian, gay, bisexual student leaders in and out of the classroom. In K. L. Guthrie & V. S. Chunoo. (Eds.). *Shifting the mindset: Socially just leadership education* (pp. 53–64). Information Age Publishing.

Shah, V. (2021, September 14). *Queering leadership* [Audio podcast]. The Unleading Project, York University. https://www.yorku.ca/edu/unleading/podcast-episodes/queering-leadership/

Sharman, Z. (2019, March 30). *Queering leadership*. https://zenasharman.com/blog/queering-leadership

Spencer, D. (2021). Narrative: Amplifying voices through narrative inquiry and culturally relevant leadership learning. In C. C. Beatty & K. L. Guthrie (Eds.), *Operationalizing culturally relevant leadership learning*. Information Age Publishing.

Squire, D. D. (2020). The eradication of the ally complex. In E. M. Zamani-Gallaher, D. D. Choudhuri, & J. L. Taylor (Eds.), *Rethinking LGBTQIA students and collegiate contexts: Identity, policies, and campus climate* (pp. 186–203). Routledge.

Taylor, J. L. (2020). Assessing the classroom "space" for LGBTQ+ students. In E. M. Zamani-Gallaher, D. D. Choudhuri, & J. L. Taylor (Eds.), *Rethinking LGBTQIA students and collegiate contexts: Identity, policies, and campus climate* (pp. 61–77). Routledge.

Woodford, M. R., Joslin, J., & Renn, K. A. (2015) Lesbian, gay, bisexual, transgender and queer students on campus: Fostering inclusion through research, policy, and practice. In P. Pasque, N. Ortega, J. C. Burkhardt, & M. P. Ting (Eds.), *Transforming understandings of diversity in higher education: Demography, democracy, and discourse* (pp. 57–80). Stylus.

CHAPTER 12

IT'S ALL A SOCIAL CONSTRUCT

Socially Just Leadership for International Students

Laura Vaughn

Many of us may envision leadership similarly when we start to imagine it as embodied through higher education professionals in the United States. Differences among leaders and leadership might come to mind or we may be reminded of distinctions between leadership and management. However, what, if anything, do these mean if your conceptualizations of leaders and leadership do not match your students' notions? How might a view of leadership change if one's culture is more collectivist? What if it is more individualistic? These are among the questions socially just leadership educators explore as they strive to more deeply connect with their international students. This chapter delves into cultural and social barriers to international student (i.e. non-U.S. domestic) leadership learning and suggests how to navigate these barriers using the culturally relevant leadership learning (CRLL) model as a starting point (Bertrand Jones et al., 2016). As Cecil and Hu (2021) described international student engagement as spanning from leadership program involvement to being a part of student organizations, this chapter's purpose is to take their foundational emphasis on the importance of international student engagement and expand upon how socially just leadership educators can incorporate research on cultural differences to address international student leadership education.

Committing to Action: Socially Just Leadership Educations, pp. 141–153

POSITIONALITY STATEMENT AND CLARIFICATION OF TERMS

It is important for me to claim my own positionality on this subject. I am a White woman who was born and raised in the United States. I have studied abroad in Japan and England, and I worked in Japan as an English teacher for two years. I was also an International Student Advisor at the University of Mississippi for eight years before going back to school as a full-time doctoral student. I am currently working in the Leadership Learning Research Center at Florida State University. My experiences working with international students, and my interest in leadership development among undergraduate students, are my inspirations to research international students, and how educators can support their leadership development. To decenter the emphasis on historically and stereotypically racially White perspectives within higher education, I would have preferred to not capitalize the term white in reference to race in this chapter. However, current writing standards are not always open to deviating from set guidelines.

For my purposes, *international students* are defined as individuals enrolled in classes on a United States-based higher education campus and who hold nonimmigrant student visas, in accordance with Cecil and Hu (2021). According to the Institute of International Education's (2021) *Open Doors Report*, the number of international students in the United States plateaued in the 2015-2016 academic year, remaining between 1,043,000 and 1,075,000 until the 2019–2020 academic year. This number plummeted by 15%, to around 914,000 students, in the 2020–2021 academic year, mainly due to the impact of the COVID-19 pandemic (Institute of International Education, 2021). No matter their percentage, the influence and importance of international students in American higher education cannot be understated.

WHY FOCUS ON LEADERSHIP EDUCATION FOR INTERNATIONAL STUDENTS?

With almost one million international students in American postsecondary educational institutions, members of these populations need more specialized assistance than currently exists. Research demonstrates several benefits of international student engagement (Glass, 2012; Cecil & Hu, 2021; Mamiseishvili, 2012). For example, international students who participated in leadership programs and took courses where professors facilitated intergroup dialogue perceived campus climate more positively than those who did not (Glass, 2012). Among those international students who participated in leadership programs, campus-organized diversity discussions and interacted with those from diverse cultural backgrounds

exhibited gains in learning and development when measured against otherwise comparable students. (Glass, 2012). Social groups, positive peer
interactions, and supportive academic advising were all associated with
greater international student retention (Mamiseishvili, 2012). Furthermore, the benefits of international student engagement not only affect
international students; cross-cultural engagement has helped dismantle
the "walls of Whiteness" within U.S. higher education (Mahoney, 2016).
These walls are both physical and metaphorical barriers preventing White
students from seeing the broader racial contexts and experiences in the
world, and they demote non-White students to a losing side of contexts and
experiences (Mahoney, 2016). These barriers to cross-cultural communication, learning, and student development take varied forms across various
types of postsecondary educational institutions.

Although there are several benefits to international student engagement
and involvement, higher education administration, faculty, and staff do not
always create welcoming environments for international students, and these
actions can negatively impact international student engagement in and
involvement with leadership; both positional and non-positional. International students are often viewed as a commodity by administrators since
they, generally, pay more tuition and fees than domestic students (Yao &
Viggiano, 2019). Some institutions cluster international students together
in housing, which upholds walls of Whiteness when domestic students are
not given opportunities to have international student roommates (and
vice versa). This segregation of international students also gives them a
feeling of othering; the exact opposite from the sense of belonging many
student housing systems claim to create. One experience shared from an
international student enrolled at a four-year institution in the United States
discussed how all the international students were assigned to live together
in one residential hall separate from the domestic students. Although this
living situation did allow for the international students to connect with
each other, they were cut out from the larger campus community, which
made cross-cultural learning more difficult. Having discussions concerning
sociocultural issues was found to be a strong predictor of leadership efficacy
(Dugan & Komives, 2007), and failing to facilitate these types of discussions
within campus housing blocks chances for leadership learning among both
international and domestic students.

Higher education often frames international students from a deficit perspective, which focuses on "dealing with the extra supports" these students
may need, especially when they might not have complete fluency in English,
or have non-Western dietary restrictions and experiences (Glass, 2012;
Mamiseishvili, 2012). Personally, I have seen teachers and administrators
focused on how to make international students acculturate to the United
States instead of looking for the benefits international students provide

by adding alternate perspectives needed for cross-cultural interactions among students. Socially just leadership educators who work with international students seek to deconstruct deficit-oriented views and reorient their energies toward asset-based approaches (Smit, 2012). However, the barriers to socially just leadership education, involvement, and engagement among international students can come from a variety of sources, including both the institutional structure and interpersonal dynamics among students.

Barriers to Engagement

Cecil and Hu (2021) delineated several barriers to international student engagement, which should be revisited and expanded upon from their previous work:

1. *Focus on academics*—international students are often focused on attending United States higher education institutions to get specific degrees (Cecil & Hu, 2021). Many international students are focused on their academics in a way that does not give themselves time or motivation to get involved in leadership programs if they see no benefit.
2. *Discouraging campus environment/culture*—microaggressions from other students, staff, and faculty create an unwelcoming campus climate where international students who might be interested in getting involved on campus no longer feel like they can be involved (Glass, 2012).
3. *Language barriers*—socially just leadership educators strive to meet their students where they are when it comes to language learning. The communication barriers often stem from educators not creating understanding with their students.

One example of an educator creating a barrier to classroom engagement occurred a few years ago at a major research institution. There was a professor who reached out to the director of the English as a Second Language program, saying one of their students needed to take more English classes because they did not speak at an appropriate level. After meeting with both the professor and the student, the director discovered root causes of: the teacher using slang in class, possessing a strong regional accent, speaking too quickly, and failing to use alternative terminology when the international student misunderstood their slang usage. The communication barriers were not caused by student; they otherwise displayed the fluency needed to succeed in the class. The root of the issue was the professor who failed to reflect on their own language and communication skills when working with students who were not native English speakers. Socially just leadership learning calls for leadership educators to examine their own positionalities and backgrounds while attending to how those factors impact students (Beatty & Guthrie, 2021). In the example, it was clear the instructor in question failed to critically examine their own views and biases before interacting with an international student and these types of microaggressions impact how students learn and grow.

THE INTERNATIONAL STUDENT VIEW OF LEADERSHIP

When leadership educators surface topics of leadership and leadership learning with international students, it is important to leadership's essential nature as a social construct (Beatty & Guthrie, 2021). What people in the United States view as leadership can be different from how other members of societies around the world view as leading, since conceptualizations of leadership can vary across cultures. Research routinely demonstrates, "[l]eadership is culturally contingent" (House, 2004, p. 5). The Global Leadership and Organizational Behavior Effectiveness Research Program (GLOBE) is a longitudinal research project, started in the early 1990s, examining how 62 societies scored on nine attributes of culture and six leader behaviors (House, 2004). The study found some countries and cultures tend to romanticize leaders and leadership by viewing it as something positive to have, while other countries have a fear of the term leadership, and students from those cultures may be repulsed by programs with the term leadership in them (House, 2004).

In general, the cultural groups who regarded leadership as positive included, "Americans, Arabs, Asians, [the] English, Eastern Europeans, [the] French, Germans, Latin Americans, and Russians" (House, 2004, p. 5). Those who viewed leadership negatively included, " [m]any people of German-speaking Switzerland, the Netherlands, and Scandinavia" (House, 2004, p. 5). These differential and culturally-based perspectives on leadership are important for educators when working with international students and while encouraging them to attend leadership programing. The United States approaches leadership education from a White, Anglo-Saxon point of view and this colonizing approach is not always viewed in a positive light by students from different countries and cultures (House, 2004; Mahoney, 2016).

Collectivism's Role in Societies

Another important factor when working with international students is many of them come from more collectivist societies (than the U.S.) which can impact their views on leadership. When considering collective societies, as compared with individualist societies, it should be noted how cultures of birth can impact a student's perception of leadership. Geert Hofstede was one of the first researchers to formally consider cultural values, such as collectivism within his cultural dimensions theory that addressed cross-cultural communication (Gelfand et al., 2004). Although Hofstede's research on collectivism and individualism was groundbreaking for its time, it also had validity and generalizability issues (Gelfand et al., 2004). The GLOBE study was more nuanced by separating collectivism and individualism for countries, and by differentiating the impact of collectivism on individuals as different from that of organizations (see Table 12.1).

Table 12.1

Collectivism Practice Scores by Country

Societal Institutional Collectivism Practices Scores		Societal In-Group Collectivism Practices Scores	
Country	Score*	Country	Score*
Sweden	5.22	Philippines	6.36
South Korea	5.20	Georgia	6.19
Japan	5.19	Iran	6.03
*Higher scores show greater collectivism			

As shown in Table 12.1, within the GLOBE study, countries like Sweden, South Korea, and Japan show greater collectivism in their societal institutional practices scores, but the Philippines, Georgia, and Iran are more collective in their societal in-group practices scores (Gelfand et al., 2004). What this means is while a country like Sweden is highly collective in their institutional practices, they are not at the same level of collectivism within social groups. Using the same set of scores, Greece, Hungary, and Germany ranked low on collective institutional practices and Denmark, Sweden, and New Zealand ranked low on collective in-group practices. From this data, collectivism practices for those in Sweden and New Zealand might be high institutionally, but are extremely low socially. The United States was placed around the middle for institutional collectivist practices and low in in-group collectivism.

Cultural Clusters

Through patterns found by GLOBE study, individual countries were organized into cultural clusters of: Anglo, Middle East, Confucian Asia,

Eastern Europe, Germanic Europe, Latin America, Latin Europe, Nordic Europe, Southern Asia, and Sub-Saharan Africa (Gelfand et al., 2004). By cluster, Nordic Europe (Finland, Sweden, and Denmark) had the highest values for institutional collectivism practices and Latin America (including Argentina, Brazil, Ecuador, Mexico, and others) had the lowest values for institutional collectivism (Gelfand et al., 2004). Regarding in-group collectivism practices, Southern Asia (including India, Philippines, Thailand, Iran, etc.) scored the highest and Nordic Europe scored the lowest (Gelfand et al., 2004). These researchers also found the focus on the individual is heavily impacted by family and society which also influences their views on leadership among collectivist cultures.

When applying these clusters to culturally endorsed implicit theories of leadership's leadership dimensions, all but the Eastern Europe and Middle East clusters had highest scores in the charismatic/value-based dimension. For the Eastern Europe and Middle East clusters, their highest scored dimension was "team-oriented" (Dorfman et al., 2004). This view of the most important dimension of leadership shows how much importance is placed on charismatic leadership, which does not fully match how many American leadership educators view the leadership process; as something anyone can do regardless of charisma. This trait-based view of leadership is something United States-based leadership educators will need to keep in mind when approaching international students about leadership development programming.

International students' understanding of leadership is often dependent on the social construction of leadership within their countries and cultures or origin. For more collectivist cultures, leadership can be associated with saving face, charisma, and paternalism. In more individualistic cultures, autonomy and task accomplishment are typically associated with leadership (Gelfand et al., 2004). Some Western research has been conducted by separating leaders as people, leadership as a process, and management as different from both (Beatty & Guthrie, 2021; Bertrand Jones et al., 2016; Day, 2000). However, students from other cultures may place greater emphasis on being a leader as opposed to the process of leadership due to their understanding of leadership. As seen earlier, management traits, such as paternalism or task accomplishment are associated with leadership, as evidenced by GLOBE study findings.

In general, the GLOBE study found the highest scores in team-oriented among members of the Latin American cluster. For charismatic/values-based leadership, the Anglo, Latin American, and Southern Asia clusters scored high, while the Eastern Europe cluster scored the highest in autonomous leadership (Gelfand et al., 2004). When applying these findings to students, socially just leadership educators can use these results to understand how international students view leadership, and therefore may or may not engage with leadership learning offerings. Some students may seem uninterested in leadership positions because they do not view themselves as 'a leader'; they may view leadership as authoritarian, and trait based. Socially just leadership educators do not stereotype our students based on the GLOBE findings since while some students might match the findings associated with their cultures, but different students have differential backgrounds which can impact who they are and how they relate to leadership.

RECONTEXTUALIZING THE
LEADERSHIP EDUCATOR MINDSET

Socially just leadership educators recontextualize how they view leadership for students from different cultures. A starting point for this is by applying the culturally relevant leadership learning model to the experiences built for international students (Beatty & Guthrie, 2021; Guthrie et al., 2016). By applying CRLL to international students, educators reflect on students' backgrounds as well as our own as means to derive common understanding. The research represented by the GLOBE studies validates CRLL's application to international students. Table 12.2 shares historical context and offers questions to ask when thinking about our students' backgrounds. This is not a comprehensive list and should be only used as a starting point for educators to then do more targeted research on their specific international student populations (see Table 12.2).

The impact of the five dimensions listed above on international student identity, capacity, and efficacy within the CRLL model play a large role in how international students interact on campus, and how domestic students, staff, and faculty interact with international students. Use of the CRLL model to contextualize how international students engage with campus helps leadership educators adjust their beliefs and behaviors while addressing injustices they might encounter. Cross-cultural communication with international students can uncover CRLL dimensions facing individual international students, while critical interrogations of the campus environment illuminate other factors influencing international student experiences.

RECOMMENDATIONS FOR ACTION

Confronting and Interrupting Our Biases

A number of meaningful steps can be taken to confront and interrupt deficit-oriented biases toward international undergraduates. First, we can

Table 12.2

Culturally Relevant Leadership Learning Questions by Dimension

Dimension	Questions to ask concerning International Students
Historical Legacy of Inclusion/Exclusion	–What are the historical immigration bans in the United States? –How difficult is the visa application and approval process? –How are students impacted by politicians claiming immigrants are stealing American jobs? –Are students coming from homogenous cultures where they have never been the minority? –Are international students coming with set gender expectations?
Compositional Diversity	–Are international students included in campus organizations or student government? –How many international students are involved in leadership programs? –How many leadership educators are international?
Psychological Dimension	–How do those on campus react to international students? –Is there a pattern of discrimination and racism on campus? –Is there discrimination towards certain international populations based on 9/11 and COVID-19?
Behavioral Dimension	–How do people interact with international students? –Look for microaggressions around you - are they targeted toward international students?
Organizational/Structural Dimension	–What is the university's structure and policy when handling international students? –Do people try to help them or are they sent to international office for everything? –There are barriers to specific roles due to labor laws such as student government leadership sometimes being a paid position

increase the number of staff members, faculty, and leadership students who experience CRLL and cultural competencies training. When international students are not represented in our programs and services, the responsibility to repair this should not be solely placed on students the systems in place are creating access barriers. Socially just leadership educators being by looking for barriers at their institutions and strategically investigate how they can be removed or reduced. Sometimes, domestic students need to be pushed into situations where they interact with international students

(Tavares, 2022). Collaborating with advisors and the international student office on campus can connect you to members of international student groups if you do not know where else to start. Although many leadership educators want international students to be involved in leadership learning, we also remember not all international students view leadership as we do. When students come from cultures where leadership is not a desirable social characteristic, it becomes important to recontextualize leadership in the United States context and subsequent mismatches in understanding. Socially just leadership educators also recall the impact of colonialism in world history and consider how their approaches may reinforce imperialist norms if they are too direct. If students remain uninterested in leadership learning after attempt to translate it across cultures, that choice should be respected as an expression of knowledgeable agency.

Making Connections

Many campuses would benefit from transparency on how to find student organizations and ways to get involved. International students some forms of social and cultural capital their domestic peers may possess, and therefore, need extra help finding meaningful memberships. One way of increasing transparency is by getting organizations to recruit international students through orientation and involvement fairs. Other ways to encourage involvement is to teach faculty and staff how to attend to international student needs inside and outside of the classroom. Increasing listening and empathy towards international students fosters inclusion within the campus and can provide influence when it comes to policy and practice as structures of institutions change to meet the needs of their increasingly diverse student population. Faculty members shape students experience campus climate (Glass, 2012), therefore; their actions are crucial in the lives of students. Instructors can encourage participation from students of collectivist cultures by starting assignments with groupwork as a precursor to individual tasks instead of starting with individualized activities which lead into teamwork. Working in a group first can allow those who are shy to be more confident sharing with the wider class.

Socially just leadership educators operating in an individualistic, Western society, shift our mindsets toward how international students are viewed within higher education and change our courses of action. Instead of looking at what additional things international students might need for success, we appreciate the diverse perspectives they add to our campuses.

International students are not simply revenue generators; they are valuable assets for our campus culture that help to bridge cultural gaps of understanding through interactions both inside and outside of the classroom. Keep the CRLL foundations in mind when working with international students to have more empathy with how they may view and approach the idea of leadership. If a student says "I can't be a leader," see what they mean first before pushing your western viewpoint of leadership on the student. What you mean by leadership and what the student hears can be different and it is important to work to bridge the gap of understanding with compassion.

COMMITTING TO ACTION FOR INTERNATIONAL STUDENT LEADERSHIP LEARNING

This chapter has shared important factors of international student leadership development including campus barriers blocking international student engagement, views on leadership, and what educators creating leadership learning opportunities need to know about the social construction of leadership. Change can be challenging, so when looking at your own institutions and programs, consider the following questions to drive future actions:

1. What are the systems in place on your campus international students deal with?
2. Who is helping international students grow their social capital on campus?
3. Where are your international students housed?
4. How many international students are in your leadership curricular/co-curricular programs?
5. If you don't have many, or any, international students in your programming, which barriers can be reduced or removed?

Social justice is not only for domestic students and the treatment of international students by leadership educators can make a large difference in how those students engage with the campus environment. Leadership is a social construct and it is important to remember not everyone views leadership in the same way. This does not mean any specific view is right or wrong, just different. I empower you to commit with others within higher education to treat international students as more than an economic benefit; they provide wonderful and diverse perspectives to campuses struggling to tear down their longstanding walls of Whiteness.

REFERENCES

Beatty, C. C., & Guthrie, K. L. (2021). *Operationalizing culturally relevant leadership learning*. Information Age Publishing.

Bertrand Jones, T., Guthrie, K. L., & Osteen, L. (2016). Critical domains of culturally relevant leadership learning: A call to transform leadership programs. *New directions for student leadership*, *152*(2016), 9–21. https://doi.org/10.1002/yd.20205

Cecil, B., & Hu, P. (2021). Redefining engagement. In K. L. Guthrie & V. S. Chunoo (Eds.), *Shifting the mindset: Socially just leadership education* (pp. 39–52). Information Age Publishing.

Day, D. V. (2000). Leadership development: A review in context. *The Leadership Quarterly*, *11*(4), 581–613. https://doi.org/10.1016/s1048-9843(00)00061-8

Dorfman, P. W., Hanges, P. J., & Brodbeck, F. C. (2004). Leadership and cultural variation: The identification of culturally endorsed leadership profiles. *Culture, leadership, and organizations: The GLOBE study of 62 societies* (pp. 669–719). SAGE.

Dugan, J. P., & Komives, S. R. (2007). *Developing leadership capacity in college students: Findings from a national study*. National Clearinghouse for Leadership Programs.

Gelfand, M. J., Bhawuk, D. P., Nishii, L. H., & Bechtold, D. J. (2004). Individualism and collectivism. *Culture, leadership, and organizations: The GLOBE study of 62 societies* (pp. 437–512). SAGE.

Glass, C. R. (2012). Educational experiences associated with international students' learning, development, and positive perceptions of campus climate. *Journal of Studies in International Education*, *16*(3), 228–251. https://doi.org/10.1177/1028315311426783

Guthrie, K. L., Bertrand Jones, T., & Osteen, L. (Eds.). (2016). *Developing culturally relevant leadership learning: New directions for student leadership, Number 152*. John Wiley & Sons.

House, R. J. (2004). Illustrative examples of GLOBE findings. *Culture, leadership, and organizations: The GLOBE study of 62 societies* (pp. 3–8). SAGE.

Institute of International Education. (2021). International student enrollment trends, 1948/49–2021/21. *Open Doors Report on International Educational Exchange*. http://www.opendoorsdata.org

Mahoney, A. D. (2016). Culturally responsive integrative learning environments: A critical displacement approach. *New Directions for Student Leadership*, *2016*(152), 47–59. https://doi.org/10.1002/yd.20208

Mamiseishvili, K. (2012). International student persistence in US postsecondary institutions. *Higher Education*, *64*(1), 1–17. https://doi.org/10.1007/s10734-011-9477-0

Smit, R. (2012). Towards a clearer understanding of student disadvantage in higher education: Problematising deficit thinking. *Higher Education Research & Development*, *31*(3), 369–380. https://doi.org/10.1080/07294360.2011.634383

Tavares, V. (2022). "Lock us in a room together": Local students' suggestions for improving socialization with international students. *Journal of Comparative & International Higher Education*, *14*(4), 22–36. https://doi.org/10.32674/jcihe.v14i4.4280

Yao, C. W., & Viggiano, T. (2019). Interest convergence and the commodification of international students and scholars in the United States. *Journal Committed to Social Change on Race and Ethnicity (JCSCORE)*, *5*(1), 82–109. https://doi.org/10.15763/issn.2642-2387.2019.5.1.81-109

CHAPTER 13

TOP OF THE "CLASS"

Socially Just Leadership Identity Development for High-Achieving College Students

Amy Haggard

The purpose of this chapter is to discuss the importance of the multilayered and complex identities of high-achieving students, while critically examining their leadership identity development, and monitoring the relationship of that development with their social class identity. Using effective leadership identity models, such as culturally relevant leadership learning model (Owen et al., 2017) and the leadership identity development model (Komives et al., 2006), I will explore the development, intersection, and importance of multiple identities in this specific student population. There will also be a direct emphasis on the social class of high-achieving students, including how the high-achieving identity directly influences the student's social class, and how interactions of both affect leadership identity development.

This student population is important for socially just leadership educators to consider because attending to the student's varied backgrounds is core to developing them as leaders who are prepared to make the world a fairer and more equitable place. Researchers have already expressed the importance of social justice supporting the work of educational leaders who have an obligation to create equitable practices and spaces for such identity groups (Jean-Marie et al., 2009). The understanding of the high-achieving

Committing to Action: Socially Just Leadership Educations, pp. 155–162
Copyright © 2025 by Information Age Publishing
www.infoagepub.com
155

identity, and its connection to leadership identity development, should be one of interest for socially just leadership educators.

It is important to focus on high-achieving student identity because of the various experiences that play a role in this identity development. Most characteristics that play a role in the makeup of a high-achieving students can cause positive reactions from peers, professors, and individuals in leadership roles, which can engender leadership qualities in the student (Shoenberger et al., 2015). General recognition for high performance in academic settings creates positive rewards and behavior which leads to new leadership identity development.

I will highlight expectations and performance of high-achieving students and the relationships between those expectations to leadership identity development. I will also reiterate the importance of understanding leadership identity and how it is developed through the lens of high-achieving students. Staying grounded in theoretical framework that guides overall importance of incorporating high-achieving students into social justice leadership education.

HIGH-ACHIEVING STUDENT IDENTITY AND EXPECTATIONS

A noteworthy factor when analyzing the high-achieving student population is how expectations hinder students' academic performance. Thus, an important goal would be to analyze any correlations from those greater expectations to leadership identity development and meaning making of that identity. Findings from recent studies suggest while high-achieving college students are not expected to perform well in all activities, in less academically rigorous activities, they may feel constrained and perform poorly (Wu et al., 2019). Examples of these activities include social activities without commitment to a role. This questions if high-achieving students presume leadership due to their academic status, instead of developing self-efficacy. This creates the argument that leadership roles are needed for these students to be successful.

Owen et al. (2017) demonstrated the centrality of leadership self-efficacy in the development of leadership identity. This self-efficacy can be actualized through involvement in academic enrichment opportunities as well as co-curricular organization activities and programming. Furthermore, leadership identity can develop when one is engaged with learning opportunities in their specific environments (Komives et al., 2006). With an intentional focus on how leadership identity is developed through programming, environments, and self-efficacy, we can better understand the meaning-making process behind leader identity. Owen et al. (2017) also reminded us how students' leadership abilities increase as they develop multifaceted ways of learning. Thus, increased academic focus and success can jumpstart leadership identity development. Shortly, I will discuss how culturally relevant leadership learning can influence these dynamics, but it is important to reference leadership as learned through a process that integrates components of high-achieving identity, knowledge, experience, and skill.

When attempting to conceptualize high-achieving students' identity and the differential impact of expectations in leadership identity, it is important to remember students' views on leadership when they join a campus community. There will be subsequent discussion around the leadership identity model and its importance in understanding the view of self in relation to others and how that view is independent (Komives et al., 2006). However, it is important to note how high-achieving students may use the language of *leadership* and *leader* interchangeably and once these terms are differentiated, that shift can alter students' views of both. In the population of high-achieving students, the development and understanding of one's self-efficacy in relation to leadership assists with overall leadership identity development.

LEADERSHIP IDENTITY DEVELOPMENT

Scholarly work on leadership identity development models depict how college student growth occurs through collaboration with other students who intend social change outcomes and processes (Komives et al., 2006). Based on this premise, leadership identity can develop from participation within the community of high-achieving academic students on a college campus. There is ample information on the process of students developing leadership identity from Komives et al. (2006), who also highlights possible influences from the emerging theory lending to the greater understanding of leadership identity. There are four specific influences that are found to contribute to the development of leadership identity that could be influential in understanding the leadership identity development in the high-achieving population: meaningful involvement, reflective learning, and adult and peer influences (Komives et al., 2006). High academically achieving students tend to engage in educational enrichment opportunities, therefore; leadership educators who work with such students have a responsibility to use socially just frameworks to grow their leader identity in culturally relevant and responsive ways.

Specifically looking at leadership identity development, it is important to frame teaching and learning through the lens of the leadership identity development model (LID) from Komives et al. (2006). LID's stage-based approach describes students' development as progressive yet punctuated.

However, Komives et al. (2006) was purposeful in the observation of these punctuations as both linear and cyclical. The stages of the LID model are *awareness, exploration and engagement, leader identified, leadership differentiated,* and *generativity* (Komives et al., 2006). This model and its stages account for necessary observations and collective experiences as students become aware of their leadership identity through their engagement with and exploration with enrichment opportunities. Including this model as a framework is critical for understanding the different definitions of leadership identity.

The most significant component of the LID model is role modeling in organizations, which assists in identifying aspects of leadership identity. Sims and Manz (1982) highlighted three specific individual identifications: the establishment of new behaviors, changes of frequency in current behaviors, and appropriate behavioral cues. These factors lend value to the LID model; especially in the transition from leader identified to leadership differentiated.

In addition to the LID model, the culturally relevant leadership learning model, or CRLL (Bertrand Jones et al., 2016), incorporates identity, capacity, and efficacy in leadership learning. Guthrie and Beatty (2022) reminded us that what is necessary for the CRLL models' effectiveness is the individual's journey to understanding their own identity, capacity, and efficacy. As high-achieving students have varied associations in and out of the classroom, and across leadership roles, their identities, capacities, and efficacies are enhanced through these factors, which deepen their engagement. This continual cycle of engagement and enhancement engenders leadership identity. There are five environmental dimensions through which this cycle occurs: *historical legacy of inclusion/exclusion, compositional diversity, psychological climate, behavioral climate, and organizational/structural aspects* (Bertrand Jones et al., 2016). High-achieving students have lived experiences which can be discussed through all five environmental domains that have created space and opportunity for leadership identity growth and learning.

CRLL is important to high-achieving students' leadership identity development due in part to the interconnection of academic success and the *capacity* domain. While it is evident that identity, capacity, and efficacy are entwined, students' understanding of the combination of all three as change agents through development is critical (Bertrand Jones et al., 2016). The high-achieving students' environment on college campuses fosters considerable engagement in and out of the classroom. This engagement could lead to specific leadership opportunities. CRLL offers a reciprocal learning and engagement process visual to assist with a better understanding of how identity, capacity, and efficacy interact with the individual and their leadership identity process. This model could assist with high-achieving students making meaning of their leadership identity development process, because it creates the space to understand their leadership identity through the lens of their multiple identities, most notably in this context, their high-achieving identity (Bertrand Jones et al., 2016) (see Figure 13.1).

Figure 13.1

Culturally Relevant Leadership Learning Model

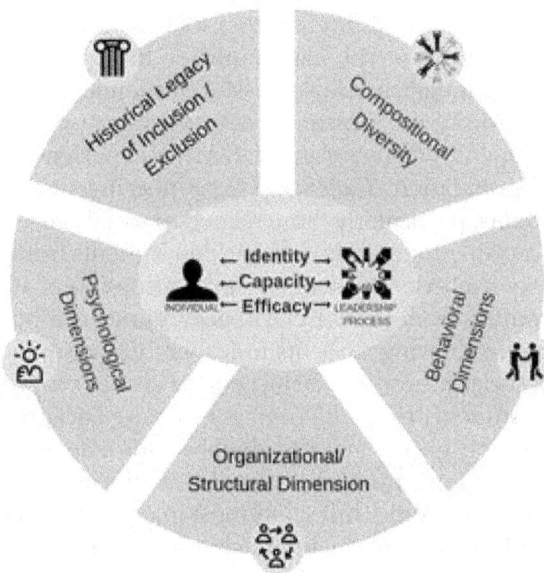

Source: Beatty & Guthrie (2021).

Leadership models play an important role in the understanding and summarization of leadership identity development. Models not only assist with understanding, but also with the framework needed to understand the different leadership learning environments (Guthrie et al., 2021). Both the LID and CRLL models are intentional in the observation and engagement from the identified populations. As discussed previously, high-achieving students have multiple identities and come from many different backgrounds, highlighting saliency that fluctuates throughout the high-achieving community. This is important for social justice leadership educators to consider when thinking about high-achieving students and how those differences and aspects are situation in their leadership identity.

RECOMMENDATONS FOR LEADERSHIP EDUCATORS

Socially just leadership educators are committed to furthering growth and development across their students' multiple identities, and high-achieving students should be included in those plans. Guthrie et al. (2021) underscored the importance of providing guidance to make meaning of personal and collective experience; especially among high-achieving students who may struggle to find peers who have the same types of lived histories and social backgrounds.

In addition to incorporating social class identity into leadership identity development, and providing guidance to make meaning of shared experiences, socially just leadership educators identify and create leadership experiences in and out of the classroom for high-achieving students. Members of this population are successful academically, but leadership experiences outside of the classroom can still increase their leadership identity development. When crafting leadership experiences for members of this student population, I advocate remembering the different backgrounds of students, particularly those related to social class; not alienating or preventing certain groups of high-achieving students from participating in leadership experiences. The common misconception of all high-achieving students coming from similar class backgrounds can be disrupted by involving all high-achieving students in leadership learning. One recommendation for social justice leadership educators is to specifically recruit high-achieving students from different social class backgrounds, specifically first generation historically marginalized student populations. This strategy could develop understanding of how these students not only develop their social class identities, but most importantly their leadership identities through the lens of the high-achieving student.

In addition to the previous recommendations, leadership identity should be addressed in intertwined ways when analyzing its development in the high-achieving student population. This is due to the need for high-achieving students to go beyond their own individualized learning. As social justice leadership educators continue to build upon existing leadership models and create new and transformative frameworks, high-achieving students should be included in the process due to their opportunities for growth that are afforded to them in the educational setting. High-achieving students' identity can assist with designing future educational programs that specifically foster their leadership identity development. As educators continually strive to create the best learning opportunities, incorporating high-achieving students into those plans assists in maximizing the learning potential for all students involved.

The impact of intersectionality of identities continues to increase in the postsecondary education setting, and high achieving students should be incorporated into those dynamics. This inclusion of high-achieving students' identities could assist with better understanding the lived experiences of the different students that make up the shared identity group of high achieving. The intersectionality and multiple perspectives of lived experiences could then influence future socially just leadership education. High achievement can be regarded as a positive quality but breaking down the experiences contributing to that identity development, and the space for engagement and the intersectionality of leadership identity, could increase perceived positive qualities. Given the robustness of social justice educators when incorporating high-achieving students into their praxis, it would also be effective to provide relevant experiences from the educators themselves in the realm of high achievement, specifically educational enrichment opportunities. The opportunity to connect lines of inquiry from educator to learner could be significant with this population, creating even more opportunities for shared experiences.

CONCLUSION

Like all students, those who are high academic achievers have multiple social identities that culminate in a complex and multilayered individual. However, their status as high-achieving may complicate their leadership identity development as they strive to become socially just leaders. Understanding the importance in the makeup of these identities, and how high-achieving students uniquely make meaning of their leadership identity, is an important focus for social justice leadership educators. The various experiences that contribute to high-achieving identity can be explored through the lens of social class and contribute to the overall meaning making of leadership identity development. Approaching leadership development for these students in socially just ways leads not only to prosocial outcomes for society, but also produces individuals capable of leveraging their identities in responsible ways.

REFERENCES

Beatty, C. C., & Guthrie, K. L. (2021). *Operationalizing culturally relevant leadership learning*. Information Age Press.

Bertrand Jones, T., Guthrie, K. L., & Osteen, L. (2016). Critical domains of culturally relevant leadership learning: A call to transform leadership programs. In K. L. Guthrie, T. Bertrand Jones, & L. Osteen (Eds.), *Developing culturally relevant leadership learning*. (New Directions for Student Leadership, No. 152, pp. 9–21). Jossey-Bass. https://doi.org/10.1002/yd.20205

Guthrie, K. L., Ardoin, S., & Purita, R. (2021). Expanding influence of social class in leadership development. *New Directions for Student Leadership, 2021*, 121–131. https://doi.org/10.1002/yd.20428

Guthrie, K. L., & Beatty, C. C. (2022). Centering socially just leadership: An integrated model for contextualizing leadership learning. *Journal of Leadership Studies, 16*(3), 22–27. https://doi.org/10.1002/Jls.21825

Jean-Marie, G., Normore, A. H., & Brooks, J. S. (2009). Leadership for social justice: Preparing 21st century school leaders for a new social order. *Journal of Research on Leadership Education, 4*(1), 1–31. https://doi.org/10.1177/194277510900400102

Komives, S. R., Mainella, F. C., Longerbeam, S. D., Osteen, L., & Owen, J. E. (2006). A leadership identity development model: Applications from a grounded theory. *Journal of College Student Development, 47*(4), 401–418. https://doi.org/10.1353/csd.2006.0048

Owen, J. E., Hassell, G. S., & Yamanaka, A. (2017). Culturally relevant leadership learning: Identity, capacity, and efficacy. *Journal of Leadership Studies, 11*(3), 48–54. https://doi.org/10.1002/jls.21545

Shoenberger, N., Heckert, A., & Heckert, D. (2015). Labeling, social learning, and positive deviance: A look at high achieving students. *Deviant Behavior, 36*(6), 474–491. https://doi.org/10.1080/01639625.2014.944066

Sims, H. P., & Manz, C. C. (1982). Social learning theory: The roles of modeling in the exercise of leadership, *Journal of Organizational Behavior Management, 3*(4), 55–63. https://doi.org/10.1300/j075v03n04_06

Wu, A., Li, X., Wang, J., & Li, D. (2019). Why are high-achieving students susceptible to inhibition? An idiographic analysis of student self-identity in China. *Frontiers in Psychology, 10*(1918), 1–14. https://doi.org/10.3389/fpsyg.2019.01918

CHAPTER 14

HIDDEN LEADERSHIP

Foster Care Alumni as Socially Just Leaders

Lisa Jackson

Historically, child welfare systems in the United States have overlooked foster youth's insight, experience, and input while making life-altering decisions on their behalf. Recognizing the injustice perpetrated by ignoring youth perspectives, state foster care agencies launched youth advocacy boards to incorporate youth feedback into decisions related to child welfare policy and practice (U.S. Department of Health and Human Services, n.d.). An increasingly popular advocacy and leadership mechanism by and for youth with lived experience in foster care, youth advocacy boards take various forms and have been found to create a space for participants to reframe their experiences in a fashion that amplifies the positive aspects of their identities (Havlicek & Samuels, 2018).

While the youth advocacy board model is considered a promising practice in child welfare, a similar approach to making meaningful changes to higher education policy and practice to support college-going of foster care alumni is virtually non-existent. This chapter explores the use of a foster care alumni student advisory board in collegiate spaces to leverage the strengths perspective (Saleebey, 1997) and culturally relevant leadership learning (Guthrie et al., 2017) to improve their postsecondary education outcomes. By acting upon foster care alumni leadership and advocacy efforts, postsecondary educational institutions can better support

Committing to Action: Socially Just Leadership Educations, pp. 163–177
Copyright © 2025 by Information Age Publishing
www.infoagepub.com

the collegiate experience of students with lived histories in the foster care system. A specific context example highlighting the effectiveness of this approach is included.

POSITIONALITY OF AUTHOR

My identity as a first-generation college graduate who experienced periods of informal relative care during childhood, my training as a licensed clinical social worker who utilizes a strengths perspective, and my continued studies as a doctoral candidate pursuing a PhD in higher education, strongly influence the composition of this chapter. My fascination with emerging adults' transition to and through postsecondary school motivated me to study human behavior and seek a higher-education career. My area of practice and research became clear during a graduate assistantship in 2014 when I first learned of the unique challenges former foster youth encounter while pursuing a college degree. Literature at that time demonstrated how youth exiting the child welfare system are far less likely to attend and graduate college than their non-foster care peers (Courtney et al., 2007; Pecora, 2012). Guided by the belief those postsecondary outcomes would improve by empowering foster care alumni to lead campus support initiatives, I searched for asset-based strategies built upon the leadership of students with lived experience in foster care. Few existed, but I discovered that a few institutions had created programs to serve foster care alumni, including my own, Florida State University.

In 2012, Florida State University established the Unconquered Scholars Program to serve former foster youth as well as students that experienced homelessness, relative care, and those considered wards of the state (Samarah et al., 2023). In 2014, I was hired to direct the Unconquered Scholars Program and develop a comprehensive infrastructure for its operations. Since then, I have spent nine years advocating for this population nationally to reshape the deficit-based narrative of these remarkably resilient students by encouraging institutions to remove structural barriers that unintentionally limit their retention and graduation. I argue that foster care alumni are more likely to complete a college education when their institution recognizes their strengths, acknowledges their struggles, and adjusts systems to provide holistic support during their educational journey. I believe amplifying the voices of former foster youth through their leadership of an identity-based campus support program, established upon a strengths-based perspective (Saleebey, 1997) and culturally relevant leadership learning (Guthrie et al., 2017), contributes to improved educational outcomes. I hope you come to share this view and are inspired to take a similar approach at your institution.

HIGHER EDUCATION: A MEANS TO A "BETTER LIFE"

The American Dream (Adams, 1931), a deeply embedded concept in our society's collective psyche, is based on a long-held belief that everyone can improve their professional and social mobility with advanced education and a strong work ethic. That belief is supported by research indicating college degree completion is associated with significant health, social, and economic benefits. On average, those with a bachelor's degree earn over $2.7 million more than others with a high school diploma as their highest academic credential over a lifetime (Day & Newburger, 2002; Carnevale et al., 2011). In addition to being financially advantageous, bachelor's degree holders also report a healthier lifestyle, increased civic activity, more secure employment, and additional involvement in the activities of offspring (Ma et al., 2019).

Perhaps the financial and lifestyle benefits of a college education inspire foster care alumni's dreams of attending postsecondary school. Approximately 70% of foster care alumni report a strong desire to attend college (Martin, 2003). However, the desire to earn a college degree far exceeds the degree completion rates. Estimates suggest only 3 to 11% of foster care alumni complete a four-year degree in comparison to the approximately 24% degree completion rate of the general population (Casey Family Programs, 2010). While these data paint a bleak picture, we must consider the context in which they occur.

Tailored to continuing-generation, traditional students who can rely upon familial support and guidance to meet their financial and emotional needs, higher education often overlooks students without those supports, specifically those with foster care experience. One has to wonder whether college campuses acknowledge the distinctions between students with familial support and those without. Do administrators realize how campus policies and practices may inadvertently create barriers for foster care alumni instead of enhancing their collegiate experience? When institutions engage foster care alumni through campus leadership opportunities, can robust campus support be provided to meet their needs?

Yes, when institutions engage foster care alumni in the leadership process, they gain the knowledge necessary to provide targeted student support to ensure adequate food, shelter, community, and academic services are available to improve retention and graduation rates. Chunoo and Osteen (2016) noted how mission-based leadership education programs benefit from a supportive campus system by leveraging higher education's theory-to-practice environment to develop students' leadership capacities. As socially just college and university educators, we must acknowledge how the structure of our institutions contributes to similar academic underperformance for foster care alumni. Providing leadership learning in a supportive campus environment for foster care alumni is essential to their retention and graduation.

HIGHER EDUCATION LEADERSIHP LEARNING

From the outset, higher education's mission included developing future leaders (Devies & Guthrie, 2022). During the U.S. industrial economic era of the late 1800s, leadership was considered a sacred process to which only a few men belonged. Great man theory postulated that leaders are born, not made; are male, not female; and must possess heroic qualities to be successful (Ahmed Khan et al., 2016). For decades, this philosophy and approach to leadership was accepted as fact and reified the academy's exclusionary origins of leadership education. Additionally, higher education has a long history of privileging those with White, upper or middle-class, and male identities (Landreman & MacDonald-Dennis, 2013, as cited in Teig, 2018). Guided by great man theory conceptualizations of a leader, students outside the privileged White, upper-class, and male identities were excluded from leadership. Students possessing minorized identities were, and may continue to be, viewed as deficient and not fit for leadership (Guthrie et al., 2021). As leadership theories progressed, assumptions about a "good"' leader's characteristics changed significantly. Postindustrial leadership promoted views that everyone is capable of leadership, that leaders are not born but made, and that environments must shift to support all aspiring leaders. This era promoted views of shared responsibility of those leading and those following while collaborating on shared goals through various approaches, including transformational leadership, servant leadership, authentic leadership, and chaos/systems leadership (Rosch & Anthony, 2012).

In today's academic world, strategic social change leadership "offers a perspective that challenges dominant assumptions on multiple levels ranging from its deep infusion of principles of social justice to its movement away from a prescriptive, leader-centric emphasis on behaviors" (Dugan, 2017, p. 11). Based on social justice values, social change leadership promotes organizational actors engaging in activities that produce collective power and socially just outcomes (Ospina & Foldy, 2005). Affirming society's diversity, leaders and leadership educators identify and critique oppressive structures and processes at our respective institutions and integrate socially just education into leadership learning (Teig, 2018). Youth who "age out" of the foster care system embody a marginalized and disempowered group (Paul-Ward, 2009; Forenza, 2016). To a considerable degree, their presence on campus is a forgotten topic (Kenton, 2018); they are a hidden population. As such, foster care alumni are challenged to lead in spaces that do not acknowledge their existence on campus, lived experiences, strengths, and input.

By pursuing social justice alongside leadership, educators establish opportunities for foster care alumni to become advocates for systematic change through leadership processes. Empowering systems and processes cultivate more control over life (Rappaport, 1981). As leadership educators seek and act upon input from foster care alumni, students' development of identity, capacity, and efficacy in the leadership process advances. Through socially just leadership learning, members of this hidden population engage in leadership to reform postsecondary educational institutions toward inclusive and supportive policies and practices.

LEADERSHIP LEARNING FOR FOSTER CARE ALUMNI

This overlooked population can be included in the development of campus policies and practices impacting their collegiate journey by employing an interdisciplinary approach to leadership learning for foster care alumni. In this chapter, Saleebey's (1997) strengths perspective, and the culturally relevant leadership learning model (Osteen et al., 2016), serve as two critical elements to develop socially just leadership learning for foster care alumni.

Strengths-Based Perspective

When considering foster care alumni's higher education outcomes, we must contemplate how postsecondary structures, built for traditional student populations, negatively impact their retention and graduation. Valuing the strengths of an overlooked student population is impossible. Perhaps worse than being unseen, foster care alumni are often viewed through a deficit-based lens. Former foster youth, who are themselves aware of this bias, expressed the need for higher education administrators to be mindful of foster care alumni on campus and to view them as human beings, not pity cases (Kenton, 2018). By recognizing foster care alumni as experts in their college experience, higher education can activate their unique and valuable knowledge to engage in leadership to improve campus culture and climate.

The principles of the strengths-based perspective include: acknowledging each person, group, family, and community has strengths; struggle can be harmful while providing an opportunity; not to assume the upper limits of capacity to grow and change for another; we serve others in collaboration with them; and every environment is full of resources (Saleebey, 1997). In addition, one must genuinely be interested in, and respectful of, the lived experiences of our students and recognize that their identities do not come from "a ritual litany of troubles, embarrassments, snares, foibles, and barriers ... [but rather to] ... assume that they know something, have learned lessons from experience, have hopes, have interests, and can do some things masterfully" (Saleebey, 1997, p 12). By listening, we learn how to better serve them in higher education by leveraging their strengths. Leadership educators are uniquely positioned to empower foster care alumni and improve services to this population by utilizing a strengths perspective in leadership education.

Culturally Relevant Leadership Learning Model

The culturally relevant leadership learning model (CRLL) uses "the theory and practice of inclusion and leadership across diverse lived experiences in order to reflect and act upon the world" (Osteen et al., 2016, p. 95). Responsive to the intricacies of socially just leadership learning, CRLL positions leadership educators at the center of inclusion and equality efforts through leadership learning (Osteen et al., 2016). CRLL recognizes and challenges how sexism, religious oppression, racism, heterosexism/cisgenderism, and classism, privileges and disadvantage lives (Guthrie et al., 2017). CRLL recognizes how language and institutional culture affect the identity, capacity, and efficacy of students who engage in social change (Bertrand Jones et al., 2016) and how each domain affects, and is affected by, changes and interactions within the system (Guthrie et al., 2017).

As shown in Figure 14.1, CRLL comprises multiple domains and is used as a framework to reshape organizations and leadership programs to become truly inclusive and welcoming to all (Guthrie et al., 2017), including hidden populations such as foster care alumni at college campuses. Additionally, CRLL incorporates the domains of identity, capacity, and efficacy and advocates for students to consider themselves as agents of change (Bertrand Jones et al., 2016).

Utilizing Selected CRLL Domains

The responsibility to facilitate and support the creation of socially just leadership learning environments in co-curricular spaces lies with educators and staff (Guthrie & Rodriguez, 2018). Socially just leadership learning is achieved by being intentional about how members of marginalized populations are represented in all contexts and diligent about creating socially just leadership learning spaces for all students (Guthrie & Rodriguez, 2018). Building campus support programs that implement

Figure 14.1

Culturally Relevant Leadership Learning Model

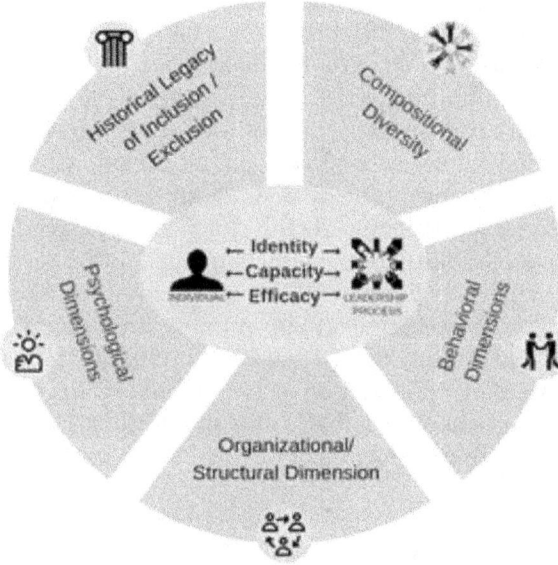

Source: Beatty & Guthrie (2021).

elements of CRLL provides spaces for foster care alumni to amplify their voices and impact, develop identity as individuals and leaders, and engage in socially just leadership for those with similar lived histories. By involving and acting upon foster care alumni students' input, campus administrators can reshape systems to improve students' well-being and academic performance.

Context. Exclusionary practices of non-White, non-male, non-cisgender, non-heterosexual, and non-affluent people in leadership education and literature have a long history (Bertrand Jones et al., 2016). Institutions create conflict for marginalized students, which can result in them going unrecognized or being discounted by other privileged students, since campus culture is experienced differently by marginalized students in comparison to their privileged peers (Bertrand Jones et al., 2016). CRLL upholds the importance of underrepresented and marginalized student populations' participation in the leadership process to meaningfully shape factors affecting them (Bertrand Jones et al., 2016).

Foster care alumni are a hidden population on most campuses and often inhabit multiple minoritized identities. As a result, they are largely excluded from the leadership process in higher education. By enthusiastically engaging them in decision-making about their well-being and education, socially just leadership educators align their practices with CRLL's mission to move from simply accounting for diverse populations to engaging them in policy and practice.

Identity, capacity, and efficacy. At the heart of CRLL is an interaction between individual and collective processes involving identity, capacity, and efficacy. One's conception of self, or identity, is informed by how one navigates and makes sense of context, self, and relationships (Abes et al., 2007). As one changes over time, so does identity. Dugan (2017) suggested capacity combines students' leadership knowledge, attitudes, and skills to form the overall ability to engage in the leadership process. Leadership efficacy, or one's belief about their ability to utilize their leadership skills and knowledge (Denzine, 1999), strongly predicts one's leadership capacity (Bertrand Jones, 2016). Dugan et al. (2013) stated the development of student leadership efficacy is empowered or discouraged by the contextual messages about what a leader should look, act or sound like, and can adversely impact members of historically marginalized student populations.

When educators reflect on these domains, they demonstrate how diverse students' experiences impact an organization (Beatty & Guthrie, 2021). CRLL frames learning environments in terms of contextual dimensions, including the historical legacy of inclusion and exclusion, compositional diversity, behavioral, organizational/structural, and psychological, which are interconnected to the identity, capacity, and efficacy of diverse learners as they engage in leadership (Beatty & Guthrie, 2021). The CRLL model recognizes the power leadership educators' possess to influence students' identity, capacity, and efficacy (Bertrand Jones et al., 2016). Through practical and efficient use of CRLL and strengths, we can work toward socially just leadership learning for all students, with particular benefits for foster care alumni.

SPECIFIC CONTEXT

In 2012, Florida State University (FSU) launched the Unconquered Scholars Program (henceforth referred to as "Program") to provide students that experienced foster care, homelessness, relative care, or ward of the state status with "guidance, continual mentor-ship, advocacy, security, and a voice to further ensure their personal academic success and long-term independence" (FSU Center for Academic Retention and Enhancement, n.d.). Grounded in strengths perspective, Program administrators value the lived experience, voice, and leadership effort of Program participants to inform every aspect of the campus support program. Scholars (i.e., students in the Program) worked with campus administration to define the Program's mission and determine where the Program would be situated on campus.

Program developers recognized that Scholars are the only people on campus qualified to inform the Program's operations from the lens of a former foster youth. Their participation in leading the Program's operations would be essential to engage and support their collegiate journey successfully. As such, a student advisory board composed of scholars was created to codify their involvement in the Program's leadership processes. Over the last decade, knowledge shared by the student advisory board through the leadership has informed program practices and campus policy changes, including those noted below.

By drawing upon Scholars' identity, capacity, and efficacy through shared leadership, FSU removed institutional barriers affecting their well-being and academic progression. For example, Scholars informed the administration that many foster care alumni had no stable place to live when the residence halls close between semesters and during winter break. In response to this information, the institution adjusted housing practices and offered temporary lodging to Scholars. In addition, the student advisory board's leaders were instrumental in overcoming the emotional distress and academic decline Scholars experienced several weeks after the annual Parents' Weekend programming on campus. By amplifying the experiences of their fellow Scholars, the institution now arranges for students in the Program to travel away from Tallahassee while Parents' Weekend takes place on campus. In the context of an institution committed to adjusting practices and removing barriers to their progress, the student advisor board's engagement in socially just leadership changed the college-going experience of fellow Program participants. Scholars now consider their trip away from campus a highlight of the academic year instead of suffering on campus during and after Parents' Weekend.

In my conversations with scholars over many years, they have shared that the student advisory board leadership structure, which incorporates elements of CRLL and strengths perspective, plays a significant role in their identity development and retention at the institution. Identity development activities are embedded in the Program's design whereby Scholars are offered a variety of methods to reflect on "who they are" and "whom they are becoming" while employing a strengths perspective narrative of self. With the Program staff's guidance, Scholars abandon internal narratives suggesting they are unqualified to lead or cannot be successful college students. Additionally, the student advisory board attends leadership learning workshops several times every semester to enhance their leadership capacity. Program administrators scaffold Scholars' leadership learning with one-on-one feedback sessions, provision of leadership resources, and reflection assignments. Scholars' sense of efficacy grows as they successfully participate in the leadership process and is enhanced through programming and consistent opportunities to lead. By engaging in activities designed to improve Scholars' awareness of their abilities, capacity, and strengths view of identity, they embrace their lived experience in foster care and celebrate their unique and institutionally valued qualities.

Undoubtedly, many contextual factors contribute to the Scholars' academic success. However, they are situated at an institution that values their perspectives and adjusts based on their leadership, with promising results. The scholars achieved a 95% first-year retention rate and attained an 84 percent six-year graduation rate, which rivals the 95% retention rate and 85% six-year graduation rate for the general student body at Florida State University.

Beyond Florida State University, by practicing the CRLL approach to leadership, Scholars advocate for foster care alumni far beyond the context of their campus and the Unconquered Scholars Program. As leaders, Scholars share their lived experiences as college students with a history of foster care at higher education and child welfare conferences nationwide. Through their leadership efforts, Scholars improve awareness of an overlooked and undervalued population to promote the development and implementation of campus support programs informed by and for foster care alumni. More specifically, Scholars urge institutions to utilize foster care alumni's identity, efficacy, and leadership capacity to create a more socially just institution. These efforts successfully led to the development of campus support programs, informed by students' lived experiences and voices, across the country. Additionally, Scholars informed state legislators about ways to improve public policy to enhance foster youth's recruitment, retention, and college graduation rates. After years of engaging in the leadership process with Scholars and observing the benefits of a strengths approach and CRLL at an institution that welcomes their leadership, I encourage administrators to consider taking a similar approach to establishing leadership opportunities for this underrepresented student population.

CALL TO ACTION

Mahoney (2017) eloquently remarked how CRLL "harnesses diverse and often overlooked leadership thought and practice to enhance all students' identity, capacity and efficacy in leadership development for social change" (p. 57). Awareness of foster care alumni on every college and university campus is absolutely essential to creating socially just leadership opportunities for this population. By recognizing the value of foster care alumni's expertise, leadership educators honor their wisdom, strength, and capacity to lead alongside administrators to transform campuses into genuinely inclusive spaces.

Create Brave Spaces for Foster Care Alumni to Lead

Campus support programs can serve as brave spaces for former foster youth. A brave space, introduced by Arao and Clemens (2013), is where students can truthfully engage and be pushed to the limits of their comfort zones to maximize learning (See also: Rezaei, 2018). Thus, campus support programs can adequately prepare and support students and staff to participate in campus-wide leadership opportunities (Farinella, 2018). Next, installing a student advisory board enhances the campus program toward being routinely and deliberately informed by the expertise and leadership of students with lived foster care experience. Finally, a student advisory board nested in a campus support program using a strengths perspective provides a setting that celebrates the collective strength in their shared identity as former foster youth and drives the Program's mission and activities in a manner that responds to students' needs.

Embedded in a supportive environment, students who engage in leadership processes enhance their identity, capacity, and efficacy through dynamic and reciprocal relationships (Bertrand Jones et al., 2016) and inform their campus about improving support for non-traditional student populations. By implementing aspects of CRLL in a student advisory board embedded in a campus support program, foster care alumni engage in socially just leadership to promote awareness of a hidden population and seek systematic changes in higher education. As a result, these students thrive as they engage in leadership processes.

Shared Leadership

Socially just leadership educators empower members of this hidden population by valuing their identity, capacity, and efficacy as leaders. Their journey to and through higher education is unique. Socially just faculty and administrators learn from them and act upon their expertise. They engage foster care alumni in the leadership process, especially regarding decisions impacting their lives as members of our campus community. The words of the institution must align with its action; it is not sufficient to assert that 'foster care alumni are valued in higher education' and then fail to engage them in leadership processes. Inclusive institutions improve based on foster care alumni's leadership. We must remove institutional barriers that impede their well-being, development, and academic journey through leadership.

Next Steps

Beatty and Guthrie (2021) offered additional guidance on operationalizing CRLL in co-curricular programs. They explained those "who develop programs must focus on the development of all students and validate their lived experiences as strengths rather than weaknesses" (pp. 85-86). Their suggestions included establishing a strong foundation of leadership learning that provides diversity in programming and creating a space where all students feel respected and diverse voices are represented. They highlighted the importance of using inclusive and respectful language in co-curricular leadership learning spaces and staying informed about changes in language across time to sustain the inclusivity of all students.

Furthermore, while reflecting on the contents of this chapter, consider how this approach can engage foster care alumni in the leadership process on your campus. For example, how does your institution identify foster youth, or are they a hidden population? Is there a campus support program in place, or is one needed? How might you help these students recognize their strengths? How can you help them understand that they are uniquely qualified to lead at the institution? How can you help them realize support for students with similar lived experiences will improve due to their leadership? How will you utilize CRLL to build brave spaces for foster care alumni to develop identity, capacity, and efficacy in the leadership process?

REFERENCES

Abes, E. S., Jones, S. R., & McEwen, M. K. (2007). Reconceptualizing the model of multiple dimensions of identity: The role of meaning-making capacity in the construction of multiple identities. *Journal of College Student Development*, *48*(1), 1–22. https://doi.org/10.1353/Csd.2007.0000

Adams, J. T. (1931). *The epic of America*. Little, Brown, and Co.

Ahmed Khan, Z., Nawaz, A., & Khan, I. (2016). Leadership theories and styles: A literature review. *Journal of Resources Development and Management*, *16*, 1–7. https://doi.org/10.1108/jmd-01-2015-0004

Arao, B., & Clemens, K. (2013). From safe spaces to brave spaces: A new way to frame dialogue around diversity and social justice. In L. M. Landreman (Ed.), *The art of effective facilitation: Reflections from social justice educators* (pp. 135–150). Stylus .

Beatty, C. C., & Guthrie, K. L. (2021). *Operationalizing culturally relevant leadership learning* (pp. 85–103). Information Age Publishing.

Bertrand Jones, T., Guthrie, K. L., & Osteen, L. (2016). Critical domains of culturally relevant leadership learning: A call to transform leadership programs. *New Directions for Student Leadership, 2016*(152), 9–21. https://doi.org/10.1002/yd.20205

Carnevale, A. P., Cheah, B., & Rose, S. J. (2011). *The college pay off.* The Georgetown Center on Education and the Workforce. https://vtechworks.lib.vt.edu/bitstream/handle/10919/83051/ TheCollegePayOff.pdf?sequence=1

Casey Family Programs. (2010, December 1). *Supporting success: Improving higher education outcomes for students from foster care.* https://www.casey.org/supporting-success/

Chunoo, V., & Osteen, L. (2016). Purpose, mission, and context: The call for educating future leaders. *New Directions for Higher Education, 2016*(174), 9–20. https://doi.org/10.1002/he.20185

Courtney, M. E., Dworsky, A. L., Cusick, G. R., Havlicek, J., Perez, A., & Keller, T. E. (2007). *Midwest evaluation of the adult functioning of former foster youth: Outcomes at age 21.* Chapin Hall Center for Children at the University of Chicago.

Day, J. C., & Newburger, E. C. (2002). The big payoff; educational attainment and synthetic estimates of work-life earnings. Special studies. Current population reports. U.S. Census Bureau. https://eric.ed.gov/?id=ED467533

Denzine, G. (1999). Personal and collective efficacy. Essential components of college students' leadership development. *Concepts & Connections, 8*(1), 1–5.

Devies, B., & Guthrie, K. L. (2022). What mission statements say: Signaling the priority of leadership development. *Journal of Higher Education Policy and Leadership Studies, 3*(1), 91–107. https://doi.org/10.52547/johepal.3.1.91

Dugan, J. P. (2017). *Leadership theory; Cultivating critical perspectives.* Jossey-Bass.

Dugan, J. P., Kodama, C., Correira, B., & Associates. (2013). *Multi-institutional study of leadership report: Leadership program delivery.* National Clearinghouse for Leadership Programs.

Farinella, J. (2018). Foster care youth alumni to collegiate leaders. In K. L. Guthrie & V. S. Chunoo (Eds.), *Changing the narrative: Socially just leadership education* (pp. 193–209). Information Age Publishing.

Forenza, B. (2016). Psychological empowerment and the pursuit of social change: Outcomes of foster youth engagement. *Journal of Public Child Welfare, 10*(3), 274–290. https://doi.org/10.1080/15548732.2016.1140698

FSU Center for Academic Retention and Enhancement. (n.d.). *Unconquered Scholars Program.* https://care.fsu.edu/UnconqueredScholars

Guthrie, K. L., Beatty, C. C., & Wiborg, E. R. (2021). *Engaging in the leadership process: Identity, capacity, and efficacy for college students.* Information Age Publishing.

Guthrie, K. L., Bertrand Jones, T., & Osteen, L. (2017). The teaching, learning, and being of leadership: Exploring context and practice of the culturally relevant leadership learning model. *Journal of Leadership Studies, 11*(3), 61–67. https://doi.org/10.1002/jls.21547

Guthrie, K. L., & Rodriguez, J. (2018). Creating cocurricular socially just leadership learning environments. In K. L. Guthrie & V. S. Chunoo (Eds.), *Changing the narrative: Socially just leadership education* (pp. 245–258). Information Age Publishing.

Havlicek, J., & Samuels, G. M. (2018). The Illinois state foster youth advisory board as a counterspace for well-being through identity work: Perspectives of current and former members. *Social Service Review, 92*(2), 241–289. https://doi.org/10.1086/697694

Kenton, D. H. (2018). *The forgotten topic: A study on the transition college experiences of former foster youth.* ProQuest Dissertations Publishing.

Landreman, L. M., & MacDonald-Dennis, C. (2013). The evolution of social justice education and facilitation. In L. Landreman (Ed.). *The art of effective facilitation: Reflections from social justice educators* (pp. 3–22). Stylus.

Ma, J., Pender, M., & Welch, M. (2019). *Trends in higher education series; Education pays 2019.* College Board. https://research.collegeboard.org/pdf/education-pays-2019-full-report.pdf

Mahoney, A. D. (2017). Being at the heart of the matter: Culturally relevant leadership learning, emotions, and storytelling. *Journal of Leadership Studies, 11*(3), 55–60. https://doi.org/10.1002/jls.21546

Martin, J. (2003, October 2). Washington University in St. Louis; The Source. *Foster youth desire college, study shows, but face roadblocks learning.* https://source.wustl.edu/2003/10/foster-youth-desire-college-study-shows-but-face-roadblocks-to-learning/

Ospina, S., & Foldy, E. (2005, September). *Toward a framework of social change leadership.* Annual Meeting of the Public Management Research Association, Los Angeles.

Osteen, L., Guthrie, K., & Bertrand Jones, T. (2016). Leading to transgress: Critical considerations for transforming leadership learning. *New Directions for Student Leadership. 2016*(152), 95–106. https://doi.org/10.1002/yd.20212

Paul-Ward, A. (2009). Social and occupational justice barriers in the transition from foster care to independent adulthood. *The American Journal of Occupational Therapy, 63*(1), 81–88. https://doi.org/10.5014/ajot.63.1.81

Pecora, P. J. (2012). Maximizing educational achievement of youth in foster care and alumni: Factors associated with success. *Children and Youth Services Review, 34*(6), 1121–1129. https://doi.org/10.1016/j.childyouth.2012.01.044

Rappaport, J. (1981). In praise of paradox: A social policy of empowerment over prevention. *American Journal of Community Psychology, 9*(1), 1–25. https://doi.org/10.1007/BF00896357

Rezaei, R. (2018). Creating brave spaces in leadership education. In K. L. Guthrie & V. S. Chunoo (Eds.), *Changing the narrative: Socially just leadership education* (pp. 213–228). Information Age Publishing.

Rosch, D. M., & Anthony, M. D. (2012). Leadership pedagogy: Putting theory to practice. In K. L. Guthrie & L. Osteen (Eds.), *Developing students' leadership capacity* (pp. 37–51). Josey-Bass. https://doi.org/10.1002/ss.20030

Saleebey, D. (1997). *The strengths perspective in social work practice* (2nd ed.). Longman.

Samarah, E. M. S., Schelbe, L., & Jackson, L. A. (2023). A photovoice study of college students who have experienced foster care, relative care, and/or homelessness. *Children and Youth Services Review, 151,* 1–12. https://doi.org/10.1016/j.childyouth.2023.107042

Teig., T. S. (2018). Integrating social justice in leadership education. In K. L. Guthrie & V. S. Chunoo (Eds.), *Changing the narrative: Socially just leadership education* (pp. 9–25). Information Age Publishing.

U.S. Department of Health and Human Services. (n.d.). *Engaging and involving youth: Youth advisory boards.* https://www.childwelfare.gov/topics/systemwide/youth/engagingyouth/advisory/

CHAPTER 15

INSTILLING AND ACTIONIZING CRITICAL HOPE IN BLACK COLLEGE STUDENT LEADERS

Darius Robinson

When reflecting on my collegiate leadership experiences, I ponder the question: "How did I manage to persist?" As a prominent Black male leader involved in Black student organizations, I found myself advocating every day for the needs of Black students and all students of color on campus. Coming into my experience early, I was "trained'" by my "elders"—seasoned, experienced third- and fourth-year student leaders of color—about two intersecting arenas that would be critical to my success on campus: the specific student organization and the larger institutional structure in which they resided. In my training, I learned I cannot have one without the other. To work on behalf of my organization is to understand that I must continually advocate for them against hegemonic norms. To know the institutional structure means that I must find and negotiate different pathways to success.

As I became a campus "'elder" myself, I came to understand and be critical of this dyadic relationship. Being a person a color at a predominantly historically White postsecondary institution (HWIs) is a task, especially as someone who recognizes how race plays a role in organizational structures. Throughout my years as an undergraduate student leader, I had learned the "tricks of the trade" and how to navigate these pathways while representing my organizations. This did not come without

Committing to Action: Socially Just Leadership Educations, pp. 179–192

resistance. I routinely faced questions like: "How is this different from what the Black student union is doing?", or, "Do you really think this is as big of an issue as you are making it?" Programs did not garner funding due to their perceived similarity with other organizations of color, despite other majority organizations getting funding for the same thing. Overall, my reflections have shown me that even with a world against me, I continued to persist. I now know that without this persistence, I would not be the leadership educator I am today.

INTRODUCTION

Reflecting on my undergraduate experience with my fellow Black student leaders, we were struck with the common role of mentoring other students of color to navigate hegemonic spaces and persistence, sustained institutional resistance. Positional and non-positional Black leaders on campus still struggle with creating pathways for Black students and other students of color to be successful. They repeatedly fight against censorship, silencing, and neglect; both malicious and benign. They toil endlessly to legitimize their leadership in spaces supposedly open to all students. Black student leaders continue to persist because they see a vision greater than themselves—one where students of color are able to participate and thrive on campus, just as their White counterparts.

This reflection had brought up the critical question: "*How did we continue to persist against all this adversity?*" I believe that I had, like many Black student leaders today have, "critical hope." This is the aspiration of a more just and equitable world within our field of higher education (Dugan, 2017). Critical hope allows Black student leaders to resist hegemonic norms, persists in invisible spaces, and thrive in an academy not originally built toward their academic growth and professional development.

Socially just leadership educators delve into critical hope and interrogate for themselves: How much do we know about leadership? How have Black student leaders learned these ideas? What can we do to actionize leadership learning for our Black student leaders? Socially just leadership educators need to find creative ways to support Black student leaders through critical hope using curricular and co-curricular leadership learning approaches. To do this, they must strive to understand the perspectives of their students as racialized beings who exist, learn, and lead within the context of historically White colleges and universities (HWCUs). This will allow them to provide students with tools to assist them in creating change in their own institutions.

BLACK STUDENTS IN COLLEGE

Historically, people of color, including Black students, have been excluded from higher education structures and processes (Thelin, 2019; Williamson-Lott, 2018). For most of American higher education's history, Black people were not allowed to attend colleges and universities; even when they could, many were barred from the same colleges as White people. However, the Civil Rights Movement helped to integrate primary, secondary, and postsecondary education nationwide (Warren & The Supreme Court of The United States, 1953). With these changes, HEIs became philosophically open, but the structural inequities upon which they were built did not disappear with the passing of *Brown v. Board of Education* (Jeffries, 2006). Instead, Black students came into institutions that were drastically underprepared to educate them and validate their unique experiences and perspectives (Beatty & Guthrie, 2021). These racist structures persist today, which disproportionately and negatively impact Black students, affecting both curricular and co-curricular outcomes.

Barriers to Black Student Leadership

A plethora of barriers negatively impact the retention of Black students at HEIs. One major barrier is the sense of belonging for Black students (Strayhorn, 2019). When students do not feel the institution values or supports them, they are less likely to engage with the institution, resulting in more negative outcomes for these students. This feeling of "invading" invisible, White, hegemonic spaces can have negative backlash for students of color, including alienation, oppression and microaggressions (Puwar, 2004). Additionally, Black students have difficulty navigating spaces that were not built with their needs in mind. This includes instances like living in residence halls named for former slave owners, or not seeing any depictions of Black alumni accomplishments on campus. Due to this sense of "invading," they may also have difficulty building social and cultural capital that can help them be at least as successful as their White peers at the same university (Yosso, 2005). Third, Black students may not encounter a great deal of other Black students on campus (Beatty & Guthrie, 2021). Lack of representation affects both role modeling for other Black students as well as minimizes potential peer mentorship and community building (Strayhorn, 2017). Without close connections, and ability to engage various opportunities, Black students have less of a chance of collegiate leadership success.

CREATING A CRITICAL HOPE FRAMEWORK

Critical Hope

Critical hope can be defined as the ability, "to realistically assess one's environment through a lens of equity and justice while also envisioning the possibility of a better future" (Bishundat et al., 2018, p. 91). Critical hope is more than a lofty goal; it is the summation of what socially just leadership education represents. However, there are many things critical hope is not. For one, it is not regular hope, which is a lofty or wishful goal of change happening. It is also not the work of an individual to make this happen. It does not separate itself from challenging problems. Critical hope does not shirk away from the responsibility of social justice due to resistance. Critical hope is not ordinary nor complacent (Bishundat et al., 2018).

Critical hope is and advocates for, liberation. It recognizes how leadership can be transformative when practiced through culturally relevant approaches (Bertrand Jones et al., 2016). Critical hope addresses issues of power, domination, and subordination (Williams, 2016). It recognizes how collaboration and collectivism make leadership stronger (Bordas, 2016). Through this, it shows how leadership educators participate in becoming as socially just as their students, especially their Black student leaders in-training. Lastly, critical hope is asset-based and recognizes there is no one right way to lead. All leaders bring their own unique forms of leadership capital from their leadership experiences (Brooms et al., 2018) to advocate for a more equitable and just world (Teig, 2018; Yosso, 2005).

Culturally Relevant Leadership Learning

While critical hope provides a theoretical orientation, culturally relevant leadership learning provides the conceptualization of how Black student leaders can use critical hope to successfully navigate predominantly White HEIs. Culturally relevant leadership learning (CRLL) is a framework that interrogates leadership programs and theories based on the advantages and disadvantages social differences create. The framework seen in Figure 15.1 centers student leader identity (who am I?), capacity (what can I do?) and efficacy (how do I feel about my abilities?) as integral to leadership learning process (Beatty & Guthrie, 2021). Under CRLL, five campus climate environmental dimensions directly impact leadership learning experiences. These domains are: (1) historical legacy of inclusion / exclusion, (2) compositional diversity, (3) behavioral, (4) psychological, and (5) structural/organizational.

Figure 15.1

Culturally Relevant Leadership Learning Model

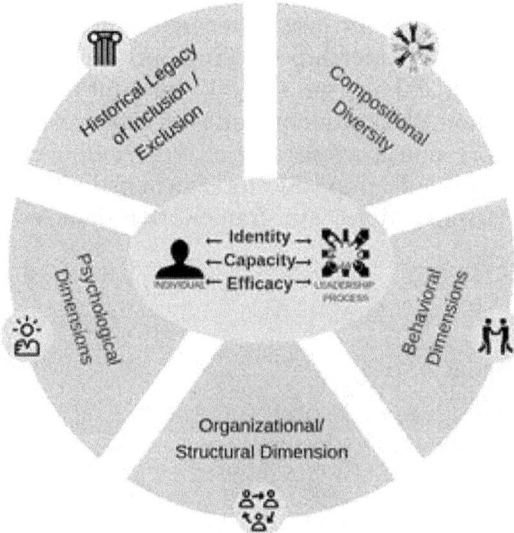

Source: Beatty & Guthrie (2021).

For critical hope to have an impact, there has to be a deep dive into the systems of oppression that comprise structures (Williams, 2016). This includes how we look at HEIs. For instance, examinations through the compositional diversity dimension allow Black student leaders to inter-rogate not only the number of Black students at the institution, but how they engage leadership programs as well (Beatty & Guthrie, 2021). This involves both quantifiable and qualifiable metrics of diversity at an insti-tution. Critical hope proponents would identify this as a major area of critique and provide solutions on how to fix it.

Creating the Critical Hope Framework

Critical hope and CRLL provide both the content and process to foster socially just leadership learning. They share many qualities: being asset-based, critically driven, and challenging of hegemonic developmental norms. However, they are distinct from one another as well. While critical hope is a transformative concept, its use has been oversimplified towards using only its definition instead of additionally incorporating one of the frameworks created by scholars, such as Quaye (2007) or Duncan-Andrade (2009). By merging the concept with culturally relevant leadership learning—a theory and framework providing a structure towards equitable leadership learning—a new framework emerges, centering the individual engaging in the leadership process as a "agent of critical hope." The various environmental dimensions of CRLL provide lenses on how to make this critical hope agent or socially just leader more attuned to their environment. By merging the leadership learning approach of CRLL, with the commitment toward action from critical hope, they provide a practical approach toward how Black students can interrupt and disrupt systematic and pervasive oppression and resistance on their campuses. It also provides a framework for how leadership educators can help their students learn and frame their leadership actions. This framework is depicted in Figure 15.2.

Figure 15.2

Critical Hope Framework

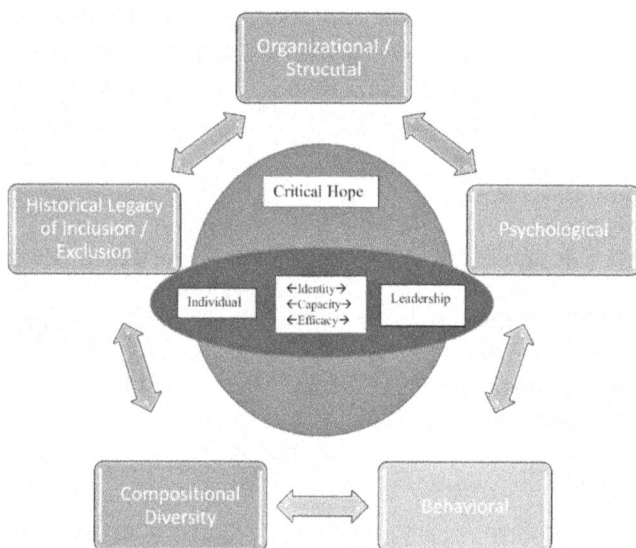

While this conceptual framework may represent an academic approach to socially just, critical hope frameworks, it can be distilled and made practically actionable for Black student leaders. Recommendations are offered on how to do so in the next section. However, given their push for equity and recognition on campus while battling racial battle fatigue (Beatty & Lima, 2021), the framework can also be metaphorized to a "student leader toolbelt." Black student leaders benefit from learning a strong and reliable set of leadership knowledge, skills, and abilities to overcome any issues that may arise in their organizations. This "toolbelt" is equipped with tools to address any situation they encounter, especially racialized incidents occurring in their leader development. Used correctly, leadership educators can use this metaphor not only to see the institution through their students' eyes, but provide them context and guidance in their leadership actions through education. Essentially, this toolkit helps students because it provides a critical filter via leadership education that recognizes a better future at HWIs through action.

ACTIONIZING CRITICAL HOPE

The framework, or metaphorical "toolbelt," allows leadership educators to provide a sturdy and reliable structure for Black student leaders to understand equity and social justice on campus. Just like the framework it embodies, there are many important qualities to this toolbelt. The quality of the toolbelt is strong, representing the depth and work of socially just student leaders and educators that helped to pave the way for a more equitable environment for today's leaders. The toolbelt also represents the ability to overcome adversity with the asset-based tools that Black student leaders have—namely, their leadership identity, capacity, and efficacy. Lastly, it shows the toolbelt is developmental, where it can be reinforced, and more tools added.

There are many tools socially just leadership educators can teach to students. Three are particularly useful for Black students' toolbelts: Yosso's (2005) community cultural wealth model, Dugan's (2017) tools of deconstruction and reconstruction, and Travers and Craig's (2021) discussion on love and healing. In the next few areas, these tools of critical hope will be reviewed, their applications for practice discussed, and Socratic questions offered "to painfully examine our lives and actions" (Duncan-Andrade, 2009, p. 187) for socially just leadership educators to reflect on and provide to their Black student leaders as a source of strength.

Community Cultural Wealth

To develop a more equitable and just world, there needs to be recognition of asset-based approaches Black student leadership has brought through leadership education. One approach to doing this is Yosso's community cultural wealth model (CCW). This model critiques long-standing ideas behind social and cultural capital, as described by Pierre Bourdieu (1977). Bourdieu (1977) argued hierarchical societies reproduce themselves to manufacture the types of capital that it finds most valuable. Social capital—the ability to build and maintain social connections—as well as cultural capital—the ability to access education and language appropriate for social movement—only served to reinforce structural racism in American society (Bourdieu & Passeron, 1977). Looking for a different path, Yosso (2005) drew on the scholarly work of critical race theorists to show how addressing racism allows students of color to bring unique forms of capital, which can be valuable in and out of classrooms. Yosso (2005) posited these forms of capital exist not only as asset-based approaches to addressing structural oppression (including, but not limited to racism), but highlight the beauty and power of critical tools students of color bring naturally with them. As shown in Table 15.1, Yosso's model consists of six forms of capital: *aspirational, familial, linguistic, navigational, resistant* and *social*.

Table 15.1

Community Cultural Wealth

Aspirational	Showcases the resiliency of Black students to maintain their dreams in the face of oppression.
Familial	Draws upon family experiences, narratives, memory and history for direction, guidance, and purpose.
Linguistic	Showcases both different language skills of Black student leaders and how they represent critical intellectual and social communicative skills.
Navigational	Recognizes how Black students develop skills that help them navigate through institutions structures not built with them in mind.
Resistant	Acknowledges the knowledge, skill, and power Black student leaders accumulate through their efforts in challenging inequity and meeting opposition regularly.
Social	Show how communities and people networks provide physical, emotional and mental support in navigating societal institutions.

Source: Adapted from Yosso (2005).

Application. As a critical tool for the student leader toolbelt, CCW helps students assess the types of capital they have, identify what types they need to expand, and understand how development of this capital can help them become successful leaders, activists, and advocates. For example, consider a Black student leader who is trying to get funding to bring a well-known Black speaker on campus, and is having a difficult time securing resources due to the "potential critique" against their institution. Leadership educators can teach on CCW and the various forms of capital through professional development workshops. Using this, educators can help student leaders maintain hope for their goal by drawing on prior instances of resistant forces from peers and university personnel in their leadership role. Through social and navigational capitals, they lean on people networks who can help them not only secure funding but help to

showcase interest convergence with the potential needs of the institution through administrators. Lastly, linguistic capital can be used when interacting with university administrators to speak directly to their concerns in their own their language. By doing this, student leaders cultivate administrative investment and funding support can be more easily gained. Additionally, successful advocacy grows their social capital, which can be used to resolve other issues in the future.

Socratic Hope Questions

- What family experiences do you remember that have been sources of strength during your time in college?
- How have you used "code switching" to navigate through leadership spaces? What was it like and has it been helpful in your work as a leader?
- Discuss a time that you met resistance for an idea that you had. What was the outcome? How did it make you feel? How have you used this experience to help you become a stronger leader in college?

Deconstruction and Reconstruction

The models of deconstruction and reconstruction are critical, powerful tools that have a wide range of applicability for looking at hegemonic norms in leadership education. Dugan (2017) advocated the incorporation of critical social theory (CST) within formal leadership theory through these models, challenging and questioning theories for its ability to reproduce inequitable knowledges and structures in society. Through this approach, and the central themes of CST—stocks of knowledge, social location, and ideology and hegemony, Dugan (2017) created a framework to dismantle and rebuild leadership theories toward equity, as described in Tables 15.2 and 15.3.

Application. These tools reinforce and support leadership educators in addressing understand inequitable structures in HEIs through leadership education. Using critical deconstruction and reconstruction also helps with both theory and as practical tools for the "student leader toolbelt." For instance, leadership educators can teach Black student leaders looking to create a living learning community space for Black students to use the commodification tool to showcase how living learning community experiences promote other forms of self-segregation, primarily benefitting White students. This means in order for "inclusive communities" to be

Table 15.2

Tools of Deconstruction

Deconstruction	
Ideological Critique	Questions the underlying core beliefs of a theory attempting to identify what is positioned as normative.
Commodification	Questions how maximizing productivity can result in dehumanization of people and diminishing of knowledge.
Willful Blindness	Questions how and why people may remain purposefully unaware to avoid responsibility and replicate hegemonic norms.
Flow of Power	Questions the degree to which power is acknowledged, how it flows, and the ways in which it shapes experiences and relationships

Source: Adapted from Dugan (2017).

Table 15.3

Tools of Reconstruction

Reconstruction	
Disrupting Normativity	Purposefully and explicitly attempts to identity, name, and address hegemonic norms.
Attending to Power	Identifies and defines power, addresses it flow and impact, and attempts to distribute it in equitable and just ways.
Cultivating Agency	Positions the development of personal and collective agency as central to the purpose of leadership.
Building Interest Convergence	Disrupts utopian perspectives, recognizes the effects of oppression, meets people where they are, and emphasizes the building of coalitions.

Source: Adapted from Dugan (2017).

built in the residence halls, a "profit" for the university must be made. This approach dehumanizes Black students by not recognizing or valuing their need for residential spaces to build community like other more "profitable" communities. They can then reconstruct this through "building interest convergence" and showcase how developing these spaces helps with student outcomes and belongingness of Black students on campus.

Socratic Hope Questions

- What are some instances where you feel you or the communities you serve are ignored by people who hold significant power on campus?
- What do you think is normalized on campus that is problematic in reality? Have you been personally affected by it?
- How can you invite people who hold power on campus into social change discussions?

Love and Healing

While multiple frameworks can be used as asset-based approaches to get the work done, leadership educators also need to attend to the users of the student leader toolbelt. With all the visible and invisible labor Black student leaders accomplish, socially just leadership educators both enact and help them recognize how love and healing as integral to their work. Although the ideas put forth by Travers and Craig (2021) were initially envisioned for Men of Color, they are nonetheless applicable to Black student leaders, regardless of gender, with appropriate adaptations. They highlighted the importance of a love and healing framework, and frame it as a prerequisite for socially just leaders. They strengthened this resolve by drawing from Black feminists like bell hooks (2004), deepening the communal perspective of this approach. To love, in this context, means making an active choice to push ourselves for the betterment of others (Travers & Craig, 2021). Healing means to recognize the silence, as well as the pain and heartbreak that happens in this oppressive world. While these are not foreign to Black student leaders, recognition of these concepts can develop an *embodied autocritography* that is used to help them be authentic, self-reflective, and vulnerable about what is happening in their worlds (Travers & Craig, 2021).

As part of this framework, Travers and Craig (2021) envisioned three forms of love: self-love, love between men, and love in action, all of which are non-romantic forms of love. *Self-love* discusses how Black student leaders need to transcend and accept themselves for who they are. It is a recognition that they are on a journey that requires "a healthy level of kindness, compassion, and patience" during it (Travers & Craig, 2021, p. 83). *Love between men* recognizes the importance of building community and developing spaces to be one's authentic self for Black men. Derived from Black feminists explicitly and expanding its use, this approach creates love and healing spaces where Black student leaders can be honest, vulnerable, and supportive of one another against the tirade of resistance in their institution. Lastly, *love in action* shows how using power and privilege in their identity, Black student leaders must be reflective as they look to enact service and social justice within their communities. These forms of love, when taken together, yield a sense of belonging and healing for Black students, and Black student leaders, which fosters the critical hope that fuels their ongoing growth and development.

Application. Equipping this tool on the "student leader toolbelt" requires a great deal of intentionality from leadership educators. Black student leaders who are constantly immersed within their work may cause them to put their own love and healing secondary to community needs. Socially just leadership educators must recognize this, push for reflective moments using the love and healing framework, and cultivate this through active, vulnerable discussions. A potential use of this framework could include explicitly naming how Black student leaders' racial battle fatigue comes from code-switching in predominantly White institutional spaces. Using self-love, Black student leaders can express kindness, compassion and patience for themselves for having to manage these dynamics while serving the larger mission to do good for others. Using love between men, they can connect with other leaders on campus to commune and support one another. Lastly, as they go out to do their work again, they can use love in action to reflect on the privileges they have and how this can continually provide perspective on how they lead to better their communities.

Socratic Hope Questions

- How have you been treating yourself in the face of resistance? What time are you taking to heal?
- How are you building community with other Black leaders on campus? Where do you create spaces of honesty, vulnerability, and supportiveness for one another?
- How do you use your power and resources as a leader on campus to enact service for communities you hold dear?

CONCLUSION

Black student leaders are some of the hardest working undergraduates in higher education. They not only have to advocate for themselves in the classroom, but outside as well, just to gain social recognition or, in some cases, survive. They embody critical hope as they lead through a critical lens for a better future. In their work, socially just leadership educators recognize the strength, resiliency and power Black student leaders bring as they work to build better, stronger, and more collaborative communities. Additionally, socially just leadership educators recognize, assess and resist hegemonic norms at HWIs, using culturally relevant approaches. Thus, they create socially just leadership learning opportunities for their students that is compassionate, guided by love, and asset-driven. As educators work with student leaders, it is imperative they recognize how helping develop a leader is also growing an "agent of critical hope"—someone who will advocate to make the world fairer, more equitable, and more just.

REFERENCES

Beatty, C. C., & Guthrie, K. L. (2021). *Operationalizing culturally relevant leadership learning*. Information Age Publishing.

Beatty, C. C., & Lima, A. (2021). Normalcy, avoidance, consciousness raising: Exploring how student leaders navigate racial battle fatigue. *Journal of Student Affairs Research and Practice*, *59*(4), 1–14. https://doi.org/10.1080/19496591.2021.1955697

Bertrand Jones, T., Guthrie, K. L., & Osteen, L. (2016). Critical domains of culturally relevant leadership learning: A call to transform leadership programs. In K. L. Guthrie, T. Bertrand Jones, & L. Osteen (Eds.), *Developing culturally relevant leadership learning*. (New Directions for Student Leadership, No. 152, pp. 9–21). Jossey-Bass. https://doi.org/10.1002/yd.20205

Bishundat, D., Phillip, D. V., & Gore, W. (2018). Cultivating critical hope: The too often forgotten dimension of critical leadership development. In J. P. Dugan (Ed.), *Integrating critical perspectives into leadership development* (New Directions for Student Leadership, No. 159, pp. 91–102). https://doi.org/10.1002/yd.20300

Bordas, J. (2016). Leadership lessons from communities of color: Stewardship and collective action. In K. L. Guthrie, T. Bertrand Jones, & L. Osteen (Eds.), *Developing culturally relevant leadership learning*. (New Directions for Student Leadership, No. 152, pp. 61–74). https://doi.org/10.1002/yd.20209

Bourdieu, P., & Passeron, J.-C. (1977). *Reproduction in education, society and culture*. Sage.

Brooms, D. R., Franklin, W., Clark, J. S., & Smith, M. (2018). 'It's more than just mentoring': Critical mentoring Black and Latino males from college to the community. *Race Ethnicity and Education*, *24*(2), 210–228. https://doi.org/10.1080/13613324.2018.1538125

Dugan, J. P. (2017). *Leadership theory: Cultivating critical perspectives*. John Wiley & Sons.

Duncan-Andrade, J. (2009). Note to educators: Hope required when growing roses in concrete. *Harvard Educational Review*, *79*(2), 181–194. https://doi.org/10.17763/haer.79.2.nu3436017730384w

hooks, b. (2004). *The will to change: Men, masculinity, and Love*. Washington Square Press.

Jeffries, H. K. (2006). SNCC, Black power, and independent political party organizing in Alabama, 1964-1966. *The Journal of African American History, 91*(2),
   171–193.
Puwar, N. (2004). *Space invaders: Race, gender and bodies out of place* (1st ed.). Berg.
Quaye, S. J. (2007). The outcomes of contemporary student activism. *About Campus,
   12*(2), 2–9. https://doi.org/10.1002/abc.205
Strayhorn, T. L. (2017). Factors that influence the persistence and success of Black
   men in urban public universities. *Urban Education, 52*(9), 1106–1128. http://
   dx.doi.org.proxy.lib.fsu.edu/10.1177/0042085915623347
Strayhorn, T. L. (2019). *College students' sense of belonging: A key to educational success
   for all students* (2nd ed.). Routledge.
Teig, T. S. (2018). Integrating social justice in leadership education. In K. L. Guthrie
   & V. S. Chunoo (Eds.), *Changing the narrative: Socially just leadership education*
   (pp. 9–26). Information Age Publishing.
Thelin, J. R. (2019). *A history of American higher education*. Johns Hopkins University
   Press.
Travers, C. S., & Craig, J. P. (2021) Exploring the intersections of love, healing
   and leadership among men of color. In K. L. Guthrie & V. S. Chunoo (Eds.),
   Shifting the mindset: Socially just leadership education (pp. 75–87). Information
   Age Publishing.
Warren, E., & Supreme Court of the United States. (1953). *U.S. Reports: Brown v.
   Board of Education, 347 U.S. 483*. [Periodical] Retrieved from the Library of
   Congress. https://www.loc.gov/item/usrep347483/.
Williams, T. O. (2016). Internalization of dominance and subordination: Barriers
   to creative and intellectual fullness. In K. L. Guthrie, T. Bertrand Jones, &
   L. Osteen (Eds.), *Developing culturally relevant leadership learning*. (New Direc-
   tions for Student Leadership, No. 152, pp. 87–94). https://doi.org/10.1002/
   yd.20211
Williamson-Lott, J. A. (2018). *Jim Crow campus: Higher education and the struggle for
   a new southern social order*. Teachers College Press.
Yosso, T. J. (2005). Whose culture has capital? A critical race theory discussion of
   community cultural wealth. *Race, Ethnicity and Education, 8*(1), 69–91.
Yosso, T. J., Smith, W. A., Ceja, M., & Solórzano, D. G. (2009). Critical race theory,
   racial microaggressions, and campus racial climate for Latina/o undergraduates. *Harvard Educational Review, 79*(4), 659–690. https://doi.org/10.17763/
   haer.79.4.m6867014157m7071

CHAPTER 16

MAKING ROOM

Leading, Learning, and Growing in Women-Only or Women-Dominated Spaces

Brittany Devies

Even after decades of exclusion from higher education, today, women make up over 58% of the undergraduate student population in the United States (U.S. Department of Education, n.d.). Although women make up the majority of the undergraduate student population (National Center for Education Statistics, n.d.), only minimal research exists on undergraduate women's leadership development. While some scholars have explored undergraduate women's leadership development (Devies, 2023; Devies & Owen, 2022; Haber-Curran & Tillapaugh, 2017; Owen, 2020; Owen et al., 2021; Rupert, 2019; Shetty, 2020; Torres, 2019), relatively little is understood about the influence of context and environment in college women's leadership development. Previous research shows how college women have a higher leadership capacity than their male peers, yet score significantly lower than those peers on leadership efficacy metrics (Dugan & Komives, 2007). This mandates more exploration of this population and phenomenon to better understand how we can encourage leadership capacity and efficacy growth in undergraduate women. These gaps in understanding led to a narrative inquiry study that sought to explore both how undergraduate women develop their leadership capacity and efficacy and examine how factors and practices shape undergraduate women's perception of their

Committing to Action: Socially Just Leadership Educations, pp. 193–204
Copyright © 2025 by Information Age Publishing
www.infoagepub.com
All rights of reproduction in any form reserved.

leadership capacity and efficacy development (Devies, 2023). This chapter explores the impact of women-only or women-dominated spaces in undergraduate women's leadership development.

GENDER AND LEADERSHIP

It is critical to understand how gender is socially constructed (Haber-Curran & Tillapaugh, 2018; Owen, 2020; West & Zimmerman, 1987), and can be thought of as "the range of mental or behavioral characteristics pertaining to, and differentiating between and across, masculinity and femininity" (West & Zimmerman, 1987, p. 126). Different from someone's sex assigned at birth (including a person's chromosomes and reproductive organs), a person's "gender identity refers to a person's deeply felt, internal and individual experience of gender, which may or may not correspond to the person's physiology or designated sex at birth" (World Health Organization, n.d., para. 3). Devies (2023) noted it is "essential to acknowledge the many contextual, organizational, institutional, and systemic influences that contribute to the development of one's gender identity" (p. 15).

Leadership is also a socially constructed, focusing on the person, the situation, and the people's perceptions (Dugan, 2017; Grint, 1997, 2005). When analyzing socialization and leadership, context is a critical component. Batliwala (2010) defines transformational feminist leadership as

> a feminist perspective and vision of social justice, individually and collectively, transforming [oneself] to use their power, resources, and skills in non-oppressive inclusive structures and processes to mobilize others, especially other women, around a shared agenda, of social cultural, economic, and political transformation for equality and the realization of human rights for all. (p. 29)

Since gender and leadership are both socially constructed phenomenon, context is deeply important to both gender and leadership (Devies, 2023; Owen, 2020). In cultivating transformational feminist leadership in campus contexts, it is important to have spaces and places where women feel empowered to lead.

Taner (2023) noted, "Concurrently, there are established and burgeoning programs on leadership in the United States, yet disappointingly, many still focus on traditional, non-transformative, corporate, and management aspects of leadership, ultimately perpetuating the status-quo" (p. 226), furthering emphasizing the importance of crafting women-only and women-dominated spaces for leadership learning. This chapter seeks to share narratives of the powerful leadership capacity and efficacy development within women-only or women-dominated spaces, in which Taner

(2023) posit these feminist leadership spaces "disrupt the status-quo and to widen the passageways for which minoritized communities and individuals have a seat at decision-making tables" (p. 227).

SIGNIFICANCE

In 2023, I conducted a narrative inquiry study of 11 undergraduate women as part of my dissertation research. This study sought to explore two research questions: (1) How do undergraduate women develop their leadership capacity and efficacy? And (2) How do factors and practices shape undergraduate women's perception of their leadership capacity and efficacy development? Data was collected in three waves: a screening tool, a brief narrative about their experiences with gender and leadership, and a semi-structured interview. The participants' narratives were in response to the prompt: *Describe a time where you noticed a connection between your identity as a woman and your identity as a leader?* The interview more specifically focused on questions around the women's leadership capacity and efficacy development.

While this study sought to explore women's leadership capacity and efficacy development, stories about leadership in women-only or women-dominated contexts came up for Nicole, Teri, Anne, Aria, Catherine Jones, Ella, and Katie in both their narratives and interviews. Participants were never explicitly asked about these contexts or spaces, but they continued to bring up women-only or women-dominated contexts as overwhelmingly positive developmental spaces. Participants expressed feelings of safety and security when they spoke and wrote of their all-girls summer camps, women-dominated internships, women's' student unions, and women's student organizations and their developmental experiences within them. When specifically looking at the past contexts she had led in, Mariah, a third-year woman studying biology, examined every job and position of leadership she had held and noted how many instances had occurred in each role. She described her reflections on some of these instances in her narrative:

> Many have the same theme that I am not as capable as a man or that a man could be doing my job better than me. I would say it is the negative events that I could make the connection the fastest with. While the more positive events, such as having our entire store/department run by women often easily get overlooked. It is more of a small achievement that we congratulate ourselves for and no one else takes note of. I personally tend to focus on the negative events as there is more to unpack and analyze there and it is a more blatant way for the connection to be thrown in my face.

Mariah's reflections in her narrative posit the question: what happens when gender becomes more homogenous for the marginalized gendered identity in a space where leadership unfolds? What happens when women spend less time, energy, and capacity unpacking and analyzing sexism in leadership and instead utilize those resources to cultivate positive social change? What is and could be the value and opportunity of women-dominated or women-only spaces to empower women leaders?

WOMEN-ONLY AND WOMEN-DOMINATED SPACES

There are many (although not enough) spaces and places where leadership occurs that are women-only spaces or women-dominated places. Within the context of higher education, many of these exist and were historically established as a response to men dominating college and university spaces in power, presence, and influence. Early involvement opportunities for women included national academic, collegiate, and class clubs, and sororities (McCandless, 1999). These women-only or women-dominated spaces still exist on college campuses today and include, but not limited to, women's colleges, sororities, and women's unions.

Katie, a third-year student involved in Best Buddies, the Catholic Student Union, and a Panhellenic sorority, explored in her narrative how her leadership was often viewed as feminine, which led her to several women-dominated or women-only leadership spaces.

> My leadership positions can be directly related to my strengths, which are generally classified as feminine. For example, some of my strengths as a leader are emotional intelligence, vulnerability, and compassion. In addition, many of the leadership roles that I fulfill are typically female-dominated.

Katie went on to share how she was a marketing intern where 75% of the office employees were women. She was on her sorority's executive board, overseeing operations for a chapter of 250 women. She also held a coordinator role in Best Buddies, an educational organization that was primarily comprised of women members.

Katie's narrative above is just a sampling of the context the participants organically offered in their narratives in interviews. Specifically, participants Nicole, Teri, Anne, Aria, Catherine Jones, Ella, and Katie shared developmental leadership experiences that unfolded in the contexts of sororities, women's student unions, all-girls summer camps, women-dominated internships, education-focused organizations, and women's in pre-professional organizations.

Women's Colleges

While none of these research participants attended a women's college, it is imperative to honor the significance of women's colleges in creating women-only spaces. These institutions created women's only spaces during a time in higher education, where women were holistically barred from other institutions. Historically, women's colleges were crafted as spaces for women to learn among one another (McCandless, 1999; Solomon, 1985). Solomon (1985) noted that on semantics, many claimed to be the first women's college, yet, "Georgia Female College, later renamed Wesleyan, was chartered by state legislature in 1836 and opened in 1838" (p. 24).

Lewis (2021) noted, "Women's colleges have a unique and successful history in fostering women's leadership relying on transformational and feminist leadership frameworks" (p. 57).

Over time, as more institutions began to allow the matriculation of women on their campuses, women's colleges suffered. Lewis (2021) claimed, "by 2020 the numbers of women's colleges shrank to 34 predominantly White (PWI) and 2 historically Black (HBCU) institutions" (p. 57).

Sororities

Shortly after the founding of the first women's college, in 1848 and 1852, the first two predominantly and historically White social sororities (National Panhellenic Council organizations) were founded at Wesleyan College, which led to these national organizations growing tremendously and spreading into co-educational institutions across the country (Devies & Haynes, 2024; McCandless, 1999; Solomon, 1985). Social sororities for women were "were originally founded as secret societies to affirm the ties of friendship" among women in higher education spaces (Solomon, 1985, p. 107). These communities were focused on connecting students of the same gender identity around a common purpose. "Many of the nation's first sororities originated on Southern college campuses" and primarily focused on building community for women within the campus context (McCandless, 1999, p. 141).

Some institutions even leveraged these organizations to attract more women to enroll at their institutions (McCandless, 1999). It is important to note that all 26 National Panhellenic Conference (NPC) sororities were founded during the first wave of feminism, between 1851 and 1917 (Devies & Haynes, 2024; National Panhellenic Conference, n.d.). The first intercollegiate historically African American sorority, Alpha Kappa Alpha (n.d.) was established in 1908 at Howard University, with the goal of creating spaces for belonging, leadership, and service for African American and

Black women on college campuses. As of 2023, the National Panhellenic Conference (NPC) includes 26 individual national social sorority organizations, represented on campuses across the United States and parts of Canada (Owen, 2020).

Four of the 11 participants in the study were members of a historically White social sorority (NPC). Nearly 175 years after the first organization's founding on a college campus, the sorority environment came up as an important context for women to develop their leadership capacity and efficacy. Anne, a third-year student, was heavily involved on campus, primarily in fraternity and sorority life. She served on a Greek council executive board, served as a programming specialist for her sorority organization, and served as a recruitment counselor for formal sorority recruitment at her institution. The sorority culture and context came up frequently throughout her interview. When elaborating on her experience in the sorority, she noted the importance of serving as a mentor for newer members, stating:

> I think my favorite form of leadership is taking a mentorship role, I do that. I have a lot of mentoring ability.... Like mentoring positions, I guess you would say. But I like to go about a leadership role in the way of how can I make this better than I left it, and I think that's kind of ingrained in women on the society. (Devies, 2023, p. 83)

Anne noted how women are engrained to be mentors in society from their own socialization. She then was exclusively involved on campus in women-dominated or women-only spaces where she was heavily relied on to mentor other women. This aligns with her enactment of the leadership process through peer-to-peer mentorship. Additionally, Anne wrote in her narrative about a time a male guest speaker came and presented to her sorority community of over 4,000 women.

> This moment where this man was speaking to us and telling us that we fall into the stereotype of sorority women and that we need to be stronger and that we can't let other people disrespect us was so pivotal for me. It made me realize that even though people will say things like that to women, they still contribute to the system. When you have a woman who is a leader in these spaces, you have a much more open and freely feeling experience as a leader and follower.

In somewhat opposition with her first quote about the value of space to engage in empowering mentorship amongst women, this male guest speaker then entered a women-only leadership space and spoke to the stereotype of women on college campuses in such spaces. Anne brilliantly reflected on, even if this speech was meant to empower women in the space, it came from the perspective of someone with identities that had historically contributed to the stereotype narratives. It is essential to note the context in which the male speaker was speaking in and how that influenced the message he delivered. Anne ended the narrative with the reflection on how important it is to hear from women in these spaces, especially when speaking about changing systems.

Building upon the idea of creating safe and brave spaces for women to lead, Katie, a third-year student involved in a sorority, wrote in her narrative, "some organizations are strictly female, set up for women to empowered each other and have a safe place to express themselves, such as sororities" (Devies, 2023, p. 94). In this quote, Katie directly addresses the inherent and foundational levels of safety that exist when women lead in spaces that are "strictly female" as she defines it. In her experiences on campus, this happened primarily in her sorority, as noted. She felt both empower and safe to express herself and lead.

Gender and Leadership Courses

Several of the participants had engaged with a gender and leadership studies course on campus, an environment and context that was salient within their narratives and interviews. One example is Mariah, a third-year student, who wrote about her experiences in this course and how it was a "space where women being leaders is encouraged and possible" (Devies, 2023, p. 95). She noted how the resources she had within the class to learn about women in leadership and leadership increased her leadership efficacy. She wrote, "Without these resources, I fear that I would have continued to be more of a follower as I was in my previous years and would have never found my confidence again" (Devies, 2023, p. 95). While leadership efficacy and confidence are not synonymous, Mariah mentioned several times her increased confidence as a leader, noting how this led her to take on new passions and leadership roles on campus.

Women's Student Unions and Student Organizations

Several of the women were involved in women-only student organizations or women's student unions. Teri identified as a third-year student studying political science who was involved in a leadership role in the women in pre-law society on campus. Catherine Jones identified as a fourth year, senior undergraduate woman studying business; she served on the executive board of a women in business organization on campus.

Catherine Jones wrote in her narrative about her experiences in the women in business organization, stating:

> Once I got to college and started to get more involved on campus, the re-lationship between my identities as a woman and as a leader became more clear. In my day-to-day life, I had to go between leading other women as an executive board member of Women in Business (WIB) and leading male classmates in group projects. Leading the members of WIB was a cakewalk compared to working with some of the men in my classes. In my group projects, I sometimes felt like men would pretend to lead the rest of the group. They would speak the most during group meetings without hav-ing anything substantial to say. They pushed most of the work on to other group members and assigned the least amount of work to themselves, but they would often not even complete the little work that they had promised to do. After a man leading a group would fall short, I found myself having to take over, and this was when I started to identify as a leader.

She wrote about how it felt like a "cakewalk" to lead and grow in the women in business organization compared to trying to lead in her male-dominated business courses. She would often have to adapt and lead out of necessity and shortcomings in others leadership. But in her interview, she elaborated on how the women in business organization was instrumental in her finding her voice and passion for business, and perhaps most important in her finding her leadership identity as a woman in business for her future career.

Nicole identified as a third-year, senior undergraduate woman double majoring in political science and social science and intended to continue at the institution pursuing her master's in social work. She was involved on the executive board of the women's student union and helped create a new society for women on campus in her final year as an undergraduate.

In her narrative, Nicole wrote about how she was initially hesitant to even run for an executive board role in a women's student union but when she decided to, "I was determined to leave the call with my interview-ers knowing my passion for empowering the next generation of women leaders." Further, Nicole noted, "During the interview I felt intensely connected to my identity of a woman and as a leader while expressing my interest in serving on WSU's executive board." Once she won the positional role and began to become more heavily involved in the women's student union, she wrote about how empowering it was to share space with other women. In her experience working with a women's student union, she wrote about the importance of her own leadership development in leading a space with and for women.

> I was eager to take on a leadership role in an organization that advocates for women's equality, rights, and issues on [institution]'s campus and in

the greater [local] community. As a woman, I felt a calling to give back and do my part in creating spaces where women could come together to learn, grow, and build meaningful relationships.

In this example, leading in a women-only space led to her own identity development as both a woman and a leader. The interconnectedness of their womanhood and their developing and emerging leader identities was reflected in her experiences. This quote inspired the title of this chapter as it is the critical role of women-only and women-dominated spaces: to be spaces where women come together to lead, learn, grow, and build meaningful relationships. At the conclusion of Nicole's writing about her experiences in the women's student union, she stated,

> I have never been in a leadership position that makes me feel so intensely connected to my identity as a woman. Every time I walk into the WSU room ... I feel instantly connected to my identity as a woman in leadership. Having the opportunity to work with an all-women executive board from different backgrounds and experiences has given me the space to grow as a woman and a leader and allowed me to explore what the interaction of these identities mean to me. I have discovered how powerful it is to lead with compassion, integrity, and love. When you genuinely care about the leaders around you, it shows, and it is evident how much the WSU executive board cares and respects each other. Being surrounded by so many strong, women leaders has led me to embrace my identity as a woman more than ever before.

Nicole's narrative about the women's student union is profound in that it evidences that not only are women-only and women-dominated spaces important for women's leadership capacity and efficacy, but also for their gender identity and leadership identity development. Being in a space with other women who shared her gender identity was affirming for Nicole, along with others throughout the study.

DISCUSSION AND IMPLICATIONS

Hartman (1999) founded the Institute for Women's Leadership at Rutgers in 1991 to promote spaces for women to lead. She reiterated the "importance of creating the conditions in which these needs can be met—in all settings where women are present" on college campuses (Taner, 2023, p. 225). Taner (2023) further emphasized that the same notion of creating places for women to effectively lead on college campuses then "translates well into women and leadership programming by building diverse women's capacities and confidence to be leaders in their communities"

(p. 225). Bunch and Gray White (2002) posited that women's leadership development programs are critical; not because they make women leaders, but further that they "can provide opportunities to enhance and support women's leadership and to make it more visible and more viable" (p. 16).

Yet, in the last decade of higher education, single identity (including gender identity spaces) has been challenged on many occasions. In the last decade, the United States saw Harvard University propose a ban on all single sex organizations on their campus, including sororities (Owen, 2020; Rosenberg, 2020). The intention of the policy was to "address discrimination on the basis of gender and, as a practical matter, to undercut the prowess of the long-established, well-endowed final clubs" (Rosenberg, 2020, para. 1). Supporters on Harvard's campus and beyond posited that gender-based social organizations were "incompatible with the College's values, policies, and norms" (Rosenberg, 2020, para. 3). Even though the policy was withdrawn in 2020, it started a divisive conversation within the higher education community around single-gender and identity spaces (Devies & Haynes, 2024). In the face of such challenges, some national sorority organizations have created programs, initiatives, and committees to evaluate their membership policies and future as single gender organizations (Devies & Haynes, 2024). Although the narratives above evidence positive outcomes from these single gendered spaces on their leadership identity, capacity, and efficacy development, it certainly sits in tension with the national conversation around the future of these spaces on college campuses, especially considering the gender binary these organizations were founded upon and which has historically been exclusionary.

CONCLUSION

What is the value of creating "safe" spaces for leadership development in a world that is anything but safe for marginalized identities? Perhaps it ties back to Nicole's narrative that creating spaces where women are surrounded by other strong, women leaders allow women the security and capacity to embrace and develop their identity as a leader. Katie stated in her narrative, "Some of my leadership roles have been an opportunity to me because of my gender, while other roles have given me the chance to excel with the assets I possess as a female." The continued theme of these women's stories is that no matter the environment, from all-girls summer camps to women-dominated internships to sororities to women's student organizations, is it gives them the space to grow, flourish, and find their voice as emerging leaders.

Taner (2023) profoundly noted, "With critical 21st century challenges at hand, integrating women and leadership programs in our academic opportunities can influence and inform a shifting paradigm for leadership and subsequently leadership education—to co-create stronger, more equitable communities" (p. 236). These spaces and places for college women continue to develop their leadership identity, capacity, and efficacy is evident and leadership educators must continue to create and nurture these spaces.

REFERENCES

Batliwala, S. (2010). *Feminist leadership for social transformation: Clearing the conceptual cloud. Creating Resources for Empowerment in Action.* https://creaworld.org/wp-content/uploads/2020/11/feminist-leadership-clearing-conceptual-cloud-srilatha-batliwala.pdf

Bunch, C., & Gray White, D. (2002). *Power for what?: Women's leadership, Why you should care?* Institute for Women's Leadership Consortium at Douglass College, Rutgers, the State University of New Jersey.

Devies, B. (2023). "Unapologetically woman": Undergraduate women's leadership capacity and efficacy development [Unpublished dissertation, Florida State University].

Devies, B., & Haynes, L. A. (2024). Connecting feminism and the sorority experience: Looking back to move forward. In P. A. Sasso, J. P. Biddix, & M. L. Miranda (Eds.), *Affirming identity, advancing belonging, & amplifying voice.* Information Age Publishing.

Devies, B., & Owen, J. E. (2022). Cultivating a systems mindset through feminist leadership. In K. L. Guthrie, & K. L. Priest (Eds.), *Navigating complexities in leadership: Moving towards critical hope* (pp. 175–183). Information Age Publishing.

Dugan, J. P., & Komives, S. R. (2007). *Developing leadership capacity in college students: Findings from a national study.* National Clearinghouse for Leadership Programs.

Dugan, J. P. (2017). *Leadership theory: Cultivating critical perspectives.* Jossey-Bass.

Grint, K. (1997). *Leadership: Classical, contemporary, and critical approaches.* Oxford University Press.

Grint, K. (2005). *Leadership: Limits and possibilities.* Palgrave Macmillan.

Haber-Curran, P., & Tillapaugh, D. (2017). Gender and student leadership: A critical examination. In D. Tillapaugh, & P. Haber-Curran (Eds.), *New Directions for Student Leadership: No. 154. Critical perspectives on gender and student leadership* (pp. 11–22). Wiley. https://doi.org/10.1002/yd.20236

Haber-Curran, P., & Tillapaugh, D. (2018). Beyond the binary: Advancing socially just leadership through the lens of gender. In K. L. Guthrie, & V. S. Chunoo (Eds.), *Changing the narrative: Socially just leadership education* (pp. 77–92). Information Age Publshing.

Lewis, A. S. (2021). The promises and challenges of women's colleges: Leadership and equity. In R. Whitney & J. D. Collins (Eds.). *New Directions for Student Leadership: No. 171. Advancing racial equity in leadership education: Centering marginalized institutional contexts* (pp. 57–66). Wiley. https://doi.org/10.1002/yd.20456

McCandless, A. (1999). *The past in the present: Women's higher education in the 20th century south*. University of Alabama Press.

National Center for Education Statistics. (n.d.). *Fast facts: enrollment*. https://nces. ed.gov/fastfacts/display.asp?id=98

Owen, J. E. (2020). *We are the leaders we've been waiting for: Women and leadership development in college*. Stylus.

Owen, J. E., Devies, B., & Reynolds, D. J. (2021). Going beyond 'Add Women then Stir': Fostering feminist leadership. In K. L. Guthrie, & V. S. Chunoo (Eds.), *Shifting the mindset: Socially just leadership education* (pp. 89–99). Information Age Publishing

Rosenberg, J. S. (2020, June 30). Harvard single-gender social-club rules rescinded. *Harvard Magazine*. https://www.harvardmagazine.com/2020/06/harvard-rescinds-single-gender-club-rules

Rupert, K. A. (2019). Shattering the collegiate glass ceiling: Understanding the experiences of women student government presidents [Unpublished dissertation, University of Maryland, College Park].

Shetty, R. L. (2020). *The leader identity of Black women in college: A grounded theory* [Unpublished dissertation, University of Georgia].

Solomon, B. M. (1985). *In the company of educated women*. Yale University Press.

Taner, S. (2023). The transformational power of feminist women's leadership education. In T. Teig, B. Devies, & B. Shetty (Eds.), Rooted and radiant: Women's narratives of leadership (pp. 223–236). Information Age Publishing.

Torres, M. (2019). *Ella creyo que podia, asi que lo hizo: Exploring Latina leader identity development through testimonio* [Unpublished dissertation, Florida State University].

U.S. Department of Education. (n.d.). *National center for education statistics, integrated postsecondary education data system (IPEDS), Number of students enrolled in postsecondary institutions annually by gender*. https://nces.ed.gov/ipeds/TrendGenerator/app/trend-table/2/2?trending=column&rid=13

West, C., & Zimmerman, D. H. (1987). Doing gender. *Gender and Society*, *1*(2), 125–151.

World Health Organization. (n.d.). Gender and health. https://www.who.int/health-topics/gender#tab=tab_1

PART III

ACTION ORIENTED COMMITMENTS TO SOCIALLY JUST LEADERSHIP EDUCATION

CHAPTER 17

ADVISING IS LEADING

Academic and Individual Advising Praxis as Socially Just Leadership Education

Holly Henning

Socially just leadership education offers critical insight into how we foster leaders among college students, and others, across identities and contexts while applying a social justice lens (Guthrie & Chunoo, 2018, 2021). Indeed, resources continue to emerge on the topic given its value and relevance in present-day academia and beyond. One additional context worthy (and, as I argue, necessary) of infusing socially just leadership education is collegiate academic advising and more broadly, advising in one-on-one curricular settings. This type of advising is common educational practice across U.S. postsecondary institutions (Pascarella & Terenzini, 2005), and it provides essential and persistent institutional support to students. As Habley (1994) aptly put it, "Academic advising is the only structured activity on the campus in which all students have the opportunity for on-going, one-to-one interaction with a concerned representative of the institution" (p. 10). In other words, it helps students navigate the complexities of academic life, especially for those who would not otherwise connect with the institution, while making the tenets of social justice and leadership applicable.

Given its ubiquitous nature, academic advising is an ideal conduit for socially just leadership education. It builds bridges between curricular and co-curricular settings and involves both what is discussed in the classroom and experienced outside the classroom in much the same way leadership

Committing to Action: Socially Just Leadership Educations, pp. 207–218

learning occurs. While helpful information already exists on general advising for leadership development in student organizations and groups (see also: Acosta, 2018; Chrystal-Green, 2018), with few exceptions, a gap is still largely present in leadership education literature about how to marry individual advising settings and socially just leadership education.

The purpose of this chapter is to address that gap by extending the body of literature on socially just leadership education into academic advising praxis. Recognizing students also turn to individuals in faculty, administrative, and staff roles on campus, who both are and are not traditional academic advisors, this material may further apply to other one-on-one advising contexts in which academic and other matters may be discussed but are not functionally designated as academic advising settings.

Important to note is my positionality, how it influences my views on this subject, and my suggestions for understanding and advancing practice. From a leadership perspective, much of what I believe about socially just leadership education emanates from my experience and education as a college student leader, then as a full-time higher education professional, and as a graduate student who continuously participates in formal and informal leadership learning. Admittedly, I am more experienced in the world of advising. For a decade, I worked as a study abroad advisor, academic advisor, and First Year Experience instructor; meeting with countless undergraduate students and aspiring leaders whose social backgrounds differed from my own in many ways. I strongly believe a good academic advisor (or anyone individually advising college students) can help make a student's challenging college years successful, given robust advisor training, advising experience, and general support.

I also recognize many advisors and leadership educators do not necessarily receive the training and professional development they need to best assist students. I hope to incorporate socially just leadership education in one-on-one advising capacities so leadership educators and advisors will have a frame of reference when cultivating student leadership development as part of their advising approach in a meaningful way. I must acknowledge that as a White, heterosexual, cisgender woman from the United States, I have considerable privilege given my identities. My expertise has been shaped in response to these, and other, social and personal identities. Furthermore, as someone whose multiple identities situate her similarly to the majority of academic advisors (typically White women) with an increasingly diverse population in the United States and higher education, I am committed to continuously assessing my privilege and investing in leadership education that is socially just. Readers may not share my background in academic advising or may approach this topic with different levels of advising knowledge; therefore, I provide a brief overview of academic advising fundamentals and then transition into the connections between academic advising and socially just leadership education.

ADVISING FUNDAMENTALS

Understanding what constitutes advising is a necessary precursor for combining socially just leadership education and the world of individual advising. From an academic advising-specific perspective, the term "academic advising" has evolved over several decades. In its most basic form, academic advising refers to "situations in which an institutional representative gives insight or direction to a college student about an academic, social, or personal matter. The nature of this direction might be to inform, suggest, counsel, discipline, coach, mentor, or even teach" (Kuhn, 2008, p. 3). While multiple definitions encapsulate the work of academic advisors in different ways, the beauty of this definition is its inclusion of the responsibilities we all bear. In other words, academic advisors are recognized for the work they do beyond academic matters, including mentoring and coaching, and those who are not academic advisors are also acknowledged for similar functions they assume without the formal title. This inclusivity is not meant to detract from the work of academic advisors specifically, but rather to highlight the complex nature of advising and numerous people who participate in advising activities in some capacity who must also be mindful of this topic. In short, plenty of people carry the work of advising, and the work of advising is plentiful.

Beyond definitions and basic purposes, academic advising is grounded in extensive theory, which subsequently informs prominent approaches to advising students in individual settings. In fact, many theories from which the field pulls are not unique to advising, but rather stem from other fields like the social sciences and humanities (Hagen & Jordan, 2008). Common historical and modern theories underpinning academic advising and other advising or student affairs roles in higher education include the humanistic, cognitive, psychosocial, and identity-based theories; though more recently, learning-centered practices have materialized to better align advising efforts with academic affairs (Hagen & Jordan, 2008). Advising approaches span these theories and range from the developmental to appreciative to integrative and more (Drake, 2013). I encourage anyone in a leadership education or advising capacity to familiarize themselves with these approaches and question how they may be used, revised, or reconstructed to promote socially just leadership education.

ADVISING, LEADERSHIP, AND SOCIAL JUSTICE INTERSECTIONS

It is also important to note the key intersections among advising, leadership, and social justice. As it stands, there is no unifying theory or model of socially just leadership education in the context of academic advising; leadership and social justice currently exist as separate concepts. These concepts are, in fact, present in academic advising literature and best practices with more recent scholarship acknowledging social justice and especially culturally relevant pedagogy in advising. The National Academic Advising Association, also known as NACADA (2017), the global community for academic advising, emphasizes the importance of social justice through two of its core values—inclusivity and respect—with the other values mirroring these. Additionally, the NACADA Social Justice committee puts structure to these values in a visible and measurable manner, encouraging advisors to live out these values during advising sessions. As for the concept of leadership in the academic advising arena, various articles outline how academic advisors can promote their advisees' leadership development tied to specific leadership theories, yet there is little or no convergence between academic advising and socially just leadership education in the way it is presented here.

Socially Just Leadership Education and Academic Advising

What, then, is socially just leadership education, and what does it look like, conceptually and pragmatically, in academic advising? In its simplest form, socially just leadership education is "the intersection of leadership education and social justice work" (Guthrie & Chunoo, 2018, p. 2). Socially just leadership education therefore translates to an, "(1) appreciation for the rights and responsibilities of individuals and associations, (2) commitment to communities and associations within which leaders act, and (3) cultivation of the individual virtue of social justice" (Promisel, 2021, p. 17). A review of the leadership learning framework shows it as "a collaborative, interdisciplinary, and campuswide endeavor that involves a wide range of students, faculty, staff, and community partners. It is an institutional commitment" (Chunoo & Osteen, 2016, p. 9). Postsecondary institutions have also long recognized the need for leadership development as part of their purpose and mission (Chunoo & Osteen, 2016). Thus, leadership learning requires greater intentionality in advising settings based on the larger role it plays in institutional capacities and individual student development.

I envision socially just leadership in the context of academic advising as depicted in Figure 17.1. Spanning across the curricular and co-curricular is the academic advising process, which ideally covers the course of students' undergraduate careers. It is both a continuous and intermittent process that occurs over the length of time the student is enrolled in college, though it may transcend this time period as advising relationships turn to long-term mentoring, advocacy, and coaching. My argument, however, is that the accepted notion of academic advising is insufficient, and it must possess a socially just leadership lens. In this way, socially just leadership is not just an "add-on" but rather a transformation in the culture, policies, and practices of academic advising. Academic advising is both a form of socially just leadership education and means of implementing it.

Figure 17.1

Conceptual Model of Academic Advising as Socially Just Leadership Education

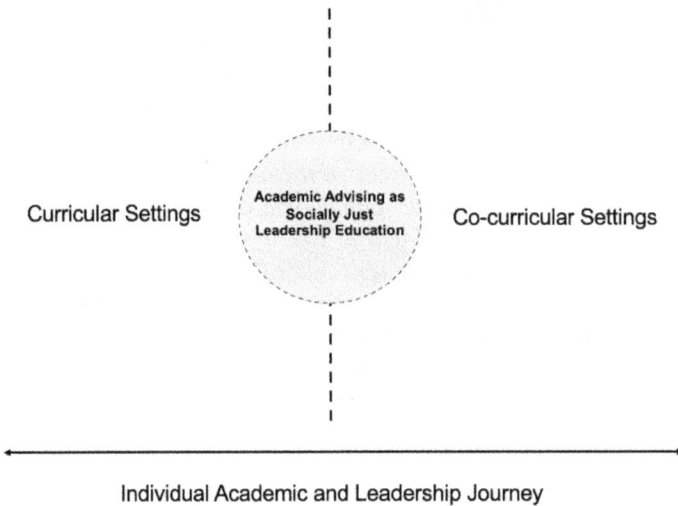

Curricular Settings

Academic Advising as
Socially Just
Leadership Education

Co-curricular Settings

Individual Academic and Leadership Journey

Culturally Relevant Leadership Learning in Academic and Individual Advising

Recognizing how socially just leadership education manifests in the context of academic advising is essential to its successful implementation. This requires greater connection to how socially just leadership education is understood, taught, and practiced. One of the most recent, and continuously evolving, additions to leadership education is the culturally relevant leadership learning (CRLL) model, which serves as the primary foundation for merging socially just leadership education and advising in this text. It acts as the mechanism that combines the "what" and "how" for the process of academic advising as socially just leadership education.

Beatty and Guthrie (2021) wrote about CRLL as rooted in the culturally relevant pedagogy of Ladson-Billings (2014) and work on campus climate by Hurtado et al. (1999), among others. One of the major benefits of this model is that it "confronts myriad ways racism, sexism, religious oppression, heterosexism/cisgenderism, and classism advantages and disadvantages individuals' lives" (Guthrie et al., 2017, p. 62). Likewise, in academic advising spaces, Museus (2021) and notable others have conducted extensive research on supporting students of color in higher education, with much of the scholarship incorporating culturally relevant pedagogy and culturally engaging advising in academic advising practices. Therefore, integrating all of these orientations advances connections between social justice and leadership.

On its own, the CRLL model infuses both the person and the environment in the leadership process, representing a complex partnership between the two. Not only is leadership learning facilitated through individual leader identity, capacity, and efficacy, but these three pieces interact with the following five environmental dimensions that also affect the leadership process: historical legacy of inclusion/exclusion, compositional diversity, psychological climate, behavioral climate, and organizational/structural domains (Beatty & Guthrie, 2021). This model therefore situates leadership learning within contextual influences whose elements are important based on students' unique positionalities. At the most basic level, each piece of the CRLL model holds substantial social justice value for academic advisors and others who fill advisor roles in one-on-one settings. Consequently, it operationalizes socially just leadership so that it can be visualized, implemented, and acted upon.

Individual Leadership Identity, Capacity, and Efficacy in Academic Advising

At the heart of the CRLL framework are the concepts of leadership identity, capacity, and efficacy. I believe the identity aspect is one of the most important and salient in the context of both leadership and advising because it starts with who individuals consider themselves to be (or how they are viewed by others) and influences the other core aspects of capacity and efficacy. As most advisors well know, students cannot leave their complex identities at the office door when they attend sessions or even speak to advisors casually outside the office in passing; much of who they are will be revealed through conversations. The same is true for academic advisors whose identities are also present, whether seen, voiced, or initially withheld during discussions with students. Interestingly, students who possess formal roles as leaders on campus are often easily recognized in the advising context. Similarly, students may recognize advisors who hold positions of authority within an advising office or on campus committees with their professors or administrative figures, which further affects advising dynamics.

Leadership capacity in CRLL refers to "the incorporation of students' leadership knowledge, skills, and attitudes, which leads to their overall ability to engage in the process of leadership" (Beatty & Guthrie, 2021, p. 23). The actionable information, abilities, and views students possess about leadership work together to make up their leadership capacity. Students' leadership efficacy stems in part from their leadership capacity. As Beatty and Guthrie (2021) noted, efficacy is related to students' beliefs about their abilities during the leadership process; students with greater capacity are predicted to have greater leadership efficacy. In this sense, academic advisors are uniquely positioned to recognize students' leadership capacity and efficacy more easily than most, as they routinely work with students and learn about their skillsets and desired competencies, both inside and outside the classroom. Academic advisors are also likely to witness explicit signs of where students may further develop leadership efficacy and capacity in terms of classes taken and grades earned in their coursework.

Recommendations for Action: CRLL Leadership Identity, Capacity, and Efficacy

Given the need to develop students' leadership identity, capacity, and efficacy, I offer the following actions academic advisors and others in similar positions can take to encourage culturally relevant leadership learning. In the context of leadership identity, advisors can inquire about, validate, and celebrate the identities of students who visit their offices. They should avoid guessing or making assumptions and judgments about who they think students are, even with outward signals or identifiers such as clothing or skin color, positions held on campus, and more. Instead, they should purposefully gather information about students' specific identities, including their preferred pronouns and how they prefer to be addressed, as well as their leader identity, to encourage a relationship built on mutual trust and respect. Integrating culturally engaging advising practices that borrow from humanistic, proactive, and holistic advising approaches also fosters a connection in these settings between academic advisors and advisees with both shared and different identities and is beneficial for overall student success (Museus, 2021).

To incorporate leadership learning related to students' identities, these initial actions, which some advisors already enact during their initial advising sessions, could be taken further. One existing practice in many academic advising offices, particularly during a student's first semester in college, is a goal setting activity where students establish what they want to achieve over that semester or year. This assignment is an ideal opportunity to intentionally ask advisees if they have any leadership-related goals and how they may program those into a larger academic goal-setting context. More so than merely goal setting, it gives advisors the chance to also consider students' mindsets about how they envision leadership and where they might be on their leader/leadership development journey such that identity, capacity, and efficacy can be enhanced through course recommendations and other avenues. It is also important to be mindful of the fact that students from different backgrounds may view the definition and embodiment of leadership in a way separate from Western leadership or cultural norms.

Additional Recommendations for Action: CRLL Environmental Dimensions

The five environmental dimensions of the CRLL grant additional opportunities for advisors in one-on-one advising settings to incorporate the individual aspects of identity, capacity, and efficacy into the leadership learning process. The historical legacy dimension of the CRLL model addresses how higher education in general, and leadership education specifically, have traditionally excluded and marginalized certain individuals from leadership experiences; formally and informally (Beatty & Guthrie, 2021). With this in mind, advisors can advocate for students to participate in campus opportunities to further enhance their leader identities through academic initiatives.

One way may be through intentionally promoting participation in scholarship programs for minoritized students or academic societies related to particular academic disciplines and are geared specifically for students from certain identity-based backgrounds within that field. Academic programs like the Gates Scholarship (n.d.) and Gilman Scholarship (n.d.), or later, the McNair Scholars Program (n.d.; for graduate students) offer actionable ways students from diverse backgrounds can connect to valuable funding, leadership opportunities, and peers from similar identities. Not only can advisors recommend these pathways to increase educational and leadership-based pathways, but they can write recommendations, review and edit entry essays, and connect students to peer mentors from the same programs.

The aforementioned recommendations also work to increase compositional diversity, another of the five dimensions in the CRLL model, in some campus academic initiatives. It is vital to address that mere attendance is not sufficient (Beatty & Guthrie, 2021). Following up with students during advising meetings to understand how their identities and ideas are being actively recognized, appreciated, and included (or not), especially when students do not represent the dominant narrative of the academic organization or initiative, is critical. The same is true in the curricular and classroom sense. As the organizational and structural dimension of the CRLL highlights, university processes and operations must also facilitate socially just leadership practices (Beatty & Guthrie, 2021). In academic advising, this may mean restructuring the entire advising session or the overall advising process, with various formats and levels of advisors, for example. These moves could ensure systemic practices are not barring students from achieving their goals due to too much time or emphasis on purely academic matters instead of other important student needs (i.e., their leadership development) related to their success.

Academic advising administrators can also break down organizational and structural barriers by fostering inclusive advising spaces not only through the hiring of advisors from diverse backgrounds, but through purposefully partnering them with students from similar backgrounds in the advising process. Museus (2021) stressed large student success benefits when students of color have advisors from similar marginalized backgrounds, and corresponding research expounds on how advisors of color relate to their students as they have had to overcome institutional organizational and structural barriers as well. Relying solely on state or federally funded programs to fulfill these goals is also not enough. Advising offices, through institutional support, should provide students, regardless of their eligibility for these government programs, the option to work with advisors not solely based on academic needs but in ways that mirror other aspects of their lives. As such, pairing up new advisors in training and/or mentorship processes with seasoned advisors who represent similar positionalities and who are educated in how to work with students in this way is also a socially just leadership education practice.

Finally, the remaining two dimensions of the CRLL model are psychological and behavioral dimensions. The psychological dimension refers to students' cognition and perceptions in the leadership learning process, which may manifest differently for students from minoritized populations given their identities and lived experiences (Beatty & Guthrie, 2021). Relatedly, the behavioral dimension accounts for visible actions, requiring leadership educators to focus on building environments that validate and acknowledge how the same situation may elicit different responses from individuals of a group (Beatty & Guthrie, 2021).

In advising settings related to these two dimensions, advisors should be aware that students who want to enhance their leadership identity, capacity, and efficacy may require classroom learning environments, campus leadership opportunities, or academic support services that differ based on students' identities and experiences. Moreover, students may excel through connections with faculty and staff outside of advising offices who share similar lived experiences, especially with institutional leaders, which advisors can facilitate. Ultimately, advisors can recommend community involvement, service-learning projects, and undergraduate research experiences to foster an action-based environment that intentionally develops student leaders. The positive psychological benefits of these steps should ideally be compounded as students move forward on their developmental, academic, and leadership journeys.

ADVISOR LEADERSHIP DEVELOPMENT AND THE FUTURE

The focus of this chapter thus far has been on leadership learning and socially just leadership education practices that are oriented toward students. While this was the primary goal, one major assumption underlying this notion is that advisors are fully knowledgeable about leadership studies and the processes of leader and leadership development. Though advisors are typically full of wisdom and experience, they, too, deserve opportunities to better understand leadership as a field of study and how they can foster leader identity development and leadership development within themselves, as well as students. Beyond teaching, advising is leading, and advisors are the key to unlocking students' leadership identity, capacity, and efficacy, and advancing institutional, as well as societal, visions of leadership.

Higher education institutions can better support advisor leadership development in myriad ways. One of the primary ways is through professional development opportunities focused specifically on leadership learning. NACADA, for example, had facilitated an annual Emerging Leaders Institute to help advisors develop as positional leaders. Financially supporting advisors to attend directly benefits advisors, and by proxy, their students and institutions. Colleges and universities should also consider incorporating incentives and rewards for advisors who participate in leadership education, as well as formal leadership roles to encourage the development of advisor capacity and efficacy. Lessons from these experiences can be shared with colleagues and students and promote an atmosphere of leadership learning on campus. Finally, as noted, institutions should not be afraid to restructure how advising takes place on their campuses to accommodate students, but also advisor leadership learning (and other related) opportunities. Not only does this show institutional commitment to advisors, but it reaffirms institutional commitment to leadership.

CONCLUSION

The purpose of this chapter was to understand how academic advising, and other forms of advising in individual settings, represent socially just leadership education. While I have offered several recommendations for promoting socially just leadership education in this context through the culturally relevant leadership learning model, these do not constitute an exhaustive list. I recognize others will have more to add to this discussion, and my hope is that the conversation continues in a positive direction. I truly believe there is room for socially just leadership education in academic advising, and together we can shape how it evolves in that space.

REFERENCES

Acosta, D. M. (2018). Infusing leadership education in advising identity-based organizations. In K. L. Guthrie & V. S. Chunoo (Eds.), *Changing the narrative: Socially just leadership education* (pp. 259–276). Information Age Publishing.

Beatty, C. C., & Guthrie, K. L. (2021). *Operationalizing culturally relevant leadership learning*. Information Age Publishing.

Chrystal-Green, N. E. (2018). The role of advising in leadership development. In L. J. Hastings, & C. Kane (Eds.), *Role of mentoring, coaching, and advising in developing leadership* (New Directions for Student Leadership, No. 158, pp. 63–72). https://doi.org/10.1002/yd.20288

Chunoo, V., & Osteen, L. (2016). Purpose, mission, and context: The call for educating future leaders. In K. L. Guthrie, & L. Osteen (Eds.), *Reclaiming higher education's purpose in leadership development* (New Directions for Higher Education, No. 174, pp. 9–20). https://doi.org/10.1002/he.20185

Drake, J. K. (2013). *Academic advising approaches: Strategies that teach students to make the most of college*. Jossey-Bass.

Gates Scholarship Program. (n.d.). About TGS. https://www.thegatesscholarship.org/about-gates

Gilman Scholarship. (n.d.). *Program overview*. https://www.gilmanscholarship.org/program/program-overview/

Guthrie, K. L., Bertrand Jones, T., & Osteen, L. (2017). The teaching, learning, and being of leadership: Exploring context and practice of the culturally relevant leadership learning model. *Journal of Leadership Studies, 11*(3), 61–67. https://doi.org/10.1002/jls.21547

Guthrie, K. L., & Chunoo, V. S. (Eds.). (2018). *Changing the narrative: Socially just leadership education*. Information Age Publishing.

Guthrie, K. L., & Chunoo, V. S. (Eds.). (2021). *Shifting the mindset: Socially just leadership education*. Information Age Publishing.

Habley, W. (1994). Key concepts in academic advising. In Summer Institute on *Academic Advising Session Guide* (p. 10). Available from the National Academic Advising Association, Kansas State University, Manhattan, KS.

Hagen, P. L., & Jordan, P. (2008). Theoretical foundations of academic advising. In V. N. Gordon, W. R. Habley, T. J. Grites, & Associates (Eds.), *Academic advising: A comprehensive handbook, Second edition* (pp. 17–35). Jossey-Bass.

Hurtado, S., Milem, J. F., Clayton-Pedersen, A. R., & Allen, W. R. (1999). *Enacting diverse learning environments: Improving the climate for racial/ethnic diversity in higher education* (ASHE-ERIC Higher Education Report No. 26–8). The George Washington University, Graduate School of Education and Human Development.

Kuhn, T. L. (2008). Historical foundations of academic advising. In V. N. Gordon, W. R. Habley, T. J. Grites, & Associates (Eds.), *Academic advising: A comprehensive handbook, Second edition* (pp. 3–16). Jossey-Bass.

Ladison-Billings, G. (2014). Culturally relevant pedagogy 2.0: A. K. A. the remix. *Harvard Educational Review, 84*(1), 74–84. https://doi.org/10.17763/haer.84.1.p2rj131485484751

McNair Scholars Program. (n.d.) About. https://mcnairscholars.com/about/

Museus, S. D. (2021). Revisiting the role of academic advising in equitably serving diverse college students. *NACADA Journal, 41*(1), 26–32. https://doi.org/10.12930/NACADA-21-06

NACADA: The Global Community for Academic Advising. (2017). NACADA core values of academic advising. https://www.nacada.ksu.edu/Resources/Pillars/CoreValues.aspx

Pascarella, E. T., & Terenzini, P. T. (2005). *How college affects students: A third decade of research* (Vol. 2). Jossey-Bass.

Promisel, M. E. (2021). Priests, progressives, and a mirage: A short history of social justice. In K. L. Guthrie, & V. S. Chunoo (Eds.), *Shifting the mindset: Socially just leadership education* (pp. 9–21). Information Age Publishing.

CHAPTER 18

FOR THE CULTURE

Socially Just Leadership Mentoring for Black College Men

Johnnie L. Allen, Jr.

Black men are faced with a complex world that does not always see them as valuable, human, and more than just their Blackness. Continually, Black men are victims of cruelty, harm, and injustice, especially in educational spaces. Even though Black men display positive leadership in various educational, occupational, familial, and community settings, the uncomfortable truth is Black men learn the value and importance of socially just leadership learning and mentorship through, not despite, their lived experiences of Blackness in society. Reoccurring instances of victimization trigger Black men and individuals with Black men in their lives to have "The Talk": an ongoing conversation on how to situate themselves within society to prevent becoming another victim of bias. *How do societal issues impact Black college men's leadership and mentorship in higher education environments?* An answer that comes to mind is largely related to how societal and community issues infiltrate higher education.

Thinking back to the U.S. presidential election in 2016, the plans Black college men were making with other Black college men were on how to prepare for the racism, violence, discomfort, biases, bigotry, and other harmful repercussions of the election. These agreements were aspects of intergenerational leadership, mentorship, guidance, and protection for individuals that look like them as their collegiate experience as they once knew it could shift. This is just one example of socially just leadership

Committing to Action: Socially Just Leadership Educations, pp. 219–234

mentoring for Black college men. In this chapter, the value of Black men's socially just leadership learning and mentorship will be outlined through the following sections: defining mentorship, Black men's cultural obligation to promote socially just mentorship, indicators of socially just leadership within mentorship for Black men, mentorship initiatives in practice, benefits of socially just leadership and mentorship, and promising recommendations for socially just leadership learning and mentorship for Black men.

POSITIONALITY

I entered the college environment in the fall of 2016, navigating the complexities of the "unknown" about higher education culture and campus communities. I felt like Will Smith in *Fresh Prince of Bel-Air* when he arrived in Bel-Air; a residential neighborhood in Los Angeles, California, to live with his aunt and uncle in an unfamiliar environment that was praised for being a space full of opportunities, access, safety, support, and learning. Similar to how my college campus experience was described to me upon my arrival, however; the untold truth carried the nuances, challenges, and questioning of my identity, capacity, and efficacy that would develop over time while navigating the environment as I practiced learning and unlearning paradigms. Being in this place of uncertainty, I felt the responsibility and urge to seek and engage in what I would now reference as socially just leadership learning and mentorship. At the time, I chose to participate in the same race-based activities because of my institutional design, a historically White institution (HWI).

I felt more comfortable, validated, loved, and appreciated in a space where someone looked like me and could understand the societal pressure of being a Black Man. I was the student who discovered all opportunities to be engaged in the campus community; I instantly connected with the Black Culture Center and expressed my interest to the director about what I was looking for during my undergraduate experience. Shortly after connecting with the director, I saw that the center developed the inaugural Leadership Academy creating a space for Black students to engage in leadership learning and mentorship. Soon as the information was posted for students to sign-up, I jumped on it. I knew I did not want to miss this space, even though I did not know what to expect. I noticed my active role in my leadership learning and mentorship experiences. I attended all sessions for my growth and development. I chose to make this sacrifice because I knew that to endure the journey, I needed a community/village of people who understood me to successfully reach my goal of graduating and obtaining my bachelor's degree. Due to this experience as an enthusiastic first-year student, I was looped into a community and village that I have been able to give back to since 2016, and it is what currently guides my passion and commitment to the work I do. As a doctoral student and graduate assistant in the Leadership Learning Research Center at Florida State University, working with students; specifically undergraduate Black men, in an instructor and teaching assistant role, I have been able to reflect on my experience in leadership learning and mentorship and critically think of ways to do the same for the culture and Black men after me. Like Will, who needed his Uncle Phil to teach him to engage in the leadership process and serve as his mentor as a Black man, so did I, and so do many other Black men. Participating in this life-changing experience has shown me that leadership learning and mentorship are at the core of Black college men's development.

WHAT IS MENTORSHIP?

Cultural norms and societal defaults are embedded in community growth as changes influence multiple facets of *existing* and *being* learned behaviors from others. From an early age, we are taught to model the behavior of family members, educators, peers, and digital media (e.g., television shows, movies, video games, etc.), similar to the cycle of socialization as it represents how individuals are socialized to view aspects of life through moments of socialization for the first time, institutional and cultural socialization and enforcements (Harro, 2000). Mentorship is tied to media which provides innovative approaches to the holistic idea of mentorship and mentoring.

Jacobi's (1991) review of mentorship literature revealed several definitions across fields of higher education, psychology, and management and organizational behavior, among others. I draw from these descriptions to frame socially just leadership mentorship as: *a collective experience that is mutually beneficial for mentors and mentees to critically support one's leadership learning identity, capacity, and efficacy through support, advice, knowledge rooted in socially just practices, and critical consciousness*. These experiences are connected to one's meaning-making within leadership contexts to achieve generativity in leadership (Guthrie et al., 2016; Komives et al., 2005; Neville, 2015). Learning from others' experiences informs our choices and thought processes toward social justice, not solely for ourselves, but for the betterment of the world around us.

ROLE IN SOCIAL JUSTICE MENTORING AS A CULTURAL OBLIGATION

Decades of literature have centered around the idea that Black men need mentorship because of a lack of positive representation in their personal lives, media, and culture—increasing the misconception that Black men are ill-advised, troublemakers, and detractors to society (Brown, 2011; Irvine, 1989; Kearney & Levine, 2020; Whiting, 2006). However, I disagree with this view of Black men needing mentorship based on deficit-framed perceptions. Instead, I describe the role of mentorship as a cultural obligation to change the long-standing negative narrative and employ a positive and asset-based approach to socially just leadership mentorship based on the previously provided definitions. Researchers have outlined core reasons why underrepresented and marginalized people of color, specifically Black men, seek mentors and mentorship. They include (1) overcoming challenges that directly impact the Black community in and outside of higher education (e.g., racism, oppression, and police brutality) (Brown, 2011); (2) developing a mutual understanding and brotherhood, which increases holistic human development (LaVant et al., 1997; Jackson et al., 2014); (3) fostering physical safety and psychological security (Brown, 2011; Fries-Britt & Snider, 2015; Jackson et al., 2014; Patton & Harper, 2003); (4) to learn critical skillsets necessary for becoming social change agents (Brown, 2011; Jackson et al., 2014); and (5) to grow self-efficacy related to academic and occupational success (Brown, 2011; Davis, 2007; Fries-Britt & Snider, 2015; Jackson et al., 2014; LaVant et al., 1997; Patton & Harper, 2003).

Equally important and connected to mentorship is the concept of leadership learning. As Spencer (2018) reasoned, the crucial values of Black men's leadership courses are to support the long-term growth and development of Black college men. The developmental need for Black men's leadership courses, and the identified core reasons Black men seek mentorship, I consider *cultural obligation;* filling a void in a cultural community experience to advance further positive experiences of those of later generations and cohorts. Spencer (2018) additionally noted:

> Higher education must assist in developing the next generation of Black male leaders and college graduates. Black male leadership courses assist in enhancing Black men's community cultural wealth. It is this wealth that helps Black men understand the world is theirs. (p. 123)

Building upon Spencer's work, I agree Black men's leadership courses increase Black men's leadership identity, capacity, and efficacy. Bonding Black men's leadership courses with effective mentoring supports Black men in navigating oppressive and harmful environments and increases their community cultural wealth.

MENTORSHIP AS AN INDICATOR OF SOCIALLY JUST LEADERSHIP

Socially just leadership education is constantly evolving. Guthrie and Chunoo (2021) offered guidance on socially just leadership education as: "preparing people to lead and creating a fairer world for everyone" (p. 2).

Engaging in socially just leadership mentorship cultivates the passing of knowledge, experience, resources, and perspectives to continue developing social change agents. Neville (2015) described social justice mentoring as "aspirational and requires one to continually reflect, challenge, change, and evaluate one's practice in an effort to create transformative spaces for people to harness their potential" (p. 162). Holding the role of a mentor as a Black man to other Black men reimagines their relationship as mutually beneficial and positive. Black men who engage in mentoring, whether as mentors or mentees, actively develop and maintain socially just leadership practices because the betterment of both individuals is the core of the relationship. Socially just leadership learning puts social justice at the center of effective mentoring strategies and practical mentoring knowledge. Black men embrace the cultural obligation to mentor for the following reasons: collaborative and collective mindsets of the Black men's identity, social responsibility, and generative nature as Black men positively influence the next generation of Black men and Black men leaders in society.

Collaborative and Collective Nature of Black Men

To understand Black men as a culture and community, consider the cultural semi-universal 'head nod" (Jones, 2017). The nature of the head nod is to let another Black man know that they are seen and protected by me. I frame the head nod as a sign of empathy with other Black men's lived experiences, which is not monolithic, but nonetheless reflects the common knowledge that it takes a community to survive and thrive. Mentoring among Black men is a collaborative process that indicates there is a "Brother" who will take you under their wing to ensure you are learning, being supported, and challenging yourself to grow.

Like the head nod, the collective nature of Black men through mentorship practices decreases dehumanization of systemic oppression, institutional racism, and isolation historically plagued Black men (Brown, 2011; Jones, 2017). Mentoring begins early in Black men's communities, ranging from Black fathers, mothers, siblings, relatives, educators, coaches, and community members (Brown, 2011). Leaning on other Black men to overcome societal obstacles is a long-standing tradition in Black men's identity development. It reflects the collaborative nature of the community, with repercussions for social responsibility and generativity.

Social Responsibility and Obligation

Black men becoming mentors or mentees represents fulfilling a social responsibility (Heppner, 2017). Socially, just mentorship for Black men prepares them to be active community members and to influence positive change. The definitions of who a Black man leader is, or the characteristics of a Black man leader, have changed dramatically over time. Traditionally, when asked, "Who do you identify as a Black man leader?," answers would vary and begin with historically prominent figures such as Dr. Martin Luther King Jr., Malcolm X, Thurgood Marshall, W.E.B. DuBois, Booker T. Washington, and George Washington Carver, among others. However, asking the question now may provide responses such as President Barack Obama, LeBron James, Jay-Z, Chadwick Boseman, and Will Smith. All who engaged in the leadership process and used their platforms and activism as a social responsibility to directly and indirectly positively affect Black men through leadership and mentorship. Often their social obligation to mentor was created by other Black men. Thus, positive representations were passed down, and they themselves will leave guidance to future Black men leaders who continue the cycle of social responsibility and obligation.

Generativity

Continuing the legacy of Black men leaders is important within the Black men's community as intergenerational leader mentoring guides future generations of Black men. The unlearning and relearning of leadership within Black men's community optimize each Black man's potential. Retaining membership in a community of individuals is necessary to ensure future generations' success is achieved through commitment, intentionality, and resources to promote socially just leadership learning (Hastings et al., 2015). Generativity in Black men's mentorship is critical to social justice practices and the enactment of core values. Using mentorship to drive the next generation of Black men leaders is important to intergenerational socially just leadership mentorship. Repeating the cycle of socially just mentorship and leadership learning will ensure that the generative nature of Black men is maintained. One example of a culturally based leadership mentorship program that promotes social justice is Indiana University's Neal-Marshall Black Culture Center. The program, described in detail in the next section, emphasizes a core of collaboration and collectivism, social responsibility, and generativity of Black men's cultural obligation to mentor.

CULTURALLY BASED LEADERSHIP MENTORSHIP

Indiana University's (IU) Neal-Marshall Black Culture Center (NMBCC) provides an opportunity for Black and African American students to engage in a year-long initiative called the Neal-Marshall Leadership Academy

(NMLA). The NMLA assists students with leadership development (e.g., leadership styles, identity, capacity, and efficacy as outlined in culturally relevant leadership learning, or CRLL, and leadership tools), transition to Indiana University, academic and social resources, and effective strategies to establish community amongst peers, mentors, NMBCC staff, and IU community. The NMLA began as a first year, first-semester, student-only program in 2016. As a student of the inaugural NMLA class, I found my home away from home within this space. The NMLA provides Black students with leadership development and mentorship from upper division and graduate students. Movement from a semester program to a year-long initiative was generated by positive feedback students from the academy provided, as they wanted more time to engage with their mentors and the NMLA.

Mentoring became a part of the NMLA, largely because Black students wanted guidance from Black students with similar experiences in navigating an HWI. Through an intentional focus on mentorship, the NMLA began framing questions to students at monthly sessions regarding mentorship. Questions such as "What does a mentor mean to you?," "Do you have a mentor?," "What do you hope to get from a mentoring relationship?" I began to observe how Black students in the community, me included, needed and relied on mentoring practices from individuals with the same or similar salient identities. Finding a mentor who could relate to some of the negative experiences ubiquitous in higher education for marginalized populations became evident through the NMLA. I noticed that the students engaged in the NMLA were better prepared for their collegiate journey through a historically White-dominant environment due to their mentors' intentional check-ins, resources, and support. Advancing from an NMLA student to a mentor, I saw the importance of incorporating socially just mentorship as a core component of our student's leadership learning because of the positive interactions with students and their mentors. The specific mentorship pairings often reflected the importance of developing students as socially just leaders and how to better advocate for themselves and Black students at the institution. Adding mentoring as a core component of the NMLA experience cultivated a culture with significant impacts on how students saw themselves as social justice leaders and change agents because students were able to see and learn from other Black students, faculty, and staff navigating potentially toxic environments. Learning how to engage despite challenges based on your identity is one step in understanding the role of a social justice leader and change agent.

Although the program is not a Black male-specific initiative, the goals and purposes are deeply aligned with how Black men engage in socially just leadership learning and mentorship (e.g., collaborative nature, social responsibility, and generativity). The initiative serves as a guide for institutions to adopt for the betterment of Black men's leadership and mentorship.

BENEFITS OF BLACK MEN'S SOCIALLY JUST LEADERSHIP LEARNING AND MENTORSHIP

Black men who engage in socially just leadership learning and mentorship are afforded benefits such as: (1) communal support, (2) role modeling, (3) champion-advocate (i.e., socially just supporter), and (4) love through challenge and support mindsets (Brown, 2011; Jackson et al., 2014). These four benefits form the socially just leadership learning and mentorship conceptual model, an evolving conceptual model rooted in two theoretical leadership frameworks: the social action, leadership, and transformation (SALT) model (Museus et al., 2017) and culturally relevant leadership learning (CRLL) model (Beatty & Guthrie, 2021).

Social Action, Leadership, and Transformation (SALT) Model

Museus et al. (2017) developed a leadership framework to advance existing leadership learning paradigms toward addressing systemic oppression, power, and privilege alongside culture and identity. The SALT model challenges transformative approaches to leadership, not to devalue commonly referenced models, such as the social change model of leadership (HERI, 1996), but to bring awareness to issues not explicitly called to question. By developing the SALT model, Museus and colleagues (2017) provided a framework that is both deeply rooted in social consciousness and actively works toward achieving equity and justice within society. The SALT model includes seven specific components for critical social justice leadership that promotes individual, community, and society equity: capacity for empathy, critical consciousness, commitment to justice, equity in purpose, value of collective action, controversy with courage, and coalescence (Museus et al., 2017).

Culturally Relevant Leadership Learning (CRLL) Model

Beatty and Guthrie (2021) interrogated CRLL to provide leadership educators and learners with tools on how to effectively understand the why, who, what, where, and when of how leadership needs to be culturally relevant to optimize social justice practices. The CRLL model is a framework that covers domains of leadership identity, capacity, and efficacy, as well as dimensions of history, diversity, psychology, behavior, and structure (Beatty & Guthrie, 2021). Embedding CRLL into leadership learning serves as a core aspect of understanding context and how context can influence individuals to either contribute or disengage with socially just leadership. Spencer (2018) summarizes CRLL by stating, "it also calls for educators to develop innovative approaches to educating students and cultivating leaders capable of challenging the status quo" (p. 116). Social justice leadership is about positively influencing environments to promote sustainable and critical change that increases equity in society, and frameworks like CRLL provide a guide toward those outcomes.

Socially Just Leadership and Mentorship Model

Social justice is an important aspect of both leadership and mentorship. I propose a conceptual framework representing the SALT and CRLL models to espouse their connections better (see Figure 18.1). The socially just leadership and mentorship model situates social justice and equity at the core of advancing socially just leadership learning to cultivate a mentoring commitment. Black men are the focal population for the socially just leadership mentorship model. As they are actively navigating environments that are often hostile toward their identities, it is imperative to enhance their socially just leadership mentorship capacities. Engaging in socially just leadership mentorship provides Black men with communal support, role modeling, champion-advocate, and love through challenge and support mindsets. The current conceptual model could be applied to explore other marginalized college-going populations; however, for the context of this chapter, Black men will continue to be the intended population.

Communal Support

Black men's supportive community is a core attribute of socially just leadership and mentorship (Brown, 2011). Fostering community is how one grows in relationship with others because the individuals who make up that communal context bring multiple ways of knowing, being, and doing, which enhances the experiences of everyone involved. Holistic mentoring offers an array of advantages not limited to the higher education environment but provides support in post-college careers, additional educational experiences, and life in modern society. Supportive measures for Black men do not take one singular form; there are multiple ways in which

Figure 18.1

Socially Just Leadership and Mentorship Conceptual Model

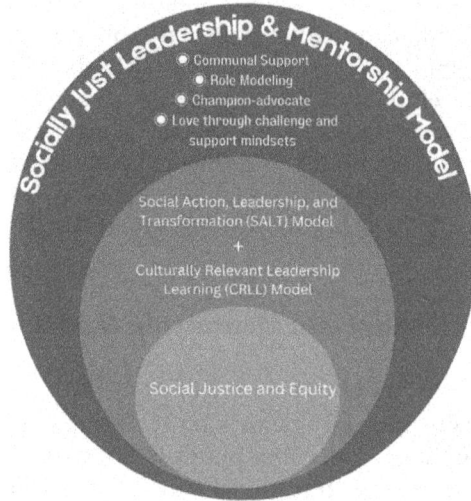

Socially Just Leadership & Mentorship Model

- Communal Support
- Role Modeling
- Champion-advocate
- Love through challenge and support mindsets

Social Action, Leadership, and Transformation (SALT) Model

+

Culturally Relevant Leadership Learning (CRLL) Model

Social Justice and Equity

Note: This figure describes the interrelationships of social justice and equity, the SALT and CRLL models to form the conceptual model of socially just leadership and mentorship. Each of the layers supports each other in cultivating a mentoring commitment that is rooted in socially just leadership learning to advance social justice and equity-centered work within Black men's leadership learning experiences.

communal support is maintained and developed. One example of maintaining and developing communal support for Black men is by establishing trust. Trust can be hard to measure or identify for individuals because it can have vastly different meanings. However, if trust is established, it can foster a community of support that contributes to socially just cultures and environments. Building trust can begin with taking the time to understand and validate the lived experiences of others, especially marginalized individuals. In addition to validating lived experiences, there also must be effective and clear communication that agrees to address injustices directly. Through trust and effective communication, communal support can serve as a promoter of socially just leadership mentorship. Communal support is connected to equity in purpose (Museus et al., 2017). To receive robust community support in social justice initiatives, the entire group's perspectives need to be equally centered and appreciated for maximum opportunities. Additionally, within communal support is the value of collective action (Museus et al., 2017) and the 'who?' of CRLL in socially just education (Beatty & Guthrie, 2021).

Role Modeling

Socially just leadership mentoring provides Black men to see positive role models with shared identities. Black men's role modeling to other Black men is done through aspects of both the SALT and CRLL models. Black men role models move beyond general aspects of modeling the way (Kouzes & Posner, 1995, 2002) to displaying how one can represent socially just leadership identity, capacity, and efficacy (Beatty & Guthrie, 2021) in addition to the development of empathy and critical consciousness (Museus et al., 2017). Black men who navigate their leadership journeys with socially just leadership mentorship experiences have a deeper understanding of their lived experiences, perspectives, and knowledge. Holding these helps them guide others while their relationship with power, privilege, and oppression equips them to become effective social justice leaders. A benefit of socially just leadership and mentorship is knowing that the effect of role modeling never ends as new role models rise.

Champion/Advocate

Black men who actively engage in socially just leadership and mentorship receive life-long champions and advocates. A champion advocate is someone who encourages an individual to stay on the path toward social justice leadership despite adversity. Social justice leadership is daunting and discouraging at times; however, Black men who practice effective, socially just leadership mentoring enter an enriched network of support that grows, and the work becomes shared. We know change can begin with one person, but deep change fails without the commitment of others. The commitment to social justice becomes shared so that the well-being of others is prioritized (Museus et al., 2017). Black men will benefit from socially just leadership learning and mentorship and receive their champion and advocate to assist in addressing issues of historical inclusion and exclusion practices that have continuously impacted Black men in environments (Beatty & Guthrie, 2021).

Love Through Challenge and Support Mindsets

Black men initiating and maintaining cultures of care for other Black men is reflected in their engagement with socially just leadership learning and mentorship. Jackson et al. (2014) discussed *reciprocal love* and an *ethos of care*. Reciprocal love means having a love for yourself and a love for others. An ethos of care is an innate characteristic of responsibility for others (Jackson et al., 2014). Socially just leadership and mentorship resemble love through challenging and supporting the mindsets of Black men. Black men who engage in socially just leadership and mentorship will have to navigate challenges, oftentimes alone, to be able to support others who may experience similar experiences down the line. The responsibility of Black men's leadership is in the hands of other Black men. Therefore, Black men embrace oppressive systems with love and care, believing that social justice benefits all groups (Museus et al., 2017). Beatty and Guthrie (2021) discussed the importance of designing and constructing purposeful leadership learning opportunities, and it is through these opportunities that social justice leadership becomes a normal practice in society. Black men loving other Black men through socially just leadership learning and mentorship is a part of leadership learning opportunities that will benefit not only Black men but social justice, equity, and society.

RECOMMENDATIONS

Socially Just Leadership Mentorship Practices for Black Men

All institutions can frame developmental opportunities by establishing socially just leadership learning and mentoring practices as a necessity for Black men's success. Intentionally providing spaces for Black men to coexist and learn from one another promotes better leadership and socially just practices. The practices can be developed in curricular and co-curricular environments. Black male leadership courses are pivotal avenues for increasing Black men's socially just leadership learning while adding mentorship. Mentorship can happen through course instructors for specific Black male leadership courses or in co-curricular spaces where mentorship may take a less formal approach. Ensuring leadership learning and mentoring are occurring for Black men through institutional resources, whether that be financial, databases to connect identifying Black men with other Black men on campus (e.g., faculty, staff, administrators, and peers), physical space, and intentional recruitment of Black students, faculty, and staff to join the institution to lead with mentorship as a core value.

Black Men Leadership Learning Culturally Based Mentorship Initiatives

After learning more about Black men's leadership classes from Spencer (2018), and the impact, it has on Black men's development; it seems clear that there must be more intentional places where Black men can be supported beyond curricular environments. Therefore, forming and maintaining Black men's mentorship initiatives for Black men can repair the misconception that Black men are ill-advised and not equipped to be positive contributors to society.

Higher education institutions can model Black men's mentorship initiatives following mentoring prototypes outlined by LaVant et al. (1997). One initiative I draw attention to from their work is *The Black Man's Think Tank* at the University of Cincinnati. The key aspects are rooted in providing African American men mentorship, space to engage in critical discourse regarding issues and concerns that directly impact Black men in and out of higher education, and a commitment to "our people" (LaVant et al., 1997, p. 47). Designing mentorship initiatives to mirror the University of Cincinnati can be important in developing Black men leaders. I challenge those who consider adopting and implementing their model to include aspects of socially just leadership learning. For example, to mentor Black men, it is critical to understand their leadership identity, as it is tied to who they are and how they show up in the spaces they enter. Through a mentoring lens, Black men's leadership capacity help mentors know what skills and abilities their mentees already hold through their lived experiences and how to strengthen them. Lastly, efficacy seems as the most important part of mentoring relationships. Mentors want to encourage and support their mentee's leadership efficacy, meaning assisting in their understanding of how they believe in themselves to engage in social justice leadership work.

Advice for Researchers and Communities

Black men in empirical research have consistently been studied from deficit-oriented perspectives. However, it is time to commit to new ways of undertaking research about Black men. Therefore, I offer the following recommendations for researchers when examining Black men's experiences: First, more positive research about Black men's experiences needs to be the basis of research questions, purposes, researchers' positionalities, and even findings. These critical points to follow when conducting research regarding Black men will contribute to more equitable knowledge and lessen knowledge gaps about Black men. Secondly, when conducting research, ensure results are framed to highlight the benefits for Black men. There should be a tangible takeaway that benefits Black men, tools to support programs specifically for Black men, and offer new knowledge to those who work with Black men. Lastly, when researchers explore the Black men population at their institutions, it is important to value Black men's lived experiences of leadership learning and mentorship that align with their community cultural wealth (Yosso, 2005) they bring to higher education environments.

Not all initiatives need to be developed because of troubling Black men's experiences or assumptions but rather can be developed to enhance and maintain positive leadership and mentorship practices for Black men. Furthermore, communities should continue to encourage Black men to embrace their experiences as they bring significance to their journey and know that the work of intergenerational leadership and mentorship does not end once they reach a certain level in their trajectory. Still, it continues for Black men to come. The work only gets more critical and important to advance equity in social justice for Black men. Communities play a vital role in shaping how Black men engage in socially just leadership mentorship because the communities provide a space to pay it forward to support younger generations. One way to continue paying it forward is by developing a community initiative connecting Black men of all ages to other Black men. Leading with these connections can promote asset-based perspectives on Black men's experiences and equip Black men with tools to become socially just leaders. Centering socially just leadership mentoring in communities that Black men live in continues the positive cycle of generative mentoring to protect and support Black men for future generations.

CONCLUSION

Black men's socially just leadership mentorship is critical to navigating oppressive systems in education and society. The benefits of engaging in socially just leadership learning and mentorship for Black men lead to (a) communal support, (b) role modeling, (c) champion/advocate, and (d) love through challenge and support mindsets as it is the social responsibility of Black men to be generative in nature. Incorporating a socially just leadership mentorship conceptual framework provides benefits for Black men and offers institutional advancements as a crucial part of institutions' success is measured by their students, specifically those from marginalized communities. Members of marginalized communities bring uniqueness and authenticity to a campus' culture and those gifts deserve recognition and celebration. Black male leadership courses, initiatives, mentoring, networks, and engagement in higher education will enhance the Black male experience across institutions. Effective leadership learning opportunities for Black men who engage in socially just leadership learning and mentorship will assist in removing barriers that historically and traditionally disadvantage Black men. Prioritizing the development of Black men will benefit them as individuals, and it is also representative for the culture as they are better equipped to make a global and socially just impact in society.

REFERENCES

Beatty, C. C., & Guthrie, K. L. (2021). *Operationalizing culturally relevant leadership learning*. Information Age Publishing.

Brown, R. W. (2011). Perceived influence of African American male mentorship on the academic success of African American males in a predominantly White institution of higher education: an institutional case study. *National Forum of Multicultural Issues Journal, 6*(1), 1–13.

Davis, D. J. (2007). Access to academe: the importance of mentoring to Black students. *Negro Educational Review, 58*(3–4), 217–231.

Fries-Britt, S., & Snider, J., (2015). Mentoring outside the line: the importance of authenticity, transparency, and vulnerability in effective mentoring relationships. In C. S. Turner (Ed.), *Mentoring as transformative practice: Supporting student and faculty diversity* (New Directions for Higher Education, No. 171, pp. 3–11). https://doi.org/10.1002/he.20137

Guthrie, K. L., Bertrand Jones, T., & Osteen, L. (Eds.). (2016). *New Directions for Student Leadership: No. 152. Developing culturally relevant leadership learning*. Jossey-Bass.

Guthrie, K. L., & Chunoo, V. S. (Eds.). (2021). *Shifting the mindset: Socially just leadership education*. Information Age Publishing

Harro, B. (2000). The cycle of liberation. In M. Adams (Ed.), *Readings for diversity and social justice, 2*, 52–58.

Hastings, L. J., Griesen, J. V., Hoover, R. E., Creswell, J. W., & Dlugosh, L. L. (2015). Generativity in college students: comparing and explaining the impact of mentoring. *Journal of College Student Development, 56*(7), 651–669. https://doi.org/10.1353/csd.2015.0070

Higher Education Research Institute [HERI]. (1996). *A social change model of leadership development, Guidebook III*. Higher Education Research Institute, University of California.

Heppner, P. P. (2017). Creating mentoring opportunities to promote cultural competencies and social justice. *The Counseling Psychologist, 45*(1), 137–157. https://doi.org/10. 1177/0011000016688781

Irvine, J. J. (1989). Beyond role models: An examination of cultural influences on the pedagogical perspectives of Black teachers. *Peabody Journal of Education, 66*(4), 51–63. https://doi.org/10.1080/01619568909538662

Jackson, I., Sealey-Ruiz, Y., & Watson, W. (2014). Reciprocal love: Mentoring Black and Latino males through an ethos of care. *Urban Education, 49*(4), 394–417. https://doi.org/10.1177/0042085913519336

Jacobi, M. (1991). Mentoring and undergraduate academic success: A literature review. *Review of Educational Research, 61*(4), 505–532. https://doi.org/10.3102/00346543061004505

Jones, J. R. (2017). Racing through the halls of congress: The "Black nod" as an adaptive strategy for surviving in a raced institution. *Du Bois Review: Social Science Research on Race, 14*(1), 165–187. https://doi.org/10.1017/s1742058x16000369

Kearney, M. S., & Levine, P. B. (2020). Role models, mentors, and media influences. *The Future of Children, 30*(1), 83–106. https://doi.org/10.1353/foc.2020.0006

Komives, S. R., Owen, J. E., Longerbeam, S. D., Mainella, F. C., & Osteen, L. (2006). Developing a leadership identity: A grounded theory. *Journal of College Student Development, 46*(6), 593–611. https://doi.org/10.1353/csd.2005.0061

Kouzes, J. M., & Posner, B. Z. (1995). *The leadership challenge: How to keep getting extraordinary things does in organizations.* Jossey-Bass.

Kouzes, J. M., & Posner, B. Z. (2002). *Leadership challenge* (3rd ed.) Jossey-Bass.

LaVant, B. D., Anderson, J. L., & Tiggs, J. W. (1997). Retaining African American men through mentoring initiatives. In M. J. Cuyjet (Ed.), *Helping African American men succeed in college* (New Directions for Student Services, No. 80, pp. 43–53). https://doi.org/10.1002/ss.8004

Museus, S., Lee, N., Calhoun, K., Sánchez-Parkinson, L., & Ting, M. (2017). The social action, leadership, and transformation (SALT) model. *National Center for Institutional Diversity and National Institute for Transformation and Equity.* https://lsa.umich. edu/content/dam/ncid-assets/nciddocuments/publications/ Museus% 20et% 20al, 20.

Neville, H. A. (2015). Social justice mentoring: supporting the development of future leaders for struggle, resistance, and transformation. *The Counseling Psychologist, 43*(1), 157–169. https://doi.org/10.1177/0011000014564252

Patton, L. D., & Harper, S. R. (2003). Mentoring relationships among African American women in graduate and professional schools. In M. F. Howard-Hamilton (Ed.), *Meeting the needs of African American women* (New Directions for Student Services, No. 104, pp. 67–78). https://doi.org/10.1002/ss.108

Spencer, D., Jr. (2018). The world is yours: Cultivating Black male leadership learning. In K. L. Guthrie & V. S. Chunoo (Eds.), *Changing the narrative: Socially just leadership education* (pp. 109–126). Information Age Publishing.

Whiting, G. W. (2006). From at risk to at promise: Developing scholar identities among Black males. *Journal of Secondary Gifted Education, 17*(4), 222–229. https://doi.org/10.4219/jsge-2006-407

Yosso, T. J. (2005). Whose culture has capital? A critical race theory discussion of community cultural wealth. *Race Ethnicity and Education, 8*(1), 69–91. https:// doi.org/10.1080/1361332052000341006

CHAPTER 19

PEER POWER

A Catalyst for
Socially Just Leadership Education

Ashley Archer Doehling

Peer education is a pivotal tool in socially just leadership education in campus settings because it engages students across multitudes of intersecting identities and functional areas. Thus, peer education should be prioritized within the institutional context as a strategy for leadership educators. Grounded in leadership theory, this chapter will contextualize peer leadership experiences and provide recommendations for practitioners seeking to create socially just educational opportunities for their student populations. By utilizing components of the integrated model for critical leadership, culturally relevant leadership learning, and relational leadership models as frameworks, I align peer education outcomes with the central tenets of these leadership models of interest to illustrate how peer leadership contributes to socially just and culturally relevant leadership education.

Preparing students as leaders has been a long-standing goal of American higher education. An overview of any institution's mission statement will highlight the attention paid to this goal through strategic plans and institutional values described in the language provided. However, it is time to reclaim higher education's purpose in leadership development with an intentional focus on socially just leadership education (Chunoo & Osteen, 2016). As access to higher education has increased, more students,

Committing to Action: Socially Just Leadership Educations, pp. 235–247
Copyright © 2025 by Information Age Publishing
www.infoagepub.com
235

especially those with historically excluded identities, can now contribute to our campus populations. Each year, student populations become more diverse and each of these identities impacts the lived experiences that influence a student's navigation of their collegiate experience (Lemon & Wawrzynski, 2022).

This increasing diversity of identities and experiences necessitates the transition to socially just leadership education. It is no longer enough to prepare students to be leaders; we must prepare them to be socially just leaders who can navigate leadership processes in culturally relevant and meaningful ways. Higher education is a vehicle for the development of student's leadership identity and practice. In order to effectively develop leadership competency, students must have opportunities to practice leadership in socially just ways to prepare them to navigate their campuses and the diverse world beyond their institutional bubble. Institutions of higher education are often described as microcosms of our larger society, which provide an experiential learning ground for leadership development. A student's undergraduate career is the opportune time to cultivate these skills and dispositions supported by so many campus professionals and dedicated student learning opportunities.

INTERSECTION OF SOCIAL JUSTICE AND LEADERSHIP

Social justice and leadership intersect substantially within higher education theory and practice, as reflected in empirical and scholarly literature. The intersection of these concepts outlines where we should be teaching leadership from, and therefore, how peer education is situated within the context of each term. To illustrate the intersection of these concepts, I offer the following distinctions.

Leadership

Bertrand Jones et al. (2016) conceptualized leadership as socially constructed within the contextual dimensions of campus climate and broader social and environmental factors to construct culturally relevant leadership learning. While a consistent definition of leadership is nearly impossible to agree upon, contemporary scholars have defined a set of assumptions or beliefs that I draw upon to construct the guiding framework for this chapter (Guthrie et al., 2021). These beliefs include anyone may engage in the process of leadership; leadership can be learned; leaders are also followers; leadership is context dependent; leaders do not have to be the loudest in a space; and leadership is ethical (Guthrie et al., 2021). Grounded in these beliefs, and the premise of leadership as culturally relevant, I contend leadership is a process where people work together toward a common goal for an ethical outcome.

Social Justice

A term originally coined by two Italian Catholic priests in the 1840s, *la giustizia sociale*—or social justice, has recently become not only a buzzword, but a polarizing phrase at that (Paulhus, 1987). For this chapter, I consider this as social justice in its purest form. Social justice refers to a state where all people may freely pursue their purpose. In this way, social justice provides a vision for promoting the common good.

This promotion is like the purpose of leadership, and I argue the two cannot exist as mutually exclusive in our society. Instead, as leadership learning evolves, so must our attention to ensuring that we are equipping students to lead for and through social justice. Considering this intersection of social justice and leadership while utilizing leadership learning frameworks informs how we create effective leadership learning opportunities for our students. One strategy to create opportunities for leadership development that honor the intersection of these concepts is the intentional design of opportunities for engagement with peer leadership. The utilization and expansion of peer education opportunities within diverse student groups will result in socially just leadership learning and practice.

Related to social justice and the pursual of the common good, cultural relevance is a dynamic and multidimensional concept that describes a leader's ability to engage with others in ways that honors the unique experiences and societal practices which surround those with whom they interact. Cultural relevance challenges dominant narratives and centers the cultural orientations of others by honoring attitudes, values, and behaviors unique to each person (Bertrand Jones et al., 2016).

Peer Education

Leadership pervades every academic discipline, and every career path requires leadership knowledge, skills, and abilities to be successful. Thus, postsecondary institutions have an obligation to prepare students for culturally relevant leadership and to provide practice space for those enrolled. Peer education is a strategy that effectively satisfies these demands. Because peers have deep and meaningful impacts on one another, there have been many attempts to harness and direct these influences over time (Colvin & Ashman, 2010).

Peer education occurs when students engage with one another within varying functional areas to enhance each other's experience or performance. "Given the powerful and ubiquitous qualities of peer influence, higher educators have begun to harness this resource in student support and service delivery by using undergraduates as leaders, mentors and educators for their fellow students" (Keup, 2016, p. 1). Peer education, or peer leadership, are used synonymously in many campus settings and, in this chapter, it describes leadership experiences for undergraduate students in which training processes and sustained supervision and support are offered by professional staff. Peer leadership programs typically transcend traditional boundaries of the academy, such as academic or student affairs, and often serve as a connective and collaborative force on campus (Wawrzynski & Lemon, 2019). Peer leaders can be in college classrooms, tutoring centers, orientation services, housing, health and wellness, fraternity and sorority life, leadership and social justice offices, and other departments within a college or university. Since peer leadership program structures vary by campus, readers should utilize the previously stated parameters when considering relevant related student opportunities.

While each of these peer leadership positions are unique in their purpose, and specific responsibilities or projects, the derived benefits are similar. Students who pursue peer educator roles reported higher self-esteem, greater leadership skills, and fewer risky health behaviors when compared to similar non-peer educators. However, peer educators did not differ on personal values and personality temperament measures (Brack et al., 2008). Scholars who investigate these students suggest most do in fact hold values and personality temperaments with a disposition for leadership. Despite this ubiquitous disposition, a lack of *efficacy* for one's ability for leadership inhibits many from pursuing peer education roles. Realized benefits of these positions are in line with the overarching goals of institutions to prepare global leaders (Wawrzynski et al., 2011). Thus, peer leadership is both a high impact practice for specific functional area responsibilities, and a valuable mechanism in applied leadership learning, generally. Peer leadership's potential for students to meaningfully bridge their goals, values, and experiences necessitates urgency for peer education to be implemented as a socially just leadership education strategy within our institutions (Wawrzynski & Lemon, 2019).

SOCIALLY JUST PEER LEADERSHIP EDUCATION

By utilizing components of the integrated model for critical leadership (Dugan, 2017) and the relational leadership model (Komives et al., 2013) as frameworks, I align peer education outcomes with the central tenets of leadership to illustrate how peer leadership contributes to socially just and culturally relevant leadership education. This connection will interrogate how peer education structures prepare students for socially just leadership in practice with implications for leadership educators across functional areas as they harness peer power as a catalyst of the leadership process.

Integrated Model for Critical Leadership

Dugan (2017) identified leadership motivation, capacity, efficacy, and enactment as central psychological constructs. In Dugan's model, each of these constructs have mutually reinforcing relationships with each other and are influenced by both social and environmental contexts. Thus, I use the core four constructs of Dugan's integrated model for critical leadership to connect tenets of peer education with leadership learning. This model also lends a socially just perspective to this learning, as it honors identity as pivotal in leadership development. In this model, there is a directional relationship between leadership motivation, capacity, self-efficacy, and enactment that is impacted by one's intersecting identities related to their work. Social identity is explored as a contextual factor that affects the relational nature between each of the constructs.

Motivation

The motivation to lead is "an individual differences construct that affects a current or aspiring leader's decisions to attend leadership training, roles, and responsibilities and that affect their intensity of effort at leading and persistence as a leader" (Chan & Drasgow, 2001, p. 482). Within the peer leadership sphere, this motivation is what initially prompts students to apply for or engage in peer education opportunities. This motivation can be classified into three areas: to get along, to get ahead, and to find meaning (Chan & Drasgow, 2001). Motivation based on self-interest is associated with students who enjoy leading and doing connect these experiences to their sense of personal identity. Those who lead to get ahead often center their career considerations and how leadership may make them competitive in their future employment. Third, students who find motivation for a higher purpose may feel a sense of duty or greater obligation that may be fulfilled through leadership (Chan & Drasgow, 2001). None of these students possess any more or less leadership capacity than others do, but rather pursue leadership opportunities grounded in varying motivations.

It is recommended that professional staff discuss these motivating components with students to assist with future recruiting and marketing efforts. In this sphere of the peer education process, students should not be expected to have the specific skills to perform their role as peer leaders, but rather the desire to do so.

Capacity

Another element of leadership growth is capacity. Leadership capacity refers to specific knowledge, skills, and attitudes necessary to engage in leader roles and leadership processes; in our case, related to peer interaction. Capacity can refer to either an individual or a group's overarching knowledge, skills, and abilities related to the leader's role or the group's leadership process (Day et al., 2004). In terms of peer education, capacity is built through formal and informal training mechanisms facilitated by professional staff. This is where socially just leadership educators dismantle damaging assumptions about the nature of leadership and instead shape how leadership capacities are perceived by students. This reframing integrates socially just skill building within leadership learning. This training is critical to our understanding of peer education in this chapter and is what allows us to consider these forms of peer leadership through this framework. Capacity, however, is just one of many pieces to the larger leadership puzzle. In other words, just because a student can do something does not mean that they will actually enact those skills to do it. Leadership capacity does not necessarily translate into leadership action.

Efficacy

Leader efficacy is connected to our internal beliefs about our ability to lead with positional power or authority. Leadership efficacy addresses beliefs associated with group processes and extends beyond specific roles or titles. Leadership efficacy explains observable gaps between students' capacity to engage in leadership processes and whether or not they actually do so. A student's belief in their preparation for an ability to engage with the leadership process is described by the efficacy construct. This construct helps to explain why there can be impactful gaps between capacity and enactment.

Enactment

Finally, leadership enactment describes what occurs when leadership capacity, motivation, and efficacy are put into action. Simply put, it is the behavioral practices of leadership. During these times, students apply the skills they have learned through training to lead peers, while feeling qualified to do so, and performing the actions they originally were motivated toward. While these specific actions vary by title, functional area, and program design among other contextual factors, enactment is the piece of the leadership puzzle where students engage leadership processes with others, including students with whom the professional staff may never interact. Enactment in peer education is the peer-to-peer interactions occurring both through formal roles and through informal leadership practices and mentoring. While the integrated model of critical leadership focuses the process of peer leadership, connections with the relational leadership model allows for the exploration of cyclical leadership experiences.

Relational Leadership Model

The relational leadership model (RLM) explains relationships formed within a group whose members intend to accomplish positive change (Komives et al., 2013). I posit this model also applies to interactions between peer educators and their fellow students. The tenets of RLM describe components that should be present in the formation of an effective team. These tenets are described to accomplish the defined purpose of the group; leaders must engage in a process that is inclusive, empowering, and ethical. To do so, individuals must possess the knowledge, attitudes, and skills for each element, also known as a model of *knowing-being-doing*, which has ideally been established throughout the capacity building training process in their peer education program (Komives et al., 2013).

This model also illustrates the cyclical nature of peer leadership, where interacting with peers may change students' view of leaders and the leadership process. This new understanding of leadership dismantles hegemonic notions of power in leadership, where students of intersecting identities are performing socially just leadership with their peers. This interaction results in the empowerment of those students and invites them into the process. This invitation can be understood as leadership generativity. Originating in the health field, this concept describes an orientation for innovation, organizational agility and high performance over time as leaders seek to empower future leaders (Disch, 2009). Witnessing this version of leadership, which is likely to be different from previous experiences, validates students so they are able to visualize themselves as leaders. Here, we find generativity in the leadership process where students are empowering one another to engage in the process in developing ways. First, as followers, and eventually as peer leaders. Generativity should be just, as students provide representation for those historically left out of the leadership process. From these interactions, students find motivation to pursue peer leadership opportunities, and we begin to engage in the integrated model for critical leadership (Dugan, 2017) with the new student population.

Aligning peer education structures with leadership frameworks allows socially just leadership educators to craft learning spaces that are inclusive of all student populations. The leadership frameworks utilized in this discussion emphasize developing relationships, exploring ways of being, solving complex problems, and creating change, which collectively facilitate learning and action for social justice while challenging traditional notions of leadership power and authority. Peer education naturally supports these endeavors and should be utilized as a strategy to provide more and different opportunities for students to engage in leadership learning in college. Using these frameworks to bound and focus peer education helps identify actionable ways to implement peer education as a strategy for socially just leadership learning.

RECOMMENDATIONS FOR PRACTICE

Peer education is an effective strategy for leadership learning that impacts students across campus. When designing peer education for socially just leadership learning, it is important to consider how it exists across campuses, and not solely as the responsibility of a diversity, equity, or inclusion focused office. To do so, I recommend the following four practices to develop socially just leadership identity in students across functional areas.

Creation of Peer Educator Roles

Broadly, the most important way of expanding leadership learning through peer education is to create peer leadership opportunities matched to student interests. Instead of asking a student interested in sport management to engage with a siloed program in another area of campus, professionals should develop opportunities for this student to engage in socially just leadership learning within their sphere of interest. Creating such experiences across functional areas provides spaces where students can enact their varying interests while engaging in socially just leadership learning. Challenging traditional notions of where leadership learning happens, and how, will create positive change beyond the metaphorical walls of an institution as students seek to enact their leader growth in career-relevant spaces.

Motivation-Focused Application Processes

Second, peer education application processes should center student motivation to lead in a given role. We should not expect students to already have built the capacity for a program's specific purpose when offering peer education through professional-supported programming with formal training measures. This approach rewards privilege and does not invite new students into the leadership development arena. Instead, evaluating potential student participants to articulate their motivations, values, and outcomes in a peer educator role allows for a more equitable selection process. In other words, our programs should not only provide opportunities for students who have already built leadership capacity, but also for those yet to build those skills. Program design can utilize the experience of students who are both adept and highly motivated in intentional mentoring or partnership experiences with their peers, who are building their capacities for leadership. This creates a peer leadership structure within a program designed to create peer leaders, a type of internal practice of purpose.

Capacity and Efficacy Reflection Requirements

Throughout the training process, socially just program managers and coordinators intentionally facilitate reflection for students to conceptualize their own sense of leadership capacity and efficacy. This strategy is twofold. First, students can credit themselves for their knowledge acquisition and identify areas for continued learning. Second, college student personnel can identify areas where multiple students share a lack of efficacy and reconsider training strategies, requirements, lessons, and other initiatives to address these challenges. Reflections can substantiate how diverse student involvement across campus expands socially just leadership learning beyond compositional diversity, or traditional leadership development and contributes to a more just campus culture overall.

Individualism During Enactment

Finally, though peer educators will perform some roles grounded in a common purpose within a program, it is important to allow students to personalize their experience. Facilitating conversations of individual purpose, growth goals, and future applicability of the peer leader experience challenges students to consider how they are unique in their role and how they can apply this experience to future opportunities. We do not want students to feel like cogs in a wheel doing what they are told, but rather active participants in a community pursuing social justice through leadership. Prompting students to share these goals also provides insight into potential areas for program growth and allows professionals a window into relational processes contributing to generative leadership. Though the peer education opportunities discussed here refer to those explicitly supported by staff and administrators, I recommend creating space for students to contribute to the design of initiatives and guide the trajectory of the program.

For those who work transformational leadership paradigm, these recommendations may look similar to Bass's (1985) four I's of transformational leadership. The four elements are used in organizational culture to create a transparent and diverse culture in which individuals are empowered and encouraged to share ideas and use their voice. For example, my recommendation of the concept of individualism during enactment parallel the individual consideration element of Bass's theory, which recognized an individual's unique contributions to an organizational culture (Bass, 1985). My recommendations are not dissimilar to transformational leadership, but are neither directly modeled after those components. However, my recommendations do highlight a shared notion with Bass' theory that if we keep rewarding contributors, or in my case, students, who have already had leadership experiences, we are both rewarding privilege and risking exploitation and burn out of students. Rather, despite which leadership theories we use to ground recommendations for leadership opportunities, the phenomenon of generativity should underscore all of our efforts. In other words, we can commit to socially just leadership by ensuring that our leaders are both supported, and our programming invites new voices and talents into leadership. We are serving multiple generations of student leaders and their peers when we create leadership programs in this way. By creating pipelines of generativity and continued leadership development for students, we are encouraging the changing of systems to be broader and more inclusive than first interactions and iteratively expand and motivate future leaders through that legacy. This iterative and cyclical leadership development is illustrated in Figure 19.1.

LIMITATIONS OF PEER EDUCATION

Developing socially just leaders begin with how we offer leadership opportunities for diverse students. While we can recognize the value added to a student's college experience by providing peer education opportunities, we must also address limitations of peer leadership. The lack of "control" over learning professionals have once peer education is in action underscores

Figure 19.1

Peer Education as a Catalyst for Socially Just Leadership Education

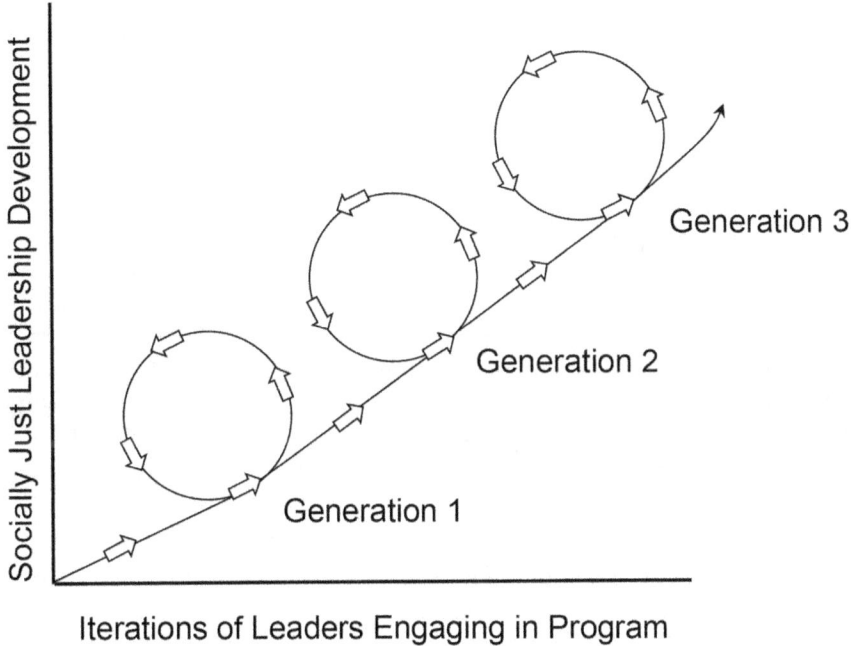

Iterations of Leaders Engaging in Program

the importance of empowering these students during training processes. Once initial capacity building has occurred, though many trainings are iterative and scaffold over time, professionals must trust their peer educators to perform without significant oversight or intervention. This trusting relationship challenges traditional notions of power and authority, and although difficult, is one of the tenets of peer education propelling the strategy toward socially just leadership.

Student affairs professionals must be careful to avoid exploiting student talent and motivation in peer leadership programming (Badura et al., 2000). While many of us naturally gravitate toward students who are highly motivated and able to contribute their time to these processes, we must balance this tendency with intentional social justice. This means recognizing the relationships between leadership motivation, capacity, and efficacy and how these factors may be embodied by individuals with different social identities. Specifically, this requires interrogating our own practice with questions like: "Which students are showing up for what peer leadership opportunities?," "Who is missing?," "What does one opportunity offer that another peer educator role on campus does not?" Grounding peer education roles within a professionally supported program on campus, and training those professionals to facilitate these programs fairly, promotes equal access to leadership learning. Despite these limitations, peer education can be a powerful vehicle for socially just leadership learning.

CONCLUSION

This chapter illustrated how peer education provides cyclical, culturally relevant leadership learning opportunities for students in both teacher and learner roles. Calling on the components of the integrated model for critical leadership, the relational leadership model, and discussions of generativity, peer education should be considered an effective strategy deserving attention across institutions of higher education seeking to facilitate leadership development for their student populations. Peer leadership can be a powerful catalyst for students of varying intersecting identities to increase their leadership motivation, capacity, and efficacy to create a structure of enactment that empowers future generations of student leaders. Higher education decision makers should pursue these opportunities for their students in curricular, co- and extracurricular settings to best prepare them to engage in the leadership process in our increasingly globalized world.

REFERENCES

Badura, A. S., Millard, M., Peluso, E. A., & Ortman, N. (2000). Effects of peer education training on peer educators: Leadership, self-esteem, health knowledge, and health behaviors. *Journal of College Student Development, 41*(5), 471–478.

Bass, B. M. (1985). *Leadership and performance beyond expectations.* Free Press.

Bertrand Jones, T., Guthrie, K. L., & Osteen, L. (2016). Critical domains of culturally relevant leadership learning: A call to transform leadership programs. In K. L. Guthrie, T. Bertrand Jones, & L. Osteen (Eds.), *Developing culturally relevant leadership learning.* (New Directions for Student Leadership, No. 152, pp. 9–21). Jossey-Bass. https://doi.org/10.1002/yd.20205

Brack, A. B., Millard, M., & Shah, K. (2008). Are peer educators really peers? *Journal of American College Health, 56*(5), 566–568. https://doi.org/10.3200/JACH.56.5.566-568

Chan, K. Y., & Dragsow, F. (2001). Toward a theory of individual differences and leadership: understanding the motivation to lead. *Journal of applied psychology, 86*(3), 481–498. https://doi.org/10.1037/0021-9010.86.3.481

Chunoo, V.S., & Osteen, L. (2016). Our purpose, mission, and context: The call for educating future leaders. In K. L. Guthrie, & L. Osteen (Eds.), *Reclaiming higher education's purpose in leadership development* (New Directions for Higher Education, No. 174, pp. 9–20). Jossey-Bass.

Colvin, J. W., & Ashman, M. (2010). Roles, risks, and benefits of peer mentoring relationships in higher education, mentoring & tutoring. *Partnership in Learning, 18*(2), 121–134, https://doi.org/10.1080/13611261003678879.

Day, D., Gronn, P., & Salas, E. (2004). Leadership capacity in teams. *The Leadership Quarterly. 15*, 857–880. https://doi.org/10.1016/j.leaqua.2004.09.001.

Disch, J. (2009). Generative leadership. *Creative Nursing, 15*(4), 172–177.

Dugan, J. P. (2017). *Leadership theory: Cultivating critical perspectives.* Jossey-Bass.

Guthrie, K. L., Beatty, C. C., & Wiborg, E. R. (2021). *Engaging in the leadership process: Identity, capacity, and efficacy for college students.* Information Age Publishing.

Keup, J. R. (2016). Peer leadership as an emerging high-impact practice: An exploratory study of the American experience. *Journal of Student Affairs in Africa, 4*(1), 33–52. https://doi.org/10.14426/jsaa.v4i1.143

Komives, S. R., Lucas, N., & McMahon, T. R. (2013). *Exploring leadership: for college students who want to make a difference* (3rd ed.). Jossey-Bass.

Lemon, J. D., & Wawrzynski, M. R. (2022). Exploring health and wellness peer educators' growth in socially responsible leadership, *Journal of Student Affairs Research and Practice, 59*(2), 149–164. https://doi.org/10.1080/19496591.202 0.1828094

Paulhus, N. J. (1987). Uses and misuses of the term 'social justice' in the Roman Catholic tradition. *The Journal of Religious Ethics, 15*(2), 261–282.

Wawrzynski, M. R., & Lemon, J. D. (2019). Understanding student learning outcomes of peer educators. In T. L. Trolian, & E. A. Jach (Eds)., *Applied learning in higher education: Curricular and co-curricular experiences that improve student learning* (New Directions for Higher Education, No. 188, pp. 61–69). https://doi.org/10.1002/he.20346

CHAPTER 20

BOUNCING BACK

Resilient Socially Just Leadership Educator

Genisis "Gen" Ramirez

It is no secret how life can throw substantial adversities in a person's path. Despite these challenges, some people rise to the occasion and thrive under intense stress. Those people are commonly considered *resilient* (Hurley, 2022). The concept, practicing, and understanding of resilience is crucial for socially just leadership educators; those who make it their mission to promote diversity, equity, and inclusion through their leadership teaching and learning practices. Socially just leadership educators aim to include members of marginalized populations, who historically, suffer from underrepresentation and injustice within higher education. Resiliency among these members is essential, as it helps individuals thrive instead of crumble.

In practice, leadership educators who prioritize resiliency can promote the development of mental health and professional development through self-awareness and intentionality. In this frame, the cultivation of resilient learning can be beneficial to educators and scholars as it fosters community, inclusivity, and influence in hopes of bringing self-awareness of one's resilient attributes when faced with adversities. This chapter emphasizes the importance of improved resiliency for socially just leadership educators. The origin of resilience will be explored, and the subsequent discussion will describe the potential value resiliency holds, especially for members of marginalized populations. After exploring theoretical frame-

Committing to Action: Socially Just Leadership Educations, pp. 249–258
Copyright © 2025 by Information Age Publishing
www.infoagepub.com

works surrounding socially just leadership educators' development, and how resiliency connects, I conclude with a call to help those socially just leadership educators who intend to become more self-aware, with recommendations on how they can model their resiliency for the benefit of others.

I acknowledge how my experiences and narratives may different from those reading this chapter, despite sharing some similar social identities with me. I will be using my identities as a spiritual, queer, and Latinx woman, to highlight my own resilience narrative and how it appears in my socially just leadership student role. Furthermore, I am aware "'Latinx" is an evolving term and most use it to ask questions about gender, language, and inclusion within Hispanic communities (Salinas, 2020). As a member of various, intersecting marginalized communities who have faced adversities, I have a unique perspective on the development of resiliency. I encourage and invite each reader to consider the shape and form resilience can take with respect to their own social location and positionality.

ORIGIN OF RESILIENCE

The history of resilience is crucial to understanding the influence it continues to hold. The term dates to the 1600s and comes from the Latin word *resiliens*. It is defined as an "act of rebounding or springing back" (Harper, n.d., para. 1). The term resilience had no evidence of lividity within scholarly work until an English engineer and author, Thomas Tredgold, used the term when describing the properties of timber in an 1818 scholarly essay (McAslan, 2010). Within the essay, the term was described by using words associated with what we would see as modernized adjectives for the concept of resilience: durability, toughness, elasticity, and strength (Tredgold, 1818). Furthermore, McAslan (2010) described the role resilience has played in the ecological system and environment. The shift from resilience being a term that described physical object attributes (i.e., Tredgold, 1818) to a concept that deepened more into a social-ecological system (e.g., McAslan, 2010) shows, perhaps ironically, resilience's conceptual and practical durability and flexibility.

When one exhibits resilience, they can bounce back from any situation they are put in. From what I have observed, through my lived experiences, others tend to use the word resilience interchangeability with the word strength. If you are similar to me, you may be wondering, what is the difference? Resilience is not an absence of weakness or presence of strength; Even the strongest among us can find themselves "knocked down" by life's challenges. Aside from strength, the phrase *growth mindset* is often conflated with resilience. To clarify distinctions, resiliency is what drives individuals to stand back up, meanwhile growth mindset is the beginning of the process that leads to resiliency. It is the ability to view adversities and failures as an opportunity for learning and growing. Embracing a growth mindset can foster resilience by empowering individuals to see challenges as opportunities for growth, learn from failures, and maintain a positive outlook in the face of adversity.

INFLUENCE OF RESILIENCE

In accordance with Iacoviello and Charney's (2014) research on psychosocial facets of resilience, I acknowledge how "resilience is broadly defined as adaptive characteristics of an individual to cope with and recover from adversity" (p. 1). As a multifaceted phenomenon, the various characteristics of resilience include, "cognitive flexibility, active coping skills, maintaining a supportive social network, attending to one's physical well-being, and embracing a personal moral compass" (Iacoviello & Charney, 2014, p. 1). Being a socially just leadership educator means fostering community, and an important variable in executing this practice involves the pillars of one's own supportive social network, especially among those educators who practice through an adaptive leadership style. Co-founders of Cambridge Leadership Associates, and adaptive leadership experts, Ron Heifetz and Marty Linsky, discussed a component of adaptive leadership as how one's ideas improve through the cogency of others point of views. The importance of this revelation influences community by describing resiliency as being critical when confronting difficult issues or conflicting values (Heifetz & Linsky, 2017). Having a supportive social network adds support to those who model resiliency.

At times, socially just leadership educators stress the importance of community and how it creates a sense of belonging. Dr. Tracy Brower, a sociologist whose work is centered around exploring happiness, fulfillment, and work-life, described the importance of a sense of belonging and community, "To truly feel a sense of belonging, you must feel unity and a common sense of character with and among members of your group" (Brower, 2021, para. 3). Growing up in my Hispanic household, I was raised by not only my parents, but by grandparents, aunts, uncles, cousins, and neighbors, among others. A common phrase my mother would use to teach the importance of community and family was: "Se necesita un pueblo para criar a un nino." This translates to "It takes a village to raise a child." Being part of a marginalized ethnic population, we are always taught that the community and support around us helps provide us a sense of belonging.

This sense of belonging drives awareness of the values and impact we, as humans, attain towards our experiences.

To clarify, whenever things fail, we look to our community to hold us together and lift us up. The support we receive when failing allows for a chance to develop resilience. Resilience can be seen as a form of self-authorship; a theory derived from Robert Kegan, who viewed the theory as phases and being associated with cognitive, relational, and psychosocial dimensions of development (Patton et al., 2016). From a communal lens, self-authorship allows us to look at our interpersonal relationships and helps us make meaning of failure to increase our sense of belonging. This is a concept supported by Baxter Magolda's (2016) revised self-authorship theory.

THEORETICAL FRAMEWORKS AND CONNECTION TO LEADERSHIP

Baxter Magolda's (2016) revised self- authorship theory provides a chance for self-aware individuals, especially socially just leadership educators, to use reflections to foster the growth of interpersonal relationships. This reflective approach might help individuals understand themselves better, identify their resilience, and utilize their knowledge and insights to support others in cultivating positive and meaningful connections with others. By focusing on three domains, three domains: cognitive, interpersonal, and intrapersonal, this theory dives into how college students reflect within themselves, analyze internal and external relationships, and develop their own ideas and beliefs through their lived experiences (Baxter Magolda, 2016; Guthrie et al., 2013). Individuals who participate in self-authorship also develop their own internal resiliency systems when by overcoming adversities and managing external influences on thinking, feeling, and outward behaviors.

Learning to develop resilience also means confronting the four principles Martin Weller, author of *Battle for open: How openness won and why it doesn't feel like victory*, outlined in his book. Weller (2014) described resiliency by focusing on four principles connected to *open education*. Using the critical pedagogy of *openness*, open education centers participation and inclusiveness in society (Weller, 2014). Through research and historical usage, it also has multiple differing definitions including, but not limited to, access, flexibility, equity, collaboration, social justice, transparency, and more (Weller, 2014). Studies revolving around the topic of open education and resilience have shown us that it offers a narrative for changes within the education system, specifically using a social justice lens. Weller (2014) named the four principles: (1) Latitude (2) Resistance (3) Precariousness, and (4) Panarchy.

Principle 1: Latitude

According to Weller (2014), *latitude* is the maximum amount of change that can occur before losing the ability to recover. It allows for the accommodation of new technology and practices. Connecting this to resilience and higher education, the role latitude plays in one teaching resiliency within the higher education setting, especially leadership, permits the leader to adjust and change technological approaches as needed without detracting from the original curriculum and educational goals. To be resilient, you must have the latitude to be able to adapt to adversities.

Principle 2: Resistance

Resistance is changing systems; regardless of complexity or challenge (Weller, 2014). When faced with a situation, those with resiliency practice resisting by acknowledging how pre-established systems that arise within higher education are built upon heteronormative frameworks as such seen in queer theory (University of Illinois, 2022). Resistance allows for those with resiliency to challenge the systems to be more diverse and inclusive, especially from a leadership point of view.

Principle 3: Precariousness

Precariousness, the third principle of resilience, focuses on approaching the limit or threshold of a system (Weller, 2014). The influence of leaders and leadership within higher education has shown us throughout history is that theories such as the cultural relevant leadership learning model (CRLL; Bertrand Jones et al., 2016) provides a framework to enhance our leadership initiatives to make them more socially just and culturally relevant. To connect resilience and precariousness within higher education through the CRLL model, this principle allows those who practice resiliency to focus on the limits such models and frameworks can enhance leadership initiatives.

Principle 4: Panarchy

Panarchy is comprised of the influences of external forces (Weller, 2014). If there is anything higher education institutions learned from the COVID-19 pandemic is that they had to adapt to change quickly. The external forces that influenced the adaptability was the pandemic, and it caused institutions to take a different approach to teaching and learning. For those practicing resiliency, it allowed for them to see the pandemic as an adversary and therefore made it possible for adaptation.

Figure 20.1

The Four Principles of Resilience

Source: Adapted from Weller (2014).

The four principles of resiliency and socially just leadership education empowers us to critically reflect on our place among these concepts. Resiliency provides socially just leadership educators the tools to accommodate, develop resistance, know limits, and possess knowledge of influential external factors. Becoming aware of one's own resiliency enhances these principles to better assist with student success through authenticity. It affects us as socially just leadership educators by bringing to our attention that students need help in realizing their own resiliency.

THE GUIDELINES

The previous section defined resilience and described how it affects us as socially just leadership educators. It discussed the impact resilience has, especially on marginalized populations. Next, I consider how and what can as socially just leadership educators can do to increase our own self-awareness with resiliency to help students realize their own resilience. The proceeding discussion will focus on important guidelines to better support students through their own resilience journey.

Recommendation 1: Use Specific Pedagogies, Purposefully

It is common for socially just leadership educators to use specific pedagogies to influence their teaching. Pedagogies allow for students to grasp ideas and beliefs through a series of activities to help with their social development. As Pendakur and Furr (2016) shared, many instructional strategies in leadership education involve reflection to identify life experiences that illuminate students' values, commitments, and fears. Some pedagogies may include case studies and/or peer facilitations. Case studies are a way to gain real-world examples when faced with a situation through a research approach. This type of pedagogy can help students critically think and analyze through a real-world context. They can take the examples from the case studies and apply them to their own experiences. This is a great way to help support students through their self-awareness resilience journey. It allows for them to analyze their experiences and think on the resilient actions they have taken. For a more collaborative approach, peer facilitations allow students to teach each other about their journeys while also receiving feedback and participating in discussion with their classmates and instructor. It gives them an opportunity to hear other viewpoints they may not have previously considered. This gives them more support in providing ways to become more resilient.

Recommendation 2: Use Meaningful and Clear Analogies

The use of analogies is a way to make sense of the self-awareness one has with their resiliency. My father has always used analogies to get his points across. There was this one analogy story where he said, "Hija, say you wanted to be a pilot. Who do you ask for validation; from your pilot teacher or from your friends? Which validation would make you feel [better] in knowing it's the right validation to help you advance into your career?" The reasonings behind his analogies never really made sense to me until I found my own analogy that made the point more meaningful.

On airplanes, flight attendants review emergency protocols and provide visual aids to enhance passenger understanding. For example, they state if the air cabin loses pressure, the oxygen mask will come down. Once they do, we are instructed to put on our own masks before assisting someone else. I always ask my students and those I have built meaningful relationships with, "Why do we put on our oxygen mask first before assisting someone else in theirs?" The answer? Because you must take care of yourself first before being able to help someone else. This analogy shows how socially just leadership educators can support their students in becoming aware of their resilience by first understanding themselves and their own capacity for resilience. Different approaches one can take to become self-aware is reflecting, journaling, having conversations with loved ones about experiences, and employing self-care techniques. Emotions from deep within will come up during these activities and these feelings will allow for authentic emotional and psychological reactions (including, but not limited to, resilience) which result in the development of self-acceptance.

Recommendation 3: Acceptance of Your Own Adversities

The Kübler-Ross grief model describes five stages of grief: denial, anger, bargaining, depression, and acceptance (Kübler-Ross, 1969). Those who pass through adversities are no strangers through this grief process. According to the model, stabilization of emotions may begin once reaching the stage of acceptance. A comparison with this stage and a socially just leadership educators' acceptance of their adversities can create a revelation that inspires a feeling of clarity that may be experienced. This allows for a development within the acquiring of self-awareness of one's own resilience by how one can accept challenges that have created a forefront of adversities and how one can move past these occurrences and be able to move forward. These acts allow us to bounce back while also creating a space that allows for discussions of vulnerability, community, and guidance. This, in turn, enables a support network for students, which manifests through dialogue and consultations from those with similar adversities. During these interactions, it is important for socially just leadership educators create brave spaces rather than safe spaces (Ali, 2017) to effectively allow feedback and guidance.

Recommendation 4: Promote Brave Spaces

In the context of higher education, safe spaces and brave spaces serve distinct purposes. Ali (2017) highlighted how safe spaces primarily aim to enhance the safety and visibility of marginalized or oppressed community members. On the other hand, brave spaces seek to embrace differences and foster open dialogue. To drive change effectively, it becomes essential to understand and empathize with those who experience discomfort and are willing to express their viewpoints. Ali (2017) explained brave spaces encompass all the characteristics of safe spaces, as recognized by various sectors, but emphasize the challenging nature of these environments, expecting students to actively engage and participate within them. Socially just leadership educators create opportunities for open dialogue and allow appropriately uncomfortable discussions to occur. This promotes inclusivity and allows for marginalized populations to feel more accepted in these spaces. It better supports students to share their adversities with others and helps develop their resiliency.

RESILIENT SOCIALLY JUST LEADERSHIP EDUCATION

Socially, just leadership educators take on the responsibility of promoting diversity, equity, and inclusion within their professional roles. To become effective in such capacities, it is important to realize the self-awareness of one's own resiliency and resilience journey. We are tasked with supporting students to become aware of their own resilient journey. The ability to bounce back from adversities not only creates personal development but also professional growth, all of which culminate in leadership. Being a resilient socially just leadership educator is an important part in student development. Doing so creates a space of inclusivity and impact, especially to those who reside within marginalized populations. This guide was made to give support to those who wish to promote resiliency while also continuing to influence and impact the next generation of socially just leaders.

REFERENCES

Ali, D. (2017). *Safe spaces and brave spaces: Historical context and recommendations for student affairs professionals*. NASPA Policy and Practice Series: Issue 2. National Association of Student Personnel Administrators (NASPA), Inc. https://www.naspa.org/files/dmfile/Policy_and_Practice_No_2_Safe_Brave_Spaces.pdf

Baxter Magolda, M. B. (2016). Remaking self-in-world. In K. M. Quinlan (ed.) *How Higher Education Feels* (pp. 53–77). Brill. https://doi.org/10.1007/9789463006361_005

Bertrand Jones, T., Guthrie, K. L., & Osteen, L. (2016). Critical domains of culturally relevant leadership learning: A call to transform leadership programs. In K. L. Guthrie, T. Bertrand Jones, & L. Osteen (Eds.), *Developing culturally relevant leadership learning*. (New Directions for Student Leadership, No. 152, pp. 9–21). Jossey-Bass. https://doi.org/10.1002/yd.20205

Brower, T. (2021, January 10). *Missing your people: Why belonging is so important and how to create it*. Forbes. Retrieved November 6, 2022, from https://www.forbes.com/sites/tracybrower/2021/01/10/missing-your-people-why-belonging-is-so-important-and-how-to-create-it/?sh=574093ad7c43.

Guthrie, K. L., Bertrand Jones, T., Osteen, L., & Hu, S. (2013). *Cultivating Leader Identity and Capacity in Students from Diverse Backgrounds: ASHE Higher Education Report, 39*(4). John Wiley & Sons.

Harper, D. (n.d.). Etymology of resilience. *Online Etymology Dictionary*. Retrieved May 15, 2023, from https://www.etymonline.com/word/resilience

Heifetz, R. A., & Linsky, M. (2017). *Leadership on the line: Staying alive through the dangers of change*. Harvard Business Review Press.

Hurley, K. (2022, July 14). *What is resilience? definition, types, building resiliency, benefits, and resources*. EverydayHealth.com. Retrieved November 30, 2022, from https://www.everydayhealth.com/wellness/resilience/#:~:text=What%20does%20it%20mean%20to,through%20emotional%20pain%20and%20suffering

Iacoviello, B. M., & Charney, D. S. (2014). Psychosocial facets of resilience: Implications for preventing posttrauma psychopathology, treating trauma survivors, and enhancing community resilience. *European Journal of Psychotraumatology, 5*(1), 1–10. https://doi.org/10.3402/ejpt.v5.23970

Kübler-Ross, E. (1969). *On death and dying*. Collier Books/Macmillan.

McAslan, A. (2010, March 14). *The concept of resilience: Understanding its origin, meaning, and utility*. Torrens Resilience Institute.

Patton, L. D., Renn, K. A., Guido-DiBrito, F., & Quaye, S. J. (2016). *Student development in college: Theory, research, and practice*. Jossey-Bass & Pfeiffer.

Pendakur, V., & Furr, S. C. (2016). Critical leadership pedagogy: Engaging power, identity, and culture in leadership education for college students of Color. In K. L. Guthrie, & L. Osteen (Eds.), *Reclaiming higher education's purpose in leadership development* (New Directions for Higher Education, No. 174, pp. 45–55). https://doi.org/10.1002/he.20188

Salinas, C. (2020). The complexity of the "x" in Latina: How Latinx/a/o students relate to, identify with, and understand the term Latinx. *Journal of Hispanic Higher Education, 19*(2), 149–168.

Tredgold, T. (1818). On the transverse strength and resilience of timber. *The Philosophical Magazine, 51*(239), 214–216. https://doi.org/10.1080/14786441808637536.

University of Illinois. (2022, August 7). *Libguides: Queer theory: Background*. Background–Queer Theory–LibGuides at University of Illinois at Urbana-Champaign. Retrieved December 2022, from https://guides.library.illinois.edu/queertheory/background

Weller, M. (2014). Resilience and open education. In M. Weller (Ed.), *The battle for open: How openness won and why it doesn't feel like victory* (pp. 171–188). Ubiquity Press. https://doi.org/10.5334/bam.i

CHAPTER 21

EMOTIONAL AND EXPERIENTIAL LEARNING

Using Table-Top Role-Playing Games as Socially Just Leadership Education Pedagogy

Antonio Ruiz-Ezquerro

A long, long time ago, in a fantasy land far, far away, a group of students entered a small mining village with inhabitants who were very different from themselves. They quickly realized the locals had different religious beliefs, political ideologies, and lifestyles than theirs, but they also witnessed commonalities the more they interacted. As these students spent more time in the town, they used empathy to establish cross-cultural relationships, and various other leadership skills to uncover and dismantle the town's oppressive systems and bring social change to the village. How would these students engage in the leadership process in the face of oppression? Will they be able to recall and apply leadership concepts learned in class? How can this activity help learners understand the lived experiences of others, promote socially just leadership practices, and help them build bridges across real-life political divides?

Socially just change requires leaders to be proficient in dealing with adaptive challenges. Adaptive challenges frequently fall outside the person's existing knowledge, or routine solutions, and often require new knowledge, innovation, or behavioral changes (Heifetz & Linsky, 2017). Leadership is

Committing to Action: Socially Just Leadership Educations, pp. 259–272

learned when students experience "changes in knowledge, skills, behavior, attitudes, and values resulting from educational experiences ... associated with the activity of leadership" (Guthrie & Jenkins, 2018, p. 57). Pedagogy that intentionally exposes students to adaptive challenges presents unique leadership learning opportunities. This chapter will explore the use of tabletop role-playing games (TRPGs) as a leadership learning pedagogy that can be customized for dealing with adaptive challenges and social justice issues while simultaneously building an inclusive learning environment. I will first present how TRPGs can be used to promote socially just leadership education. Then, I will discuss how socially just leadership educators can apply full TRPGs or adapt some of their game mechanics into their own teaching.

ROLE-PLAYING GAMES: FROM SYSTEMS TO PEDAGOGY

At their core, TRPGs are "systems of rules that allow for individual and group agency based in social interactions" (Lasley, 2022, p. 74). These rules allow players to co-create an imaginary world where they interact with complex settings and characters using narrative and decision-making. Most TRPGs have a game facilitator, who brings to life the setting and encountered problems and enforces the role-play's rules to bring consistency to the make-believe world. Adding a facilitator is one of the most significant differences between a TRPG and a traditional role-play activity, as it allows players to interact not only with each other but also with the environment. Players create characters they embody through storytelling to interact with each other and address the challenges the co-created fantasy world presents. TRPGs' adaptable nature and highly interactive game mechanics, "provide opportunities that can be used for personally meaningful role-play and enacting complex social or ethical dilemmas ripe for leadership learning" (Lasley, 2022, p. 74). Additionally, they foster the exploration of creativity, agency, and identity (Cragoe, 2016). They may act as an effective tool that fosters cooperation, diplomacy, communication, team building, and crisis management (Rivers et al., 2016).

TRPGs As Intentional Socially Just Leadership Pedagogy

Effective leadership education programs are assessed by their graduates' ability to apply leadership knowledge to the challenges they experience (Baxter Magolda & King, 2004). Therefore, it is crucial for leadership educators to prioritize student learning over teaching (Barr & Tagg, 1995), thereby shifting the role of leadership educators from knowledge distributors to facilitators of collaborative learning, personal growth, and inclusive learning environments (Guthrie & Jenkins, 2018). Moving towards a student-centered approach also challenges how we apply and think of leadership pedagogy. Real-life challenges rarely reflect the simplicity encountered in a textbook. Leaders who deal with issues of oppression, such as poverty, and racism, among other inequities, often encounter values and potential solutions that may be competing or contradictory to each other (Nelson & Padilla, 2022). Relevant leadership education cannot be separated from social justice, as meaningful social justice efforts depend on leadership knowledge, skills, and values (Guthrie & Chunoo, 2018).

According to Komives et al. (2005), leadership development opportunities during the formative college years significantly impact students' leadership perspectives. During this time, students experience a shift from seeing leadership as a leader-centric dynamic based on power and authority to a relational process that requires collaboration. Furthermore, as students engage with socially just leadership education, and learn about systemic structures of privilege and oppression, they experience cognitive, emotional, and intellectual challenges depending on their own socialization (Harro, 2010). Using games as pedagogy provides students with the opportunity to connect leadership with social justice as they navigate the transition toward a more complex understanding of leadership (Nelson & Padilla, 2022). TRPGs allow learners to use narrative, reflection, and decision-making for the exploration of themes like social identities and power structures as they bring the action needed to create change in a fictional world.

The Power of Storytelling

Dungeons & Dragons (*D&D*), perhaps the most famous TRPG of all time, has a controversial history including the irrational fears and myths that made the popular game a controversial topic during the Satanic Panic of the 1980s (Laycock, 2015). The first editions of the game were designed mainly by White men during the 1970s. The designers were inspired by Tolkien's descriptions of mythical creatures and races, such as *Orcs*, which carried heavy and deliberate racist stereotypes in their descriptions (Hodes, 2019). Additionally, the original designs catered to gratify stereotypical male power fantasies (Nephew, 2006) by using sexist imagery and rules that perpetuated systemic gender inequality within the game (Garcia, 2017). Although most of these rules have changed for the better, elements of racism and sexism still linger in the historical context of the game's creation (Lasley, 2022). I argue the oppressive historical nature of the game can bring to light similar systems of oppression to those in the real and modern world, making *D&D* and TRPGs powerful pedagogical tools which use storytelling to illustrate some of the most pressing social justice issues of our society while giving learners an educational space to engage in socially just leadership. As Parks (2005) argued, "[stories] can distill and anchor a key concept you are trying to get across" (p. 162). The cognitive effects of storytelling are amplified when they resonate with people's immediate experiences.

In *D&D*, race is typically used to describe different species and is less associated with skin color (e.g., Elves, Orcs, Dwarves, Gnomes, etc.). Traditionally, some races are associated with specific physical attributes. Dwarves and Gnomes tend to be short (four and three feet, respectively), while other races, like Orcs and Goliaths, are tall and heavy. Additionally, there is extensive lore describing the cultural characteristics of each race (their religions, traditions, culinary tastes, etc.), and how other groups may perceive them. For example, *Tieflings*, a race distinguished by their demon-like features (large, thick horns, pointy teeth, and prehensile tails) are often feared and mistrusted by others. A facilitator can create scenarios where some of the social injustices of our world appear reflected in the fantasy realm. Perhaps a Gnome player is unable to find a stool reachable for someone their size, illustrating issues of ableism. Alternatively, maybe the players witness a Tiefling character being denied service by the bartender associates because of their racist beliefs. "Imaginative fantasy games like D&D provide the additional benefit of allowing players to experience social interactions that go beyond their normal range of experiences ... creating opportunities for ethical dialogue and debate" (Wright et al., 2020, p. 102). By experiencing unfairness in a fictional world and giving learners the opportunity to address it, leadership educators can use case-in-point methodology; an effective leadership learning pedagogical tool that focuses on experiencing, identifying, and reflecting on leadership concepts as they manifest in real-time (Parks, 2005), to draw parallels with the real world. At the same time, students can practice adaptive leadership in the evolving scenario and use that experience for future reflection and meaning-making.

Identity Exploration—The Relationship Between TRPGs and Learners

The world of TRPGs is apt for the exploration of social and leadership identities (Cragoe, 2016), allowing learners to explore identities they possess but may not feel comfortable (or safe) expressing in the real world. In a TRPG, players may create and embody characters of any gender, sexual orientation, or race, among other identities. By allowing and encouraging learners to participate with authenticity, socially just educators can aim to create an environment that supports students in the development of the "critical analytical tools necessary to understand the structural features of oppression and their own socialization within oppressive systems" (Adams et al., 2016, p. 31). Different identities in-game could catalyze appreciation of human diversity and a reflection of the learners' ability to work with others toward social justice.

TRPGs as a Catalyst for Transformational Experiences

Advances in role-playing studies suggest the experiences players have within a game can impact players' real lives. Bowman and Lieberoth (2018) proposed the concepts of bleed, alibi, and steering in TRPG gameplay as factors that may influence a player's experience. *Bleed* is when real-life emotional elements unconsciously influence a played character or vice versa. The opposite of bleed, *alibi*, is the perceived distinction between the player's real life and the game's fictional events and action. Alibi strikes a conscious balance to separate the character from the self in a way that still allows for safe immersion into the game. The more alibi a player has, the less bleed they experience. Lastly, there is *steering*, the deliberate efforts of a player to direct the game's narrative towards or away from emotional experiences for out-of-game reasons. Bowman and Hugaas (2019) argued these elements are only some of the ways TRPGs lead to *transformative experiences;* where the role-play has such a meaningful effect on the participant that they integrate aspects of the experience into their lives, for example, gaining an increased sense of self-awareness, using the in-game experience to process real-life situations, among others.

Building Emotional Intelligence

Dantley and Tillman (2006) described a socially just leader as one who "interrogates the policies and procedures that shape schools and at the same time perpetuate social inequalities and marginalization due to race, class, gender, and other markers of otherness" (p. 19). I believe their definition can be easily transferred to a non-educational context by substituting the word "schools"' with "institutions," and their interpretation would remain accurate. Emotional intelligence (EI) allows socially just leaders to identify and address behavioral barriers to change, regulate their own emotions and read those of their followers and opposition. It helps leaders recognize their followers' stress levels and respond to their concerns with empathy, regulating the necessary levels of tension required for change (Heifetz & Linsky, 2017).

Emotionally intelligent leadership requires development across three areas: consciousness of self, consciousness of others, and consciousness of context (Shankman et al., 2015). TRPGs present learners with opportunities to work on all three facets, especially consciousness of others. Rivers et al.'s (2016) research suggested TRPGs may "encourage, train, and develop empathic skills in perspective taking and other empathy-related processes" (p. 293). They found TRPG players reported higher levels of empathy with others and that TRPGs aided players' ability to take different perspectives from their own. It may be partly due to TRPGs' nature of creating a highly absorbing environment where players continuously play a character. TRPG players are often placed in narrated situations where they are pushed to step in and out of other characters' worldviews (fictional or not) and immerse themselves in the co-created scenario, creating opportunities for vicarious leadership learning and leadership metacognition to occur, both of which may generate leadership knowledge in the student (Guthrie & Jenkins, 2018).

Role-played experiences, regardless of the realm where they occur, present learners with powerful opportunities where the lessons they practice are very real. Instructors can design scenarios where learners can practice EI by interacting with characters and situations where they are encouraged to use EI to succeed. Perhaps it is up to the players to listen to an argument and facilitate a dialogue where all characters can reach a peaceful resolution. Alternatively, by being able to self-regulate their behavior and thinking before acting, learners are placed in a situation where a terrible misunderstanding is clarified before it evolves into a much more destructive outcome. TRPGs give leadership educators the tools to design customized scenarios where learners can practice the leadership skills necessary to facilitate social change in the real world.

TRPGs as a Source for Experiential Learning

In addition to creating an energetic environment for classroom learning, TRPGs bring to life immersive worlds, face-to-face interaction, and a direct, shared experience" (Hays & Hayse, 2017, p. 103). Researchers have used Kolb's (2015) experiential learning (EL) framework to explain how learning happens through gameplay (check Lasley, 2022 and Whitton, 2012 for more on the topic). Kolb's (2015) framework is composed of a four-step, repeating cycle: *concrete experience, reflective observation, abstract conceptualization,* and *active experimentation* (Figure 21.1). In TRPGs, learners have in-game experiences that they reflect on, make meaning of, and lead them to modify their in-game and out-of-game behavior.

Figure 21.1

Kolb's Experiential Learning Model

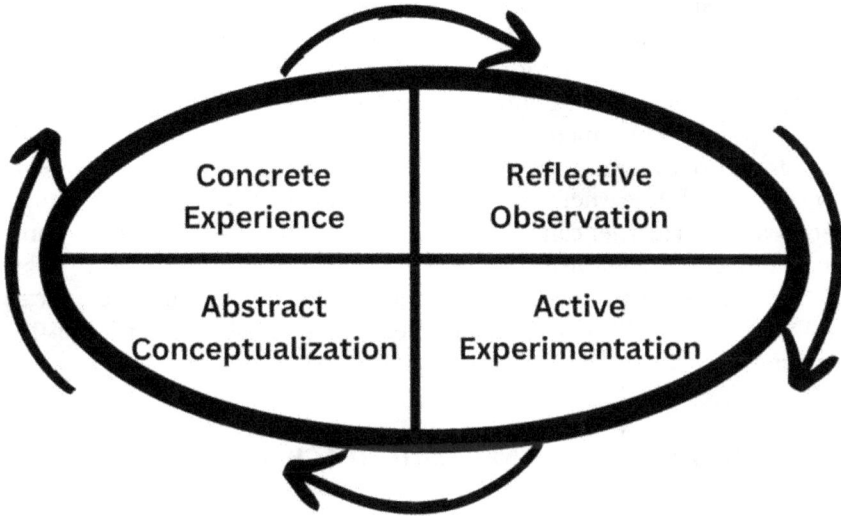

Source: Adapted from Kolb (2015).

An interesting characteristic of exercising leadership in TRPGs is the "dual layer" where the leadership process emerges, between characters making decisions to achieve their in-story goals and between players as they collaborate to co-construct a shared narrative. The dual-layer element of TRPGs gives learners and facilitators a rich repository of content from which to make case-in-point examples to reflect upon and illustrate the leadership process as it emerges. This clearly demonstrates the crucial role facilitators play in tapping into TRPG's full potential, as without a well-guided meaning-making process, the process of transforming a game into a valuable teaching tool remains incomplete. As Crookhall (2010) eloquently explained in an exploration of games as experiential learning pedagogies, "learning comes from the *debriefing*, not from the game [itself] … it reflects a fundamentally crucial part of the learning process involved in the gaming experience. *Debriefing is the processing of the game experience to turn it into learning*" (p. 907, emphasis added). Engaging in meaningful reflection after the role-played experience, with the intent of meaning-making for future experimentation, is a crucial step in using TRPGs for leadership learning (Lasley, 2022).

Bowman and Hugaas (2019) argued RPGs could foster transformation through three phases: establishing a clear vision that describes the intended impact (*design*), providing a safe-feeling environment (*implementation*), and offering support that facilitates post-game *integration*. Transformative experiences are those that impact the learner in a meaningful way beyond the game. For an experience to be considered transformational, the impact, "should expand beyond the bounds of the original experience and integrate into one's daily frames of reality and identity" (Bowman & Hugaas, 2019, para. 2). While transformational experiences are not guaranteed to occur for every player, following intentional design, implementation, and integration practices may increase the likelihood of participants going through a profound paradigm shift. Bowman and Hugaas (2019) also advocated for staying within learners' zone of proximal development (ZPD), the area between what a learner can accomplish without the need for assistance and what they can accomplish with peer or instructional support (Vygotsky, 1978). The following section will explore ways in which instructors can apply customized TRPGs or game mechanics to facilitate social justice learning.

CREATING TRPG SCENERIOS TO TEACH SOCIAL JUSTICE

Socially just leadership teaching and learning begins by accepting social justice as a core part of leadership; the same way that consequential social justice efforts require "leadership knowledge, skills, and values" (Guthrie & Chunoo, 2018, p. 2). Thus, when considering teaching social justice lessons, these lessons should be grounded in the art and science of pedagogy; otherwise, we risk our efforts crumbling like structures without foundation (Stanovich & Stanovich, 2003). The same logic applies to the use of TRPGs for socially just leadership education. The educational games or the game mechanics chosen to facilitate your lesson should still follow evidence-based practices. Below, you will find a series of steps adapted from Bowman and Hugaas (2019) and Ruiz-Ezquerro (2021) as a guide through this process.

TRPG Design Phase

1. **Vision and Learning Objectives:** Start by establishing the desired learning objectives for the participants; doing so will increase the likelihood of the experience having a profound impact on learners (Bowman & Hugaas, 2019; Ruiz-Ezquerro, 2021). Begin by answering the following questions: What learning goals are students pursuing from this activity? How does a TRPG help them achieve those goals? Is using a TRPG the best way to meet those objectives? Upon answering these questions, establish the desired impact you want on

learners. Bowman and Hugaas (2019) categorized impact as four broad groups of outcomes: "Emotional Processing, Social Cohesion, Educational Goals, and Political Aims" (para. 9). Using TRPGs can help instructors in several leadership aspects simultaneously.

2. **Develop the parameters that will govern the TRPG:** Consider the following questions when choosing or creating a TRPG for socially just leadership education:

    a. Are you using an existing TRPG, or are you creating your own? Creating a TRPG can be time-consuming and requires the creator to have plenty of experience with these game systems before creating one of their own. It is likely that an educational TRPG with similar goals that can be adapted already exists. If not, and you are determined to create your own, play a few different ones yourself to gain experience with different TRPG systems before designing your own. Like in many TRPGs themselves, experience will be your best guide.

    b. Are you using the game as a multi-session exercise or a one-and-done? Careful analysis of your learning objectives will help you answer this question.

    c. What is the world size for this role-playing game? Is it limited to a room, a building, a community, or an entire continent? Normally, the bigger the world, the more work it will take to create it.

    d. Are players interacting solely with each other, or will there be non-playable characters (NPCs) controlled by the facilitator? NPCs are great for plot development and providing in-game direction. How will these NPCs look, sound, and act? How will they contribute to your learning objectives?

Implementation of Activity and Student Safety

1. What are the rules that will govern the engaging learning environment? Will there be luck-based elements to determine decision outcomes, e.g., dice-rolling, or card drawing? Are these play mechanics inclusive and accessible to all players? Like any other educational activity, it requires a certain degree of structure. Having clear systems will help learners understand the rules that govern the world and ease their navigation of it; making it easier for them to focus on their experience.

2. What tools are you providing in-game to aid students in navigating the discomforts often experienced when learning about social

justice? How are you establishing and respecting important boundaries set by the facilitator or learners? Aside from the engagement benefits of a game, this is a pedagogical tool to teach social justice. The facilitator's job is to create a *brave space* where meaningful learning can happen (Guthrie & Jenkins, 2018). Brave spaces acknowledge that discussions surrounding diversity and social justice topics pose a higher level of risk to students with minoritized identities, making it up to the leadership educator to create a learning environment that encourages authenticity and vulnerability (Arao & Clemens, 2013).

Debriefing of Activity and Integration of Knowledge into Students' Lives

Debriefing plays a critical role when using TRPGs as pedagogy (Crookall, 2014). As Bowman and Hugaas (2019) discussed, many learning processes continue beyond the extent of role-playing, potentially having a transformative effect on learners if they achieve integrating learned lessons in their real life. Integration happens at different degrees for those who experience it, ranging from small realizations that alter one's paradigm to having profound alterations in one's identity. Facilitating a space for reflection drives learners to engage in the cognitive processes that allow meaning-making to happen (Volpe White & Guthrie, 2016). Additionally, the process gives learners an opportunity to practice critical thinking and visualize how these lessons and similar scenarios could manifest in their daily lives.

While there is no one-size-fits-all design for post-game debriefs in TRPGs (Bowman, 2014), there is similitude across several proposed models. To start, post-game debriefs should begin by validating the player experience, which gives players a space to recount the game's memorable events and share any impactful emotional experiences players experienced while playing (Bowman, 2014; Jensen, 2022; Westborg, 2018). Following validation, players are recommended to reframe the game experience (Bowman, 2014). According to Westborg (2018), when reframing, players co-create a shared narrative of the game's events that everyone can use as a point of reference and hopefully clears any content misunderstandings players may have. Further, reframing serves as a straightforward transition to the *real world*, leaving the role-playing portion of the exercise on the table.

After reframing, a debrief should contextualize the experience by giving players an opportunity to share with the group any insights about the experience (Bowman, 2014; Jensen, 2022; Westborg, 2018). Contextualizing the experience can take many forms. For instance, players may focus on character qualities they would like to adopt in their real lives or compare the role-played experience to real-world examples. In this step, players may explore questions regarding the game's content, setting, plot, how leadership was exemplified, among others. Lastly, Jensen (2022) recommends ending the post-game debrief with a space for open discussion where players may engage in further meaning-making.

Example Debrief Questions

Below are some questions worth exploring during a post-game debrief.

Character Reflection. How did you craft your character? Which elements were common to your out-of-game life, and which were selected to try something new? What made you pick certain elements over others?

Setting. What did you think of the game's setting? Were there features of the world you found comforting? Disturbing? Did playing in this world help you see anything in our world differently?

Plot. What did you think of your adventure? Were you happy with the decisions you made? Did any of your choices reflect how you live your out-of-game life?

Social Justice. How did you approach the conflicts in this scenario? Are there differences or similarities in how you approach conflict in real-life? If you were to apply something you learned in-game to your life right now, what would that be?

Leadership. Did you feel like a leader in this scenario? Why or why not? Did you express leadership in this activity? How or how not?

Socially Just Leadership. If you had to solve a similar situation after our session today, would anything you experienced here help in those circumstances?

CONCLUSION

TRPGs offer tremendous potential as leadership-learning pedagogy for social justice-oriented leadership learning. The experiences of playing give learners constant exposure to situations where reflection, feedback, and group process engagement is necessary to thrive, allowing for the exploration of identities, emotionally intelligent leadership, and practicing various other leadership lessons necessary to teach socially just leadership. TRPGs' robust customization provides leadership educators with the flexibility to design an ample range of experiential learning opportunities, which may provide leadership learners with experiences they would be unable to have otherwise. TRPG's adaptable features allow leadership educators to use them with almost any leadership concept (including, but not limited to, social justice leadership). Every leadership approach can fit a TRPG context when socially just leadership educators are willing and able to "play the game."

REFERENCES

Adams, M., Bell, L. A., & Griffin, P. (2016). *Teaching for diversity and social justice.* Routledge.

Arao, B., & Clemens, K. (2013). From safe space to brave space: A new way to frame dialogue around diversity and social justice. In L. Landreman (Ed.), *The art of effective facilitation: Reflections from social justice educators* (pp. 135–150). Stylus.

Barr, R. B., & Tagg, J. (1995). From teaching to learning—A new paradigm for undergraduate education. *Change: The Magazine of Higher Learning, 27*(6), 12–26. https://doi.org/10.1080/00091383.1995.10544672

Baxter Magolda, M. B., & King, P. M. (2004). *Learning partnerships: Theory and models of practice to educate for self-authorship.* Stylus.

Bowman, S. L. (2014). Returning to the real world. *Nordic Larp.* https://nordiclarp.org/2014/12/08/debrief-returning-to-the-real-world/

Bowman, S. L., & Hugaas, K. H. (2019). Transformative role-play: Design, implementation, and integration. *Nordic Larp.* https://nordiclarp.org/2019/12/10/transformative-role-play-design- implementation-and-integration/

Bowman, S. L., & Lieberoth, A. (2018). Psychology and role-playing games. In J. Zagal & S. Deterding (Eds.), *Role-playing game studies: A transmedia approach* (pp. 245–264). Routledge.

Cragoe, N. G. (2016). RPG mythos narrative gaming as modern mythmaking. *Games and Culture, 11*(6), 583–607. https://doi.org/10.1177/1555412015574195

Crookall, D. (2010). Serious games, debriefing, and simulation/gaming as a discipline. *Simulation & Gaming, 41*(6), 898–920. https://doi.org/10.1177/1046878110390784

Crookall, D. (2014). Engaging (in) gameplay and (in) debriefing. *Simulation & Gaming, 45*(4-5), 416–427. https://doi.org/10.1177/1046878114559879

Dantley, M. E., & Tillman, L. C. (2006). Social justice and moral transformative leadership. In C. Marshall & M. Oliva (Eds.), *Leadership for social justice: Making revolutions in education* (2nd ed., pp. 19–34). Allyn & Bacon.

Garcia, A. (2017). Privilege, power, and Dungeons & Dragons: How systems shape racial and gender identities in tabletop role-playing games. *Mind, Culture & Activity, 24*(3), 232–246. https://doi.org/10.1080/10749039.2017.1293691

Guthrie, K. L., & Jenkins, D. M. (2018). *The role of leadership educators: Transforming learning.* Information Age Publishing.

Guthrie, K. L., & Chunoo, V. S. (2018). *Changing the narrative: Socially just leadership education.* Information Age Publishing.

Harro, B. (2010). The cycle of liberation. In M. Adams, W. J. Blumenfeld, R. Casteñeda, H. W. Hackman, M. L. Peters, & X. Zuniga (Eds.), *Readings for diversity and social justice.* Psychology Press.

Hays, L., & Hayse, M. (2017). Game on! Experiential learning with tabletop games. In P. McDonell (Eds.), *The Experiential Library* (pp. 103–115). Chandos Publishing. https://doi.org/10.1016/B978-0-08-100775-4.00008-X

Heifetz, R. A., & Linsky, M. (2017). *Leadership on the line: Staying alive through the dangers of leading*. Harvard Business Review Press.

Hodes, J. M. (2019). *Orcs, britons, and the martial race myth, part 1: A species built for racial terror*. James Mendez Hodes. https://jamesmendezhodes.com/blog/2019/1/13/orcs-britons-and-the-martial-race-myth-part-i-a-species-built-for-racial-terror

Jensen, M. K. (2022, March 14). Larp in Leadership Development at the Royal Norwegian Naval Academy (RNNA). *Nordic Larp*. https://nordiclarp.org/2022/03/14/larp-in-leadership-development-at-the-royal-norwegian-naval-academy-rnna/

Kolb, D. A. (2015). *Experiential learning: Experience as the source of learning and development*. Pearson Education.

Komives, S. R., Owen, J. E., Longerbeam, S. D., Mainella, F. C., & Osteen, L. (2005). Developing a leadership identity: A grounded theory. *Journal of College Student Development, 46*(6), 593–611. https://doi.org/10.1353/csd.2005.0061

Lasley, J. (2022). Role-playing games in leadership learning. *New Directions for Student Leadership, 2022*, 73–87. https://doi.org/10.1002/yd.20501

Laycock. J. (2015). *Dangerous games: What the moral panic over role-playing games says about play, religion, and imagined worlds*. University of California Press.

Nelson, S., & Padilla, C. (2022). Level up: Games for socially just leadership education. *New Directions for Student Leadership, 2022*(174), 121–128. https://doi.org/10.1002/yd.20505

Nephew, M. (2006). Playing with identity: Unconscious desire and role-playing games. In J. P. Williams, S. Q. Hendricks, & W. K. Winkler (Eds.), *Gaming as culture: Essays on reality, identity and experience in fantasy games* (pp. 120–139). McFarland & Co.

Parks, S. D. (2005). *Leadership can be taught*. Harvard Business School Press.

Rivers, A., Wickramasekera, I. E., Pekala, R. J., & Rivers, J. A. (2016). Empathic features and absorption in fantasy role-playing. *The American Journal of Clinical Hypnosis, 58*(3), 286–294. https://doi.org/10.1080/00029157.2015.1103696

Ruiz-Ezquerro, A. (2021). Rollings dice and learning: Using role-playing games as pedagogy tools. *Journal of Campus Activities Practice and Scholarship, 3*(1), 50–56. https://doi.org/10.52499/2021022

Shankman, M. L., Allen, S. J., & Haber-Curran, P. (2015). *Emotionally intelligent leadership: A guide for college students* (2nd ed.). Jossey-Bass.

Stanovich, P. J., & Stanovich, K. E. (2003) Using research and reason in education: How teachers can use scientifically based research to make curricular and instructional decisions. *Partnership For Reading Project, National Institute for Literacy, U.S. Dept. Of Education*.

Volpe White, J., & Guthrie, K. L. (2016). Creating a meaningful learning environment: Reflection in leadership education. *Journal of Leadership Education, 15*(1), 60–75. https://doi.org/10.12806/V15/I1/R5

Vygotsky, L. S. (1978). *Mind in society: The development of higher psychological processes*. Harvard University Press.

Westborg, J. (2018). *Who sees what? Perceived learning areas after participating in an edu larp.* [Bachelor's Thesis, University of Gothenburg]. GUPEA. http://hdl.handle.net/2077/59234

Whitton, N. (2012). Good game design is good learning design. In N. Whitton & A. Moseley (Eds.), *Using games to enhance learning and teaching: A beginner's guide* (pp. 9–18). Routledge.

Wright, J. C., Weissglass, D. E., & Casey, V. (2020). Imaginative role-playing as a medium for moral development: Dungeons & Dragons provides moral training. *The Journal of Humanistic Psychology, 60*(1), 99–129. https://doi.org/10.1177/0022167816686263

CHAPTER 22

SUSTAINING COMMITMENT

Collectively Acting for Socially Just Leadership Education

Kathy L. Guthrie,
Vivechkanand S. Chunoo, and Brittany Devies

We have embarked on nearly a decade of engaging conversations about socially just leadership education. As with most issues plaguing our world, our efforts continually ebb and flow depending on global, national, and local contexts. Much like tides reaching the shore, focus on social justice shifts. In *Changing the Narrative: Socially Just Leadership Education* (Guthrie & Chunoo, 2018), collective voices discussed the need for leadership educators to change the conversation from often complicity in leadership to being a part of a social justice tide that was coming. A few years later, in *Shifting the Mindset: Socially Just Leadership Education* (Guthrie & Chunoo, 2021), the discussion moved to how we were among a tide of social justice. In fact, it is how we need to not only change the conversation, but the mindset to where developing leadership learning opportunities for all to fully engage because a part of the collective thought, not just conversation. However, as tides shift and conversation on social justice and socially just leadership education become more challenging, we need to continue to move forward. Move from the conversation and thought to action. The title of this book, committing to action, was intentional. Although change for equity may be slowing, it is now more important than ever to commit to action in integrating leadership learning opportunities to allow for all

Committing to Action: Socially Just Leadership Educations, pp. 273–280
Copyright © 2025 by Information Age Publishing
www.infoagepub.com

to fully engage, no matter religion, race, ethnicity, veteran status, ability, gender, and lived experiences.

Committing to action for all to engage in leadership learning is our obligation as educators. It is not to indoctrinate others into a specific way of thinking, nor is it to exclude certain people, but instead it is open the opportunity of leadership learning to all and to educate those who are dedicated to their own leadership development journey. To create opportunities where engaging in leadership learning is not about already being a leader or just about roles, but about engaging in a complex, socially constructed process. The leadership process where being a follower is as important as being a leader and knowing when, how, and why to step into certain roles is critical. To achieve this, we must collectively commit to reformulating socially just leadership education and commit to action of creating all leadership learning opportunities with various ways of knowing in mind.

ENGAGING IN SOCIALLY JUSTICE LEADERSHIP EDUCATION

To create socially just leadership learning opportunities, educators constantly question *what* they teach, *how* they teach, and the learning *outcomes* they are working toward with their students. Analyzing and deconstructing the current ways of teaching leadership is critical to amplify leadership learning for all and challenge the "story most often told" (Dugan, 2017, p. 59). Time for action is now: action to disrupt the status quo and change how leadership is taught. It is time to open up leadership to those excluded from traditional leadership programs, including those who are from historically underrepresented backgrounds and lived experiences. Authors in this text have provided useful tools in deconstructing leadership education in various contexts; however, recommendations of redeveloping leadership education to be socially just is at the heart of what this text is about.

Leadership Education Deconstruction

Authors in this text have amplified diverse voices and brought awareness to social identities, various contexts, and lived experiences to individuals whose voices are often not heard. Deconstructing learning environments is essential for educators, who are also situated in various contexts with diverse lived experiences. Included in this volume are authors who have shared useful tools in deconstructing leadership education with suggestions to revise socially just leadership education efforts.

In Chapter 2, Adrian Bitton discusses how the current landscape of higher education is influencing leadership education. With acknowledging neoliberalism in higher education, Bitton deconstructs not only current higher education practices but also leadership education, and offers some potential pathways forward. Although these pathways have been discussed before, they are critical to socially just leadership education. Continuing to disrupt the false contradiction between social justice and leadership is one pathway. Instead, educators need to continue to explore the interconnectedness of social justice and leadership. Another pathway forward is to continue to focus on a holistic student leadership development approach. It is critical to anchor socially just leadership education in human development, which will focus on development of the whole student to engage in leadership processes.

Joshua Taylor, in Chapter 3, reminds us how socially just leadership development is challenging because at some point, we all get something wrong before we can learn how to approach it appropriately. Taylor examines how leadership educators need to work with White students who may either resist or avoid conversations about diversity and equity. He helps us deconstruct this phenomenon and provides how to leverage catalyst points towards change.

As you have read in this text, each author offers various ways to deconstruct the current ways of teaching leadership, as well as offer recommendations and examples of ways to reformulate leadership education and social justice to become socially just leadership education. Many of these recommendations focus on considering students' lived experiences and how these lived experiences influence their leadership learning. Although we recognize context is critical in how these recommendations may be used in the various learning opportunities, we hope all educators will pause to think about the possibility of integrating more of these recommendations than they might have originally thought possible.

Leadership and Social Justice Redevelopment Recommendations

Action oriented commitments were the focus of this final section of the text. These action-oriented commitments are recommendations in moving forward to redevelop leadership education in socially just ways. In Chapter 16, Brittany Devies shared with us how important creating and maintaining women only spaces are for leadership capacity and efficacy development in college. Holly Henning in Chapter 17 discussed how academic advising is a missed opportunity in creating environments where socially just leadership education can occur. Johnnie Allen, Jr., in Chapter 18, provided critical insight on how committing to the mentoring of Black students can open hearts and minds to socially just leadership. Another commitment was shared by Ashley Archer Doehling in Chapter 19, which shared how social justice peer educators can be leadership educators. Resilience was the topic of Chapter 20 with Gen Ramirez sharing how important it was to acknowledge and honor resilient students as leaders. Finally, Antonio Ruiz-Ezquerro shared in Chapter 21 how gaming pedagogy is a way to introduce socially just leadership education to students who may not engage otherwise.

These commitments are critical for our collective movement toward socially just leadership education for all. As we experienced, the heart of this text is hearing the lived experiences, practices, and scholarship of those who sit at various intersections of identities and provide educators with various approaches to reducing barriers to engagement for diverse populations. Listening to voices and experiences of others allows us, as educators, to learn and work toward minimizing barriers and enhancing leadership education for all.

COLLECTIVELY COMMITING TO ACTION

Even though we continue to work to change the narrative of socially just leadership education and shift mindsets of educators, we still have a long way to go to fully integrate social justice into all leadership education spaces. We must collectively commit to action, as educators, to develop and provide socially just leadership learning opportunities for all. Although developing such learning opportunities is filled with barriers, it is critical to work together for support, idea generation, and to maximize learning potential of the generation we are working with. With committing to action in mind, we respectfully offer the following questions to support leadership educators' reflection and engagement in this work. The categories of critical challenges, critical hope, and critical innovation organize these questions. Critical challenges are to further develop opportunities for change. Critical hope continues to deconstruct barriers with a growth in mind. Finally, critical innovation is to hopefully ignite creativity in both personal and professional domains to lead to action to make positive sustainable change toward socially just leadership education.

Critical Challenges

Obstacles to engage in socially just leadership education are deeply embedded in our culture that they are, at times, challenging to identify.

These barriers are so ingrained in societal norms, organizational structures, practices, and cultures that is hard to recognize as oppressive actions. We offer the following questions for leadership educators to consider as they work to develop socially just leadership learning opportunities:

- How can we trouble the traditional boundaries of leadership education and redefine what, how, and why we teach leadership (Irwin, Chapter 6)?
- As educators, how do we facilitate learning for Desi identifying students (Bhatt, Chapter 10)?
- How can we acknowledge, honor, and create women-only spaces for leadership development (Devies, Chapter 16)?
- How can we redefine leadership learning situated in mentoring of Black students (Allen, Jr., Chapter 18)?
- As educators, how do we continue to connect social justice and leadership education through peer mentoring programs (Archer Doehling, Chapter 19)?

Developing socially just leadership learning opportunities presents critical challenges constantly. However, we hope these provided questions can support educators in developing programs. Although honest answers to these questions may lead to discomfort in both our own reflection and conversations with colleagues, it is critical to continually challenge the current ways leadership education is being developed, offered, and assessed. Hopefully, these uncomfortable reflections will lead to commitment to action in movement towards more socially just leadership education programs. In addition to identifying critical challenges, these changes also require critical hope to further deconstruct current ways of offering leadership education and critical innovation to offer new ways of leadership learning.

Critical Hope

As we see every day, resistance to change is common (Quinn, 1996). Resistance to change can in both active and passive ways and we see this in shifting frameworks for development of leadership learning opportunities. However, critical hope (Bozalek et al., 2013; Priest & Guthrie, 2022) is required on this journey of transforming leadership education into being socially just. We honor those who have been working towards socially just leadership education and hope that collectively we can join these efforts. We hope that by amplifying the diverse voices in this text that we can continue this journey with critical hope in the future. When encountering resistance, we offer the following questions in the framework of critical hope as we continue this collective journey:

- What opportunities are offered to reframe Black male leadership identity development in dominate leadership education (Daniels, Chapter 4)?
- In better understanding Caribbean students, how can we use these lessons to enhance socially just leadership education for all (Pacheco, Chapter 8)?
- How can constructs of body image be broken down so barriers to leadership education can be deconstructed (Wellington, Chapter 9)?
- What opportunities do we currently have to connect queer leadership more deeply to socially just leadership education (Kuhn, Chapter 11)?
- How can critical hope be a framework for underrepresented populations as a pathway forward (Robinson, Chapter 15)?
- How can we honor lived experiences of resilience to enhance socially just leadership learning opportunities (Ramirez, Chapter 20)?

Critical hope is essential for us to move collectively forward and commit to action. Identifying and making meaning from the critical challenges we encounter and celebrating the successes we have in implementing socially just leadership learning opportunities is important in sustaining critical hope. We acknowledge there will be setbacks from a lack of support, there will be stumbles by not getting things completely right, but having hope and leaning on those who are on this journey with you can produce influential, meaningful changes that will open the hearts and minds of students who have been searching for their voices to be heard. Being innovative in program development, offerings, and assessment will provide motivation to continual engagement in not only in the actual leadership learning, but the development of it by passing it on.

Critical Innovation

Finally, we recognize redeveloping leadership learning opportunities through programs and initiatives is a large task. This takes a considerable amount of time and energy, which often we do not have an abundance of. However, we hope that by focusing on collective action, we can harness the creativity or ourselves and others to do this work. To think creatively, we offer these questions for reflection:

- How can higher education institutions provide creative socially just leadership programs that cut across academic disciplines (Maia, Chapter 5)?
- Using systemic inquiry, how can we expand opportunities for leadership learning that are socially just (Chunoo, Chapter 7)?
- How are we attending to important factors in the development of international student leaders (Vaughn, Chapter 12)?
- By honoring foster youth's lived experiences, how can we create unique opportunities for development of leadership identity, capacity, and efficacy (Jackson, Chapter 14)?
- How can we maximize leadership learning opportunities for students in academic advising contexts (Henning, Chapter 17)?
- How can we expand and reframe pedagogy in innovative ways, for example in gaming, to maximize learning (Ezquerro, Chapter 21)?

With the shifting landscape in higher education, more complexities continue to emerge, whether it is through new legislation or budget cuts. Innovation and creativity have been required of leadership educators since the beginning of most programs. Meeting programmatic goals and student learning objectives has been known to be a passion of leadership educators, so being creative is not new. However, it is more important now than ever. As we continue to be thrown into this new landscape, we need to learn how to navigate new waters. We encourage educators to continue to use critical perspectives and infuse innovative practices to lead to reformulating leadership education with social justice at the heart of everything we do.

Socially just leadership learning opportunities need to be the paradigm we work from, not something we aspire to. Considering culturally relevant ways of leadership learning (Beatty & Guthrie, 2021) should be the standard in higher education. Collective commitment to action is needed now more than ever. We are past beginning the conversation or shifting mindsets; it is time for action. As we continue to see barriers of all kinds to action, it is long overdue for equity of *all* students. Together we can still develop leadership learning opportunities on decades of research that state how diverse voices are critical to maximizing learning. Together we can continue to push forward and collectively make a difference in this work.

Make no mistake, another sea change is coming. As we each work in our local contexts toward change, it might seem as though the forces of injustice are insurmountable. They are not. However, they do win when they make us believe we are less powerful than we are; individually and collectively. Together we can turn the tide of injustice. The time for action is now. Justice for all is on the horizon, and we can only sail there together.

REFERENCES

Bozalek, V., Leibowitz, B., Carolissen, R., & Boler, M. (Eds.). (2013). *Discerning critical hope in educational practices*. Routledge.

Dugan, J. P. (2017). *Leadership theory: Cultivating critical perspectives*. Jossey-Bass.

Guthrie, K. L., & Chunoo, V. S. (Eds.). (2018). *Changing the narrative: Socially just leadership education*. Information Age Publishing.

Guthrie, K. L., & Chunoo, V. S. (Eds.). (2021). *Shifting the mindset: Socially just leadership education*. Information Age Publishing.

Priest, K. L., & Guthrie, K. L. (2022). Parting the clouds: Navigating complexity in leadership. In K. L. Guthrie, & K. L. Priest (Eds.), *Navigating complexities in leadership: Moving towards critical hope* (pp. 1-13). Information Age Publishing.

Quinn, R. E. (1996). *Deep change*. Jossey-Bass.

ABOUT THE EDITORS
AND AUTHORS

EDITORS

Dr. Kathy L. Guthrie (she/her) is a professor of higher education at Florida State University. In addition to teaching in the Higher Education Program, Kathy also serves as the director of the Leadership Learning Research Center and coordinates the Undergraduate Certificate in Leadership Studies at Florida State University. Prior to becoming a faculty member, Kathy served as a student affairs administrator for 10 years in various areas, including campus activities, commuter services, community engagement, and leadership development. Kathy's research focuses on leadership learning, socially just leadership education, online teaching and learning, and professional development for student affairs professionals, specifically in leadership education. Kathy has developed and taught both undergraduate and graduate courses in leadership and higher education. Kathy has published over 100 publications, including co-editing five issues in the New Directions series. She has also co-authored and co-edited over 10 books. Kathy has served on several editorial boards and is currently the editor of the *New Directions in Student Leadership* series, on the board of directors for LeaderShape, Inc. and the International Leadership Association. Kathy has worked in higher education administrative and faculty roles for over 20 years and loves every minute of her chosen career path. Kathy enjoys spending time with her husband, daughter, and dog, where collectively they are affectionately known as Team Guthrie.

Dr. Vivechkanand S. Chunoo (he/his) is a teaching assistant professor of leadership studies at Florida State University. He teaches courses in leadership theory and practice, leadership in groups and communities, leadership and ethics, and leadership and change. His scholarly interests include culturality in leadership learning, socially just leadership education, and online leader development. Dr. Chunoo also serves as the associate editor for the *New Directions for Student Leadership* series. V. was also a co-host for the 2021–2022 and 2022–2023 seasons of the NASPA Student Leadership Programs Knowledge Community podcast (new episodes available now!). He presents his scholarship regularly at annual meetings of the International Leadership Association and routinely travels across the country to deliver workshops and training sessions. V. proudly co-edited (and contributed to) both *Changing the Narrative: Socially Just Leadership Education* and *Shifting the Mindset: Socially Just Leadership Education*. He currently lives in Tallahassee, Florida with his two dogs, Charley and Milo.

Dr. Brittany Devies serves as the inaugural Director for the Center for Fraternity and Sorority Organizational Wellness at Florida State University, leading their research initiatives around organizational leadership and wellness. She also serves as teaching faculty in the Department of Educational Leadership & Policy Studies at Florida State University, teaching in their Higher Education graduate programs and their undergraduate leadership studies program. She has authored and co-authored 30 book chapters and journal articles on leadership education and learning. She served as a co-editor for *Rooted and Radiant: Women's Narratives of Leadership*. She also co-authored *Foundations of Leadership: Principles, Practice, and Progress*. During the 2022–2023 and 2023–2024 academic years, she served as the co-host of the NASPA Leadership podcast. She has received several honors and awards, including the NASPA NOW Inquiry Award, NASPA Student Leadership Programs Dr. Susan R. Komives Research Award, NASPA Student Leadership Programs Outstanding Emerging Professional Award, and ACPA's Annuit Coeptis Emerging Professional Award. She was inducted into the American Association of Colleges and Universities' Future Leaders Society and named a 33 Under 33 Featured Alumni for Delta Delta Delta national fraternity. She received her PhD in Higher Education from Florida State University, her MS in Higher Education from Florida State University, and her BSEd in Early and Middle Childhood Studies with a minor in Leadership Studies from The Ohio State University.

AUTHORS

Johnnie L. Allen Jr. (he/him/his) is a PhD student in the Higher Education program at Florida State University, where he is a Graduate Research and

Teaching Assistant, as well as an Instructor in the Leadership Learning Research Center (LLRC). Johnnie is a two-time alum of Indiana University where he received his Bachelor of Science in Community Health and Public Health and a Master of Science in Education from the Indiana University Higher Education and Student Affairs program. His research interests include examining critical masculinities in Black male leadership and sociocultural influences on Black college men's gender socialization and leadership learning.

Ravi Bhatt (he/him/his) is a Higher Education doctoral student at Florida State University. He serves as the Associate Director for the Hardee Center for Leadership and Ethics and as a Graduate Researcher and Teaching Assistant for the Leadership Learning Research Center (LLRC). He is a Desi American with familial roots in India and the United States. With foundational pedagogy rooted in social justice, he approaches this work to expand cultural awareness, kindness, and collective growth.

Adrian L. Bitton is a PhD candidate at The Ohio State University. Prior to pursuing her doctorate, Adrian worked as a leadership educator and has taught classes within three undergraduate leadership programs. Her research interests include socially just leadership, leadership learning and pedagogy, and critical leadership studies. Adrian's identities as a White, first-generation, Jewish, cisgender woman who holds dual citizenship, have deeply influenced her experience in the academy and the world and guide her commitments to equity and justice.

Dr. Vivechkanand S. Chunoo (he/his) is an assistant teaching professor of leadership studies in the department of educational leadership and policy studies at Florida State University. His scholarly interests center the cultural aspects of teaching and learning leadership. V teaches undergraduate courses in leadership theory and practice, leadership in groups and communities, leadership and ethics, and leadership and change. He is also associate editor for *New Directions for Student Leadership*.

Dr. Michael A. Daniels (he/his) currently serves an Assistant Professor at Kent State University. Michael's passion is connecting with people, connecting people to their purpose, and providing individuals with the support necessary to achieve their dreams. He earned his Bachelor of Science degree in Psychology from John Carroll University, his Master of Arts degree in Student Affairs Administration from Michigan State University, and his Doctor of Philosophy degree in Educational Administration-Higher Education at Kent State University. Michael's research areas include the experiences underrepresented populations, leadership education, and diversity, equity, and inclusion policies and practices.

Dr. Brittany Devies serves as the inaugural Director for the Center for Fraternity and Sorority Organizational Wellness at Florida State University, leading their research initiatives around organizational leadership and wellness. She also serves as teaching faculty in the Department of Educational Leadership & Policy Studies at Florida State University, teaching in their Higher Education graduate programs and their undergraduate leadership studies program.

Ashley Archer Doehling (she/her) serves as the Curriculum Initiative Analyst at Kennesaw State University. In this role, Ashley supports faculty in designing and evaluating innovative academic programs that contribute to Kennesaw State University's curricular portfolio to support student success and maintain curricular relevance, quality, and efficiency. Currently, Ashley is a Doctoral Candidate in the Higher Education PhD program at Florida State University. Her research interests include educational accessibility, integrating socially just curriculum and teaching practices into classrooms, and graduate student success.

Dr. Kathy L. Guthrie (she/her) is a professor in the higher education program at Florida State University. She serves as director of the Leadership Learning Research Center and coordinator of the Undergraduate Certificate in Leadership Studies. She currently serves as the editor for the *New Directions in Student Leadership* series.

Amy Haggard (she/her) is currently the Assistant Director for Title IX in the office of Student Conduct and Community Standards at Florida State University and a Doctoral Candidate in the Higher Education PhD program. Amy's current research topic for her doctoral work is to explore how high-achieving undergraduate students reflect on their leadership identity development. Haggard is also passionate about student leadership and success, assessing LGBTQ+ inclusivity and programming, student-based services, and continued education. Before her time at Florida State, she received a Masters in Student Affairs in Higher Education from Colorado State University.

Holly Henning is a PhD student in Higher Education at Florida State University. She is also a Graduate Research Assistant in FSU's Center for Postsecondary Success where she researches developmental education reform, alternative course placement measures, and additional issues of college student access and success. For the last decade, Holly worked in international education and academic advising at multiple institutions. She holds a master's degree in Higher Education from the University of Mississippi and an MBA from the University of Alabama at Birmingham.

Dr. Lauren N. Irwin (she/her/hers) is an Assistant Professor of Higher Education at the University of Tennessee, Knoxville. She received her PhD in Higher Education and Student Affairs from the University of Iowa. Lauren leverages her experience as a student affairs professional in leadership education, housing and residence life, and social justice programs to inform her scholarship. Lauren's research interrogates racialization and whiteness across student affairs contexts, focusing on disrupting whiteness in leadership education programs.

Lisa Jackson (she/her) is an Assistant Teaching Professor at Florida State University's College of Social Work. Previously, she served as Sr. Program Director at Florida State University's Center for Academic Retention and Enhancement where she developed expertise in identifying and addressing biopsychosocial and system-level factors inhibiting the well-being and academic progress of foster care alumni and students experiencing homelessness. She serves on the Post-Secondary Education Subcommittee, and Board of Directors, for the National Association for the Education of Homeless Children and Youth. Lisa is a Doctoral Candidate in the Higher Education Ph.D. program at Florida State's College of Education, Health, and Human Sciences. She was honored as a Child Welfare Champion by Florida's Department of Children and Families in 2018.

Adam Kuhn (he/him + they/them) was born and raised in the west end of Toronto. Adam is currently serving as Director, Student Engagement at the University of Toronto. Adam is also a PhD candidate at the Ontario Institute for Studies in Education, studying the leadership experiences of queer students.

Dr. Ana Maia (she/her) is the Associate Dean of Student Affairs Program Effectiveness and Adjunct Faculty for the Leadership Studies Minor at the University of Tampa (UT). She has facilitated intentional leadership development experiences for over 13 years. Maia oversaw UT's President's Leadership Fellows program for six years. She serves as Chair for the Strategic Planning and Assessment Team in the Division of Student Affairs. Her research focus includes culturally relevant leadership learning, resilience, and leadership educator development.

Derrick Raphael Pacheco (he/him/el) is a PhD candidate in the Higher Education program at Florida State University and serves as a Graduate

Assistant in the Leadership Learning Research Center (LLRC). Derrick's research interest lies in the understanding of the lived experiences of college students who hold minoritized social identities and how they make meaning of their leader identity at historically white institutions. Derrick received his Certified Nonprofit Professional (CNP) credential from the National Leadership Alliance and a BS in Marketing, BS in Management, and MS in Higher Education, all from Florida State University.

Genesis (Gen) V. Ramirez (she/her/ella) currently works as the Leadership Programs Coordinator for The Center for Leadership and Service at Florida State University, her alma mater, where she earned her BS in Psychology and MS in Higher Education. While in her current role, she has had the opportunity to develop and facilitate a variety of leadership presentations and programs for FSU students and members of the greater Tallahassee Community. She is passionate about providing leadership resources that are accessible and inclusive.

Darius Robinson (he/him/his) is a doctoral candidate in the higher education program at Florida State University. His research interests revolve around the examination of leadership experiences of students of color, with a focus on Black males. Darius serves as a graduate research assistant for a Black male retention program in the South a week as a graduate assistant at the Leadership Learning Research Center. Prior to his doctoral journey, Darius had professional experiences working in residential life, K–12 education and service activism with disaster relief and rebuilding projects.

Dr. Antonio Ruiz-Ezquerro was born in Mexico City, Mexico, where he lived for the first 20 years of his life. He later moved to the U.S. where he got his BA in Marketing at James Madison University, his MS in Higher Education, and his PhD from at Florida State University. Antonio currently works at Colgate University. His research focuses on leadership pedagogy and game design, often mixing both topics into unique projects.

Dr. Joshua K. Taylor (he/him) is the founding Director of the Hargis Leadership Institute at Oklahoma State University and works with hundreds of student leaders every year in curricular and co-curricular environments. Joshua earned his PhD in Educational Leadership and Policy Studies at Oklahoma State University. Before working in higher education, Joshua worked as a middle school and high school teacher for 10 years. Joshua's current research interests include socially just leadership, student leadership development, civic learning and democratic engagement, and the long-term effects of university leadership development programs.

Dr. Challen Wellington is someone who is passionate about social justice in all forms. She is currently working in diversity, equity, and inclusion for the Virginia Commonwealth University Massey Cancer Center. In addition to her work at the Massey Cancer Center, she enjoys volunteering her time with undergraduate students from historically underrepresented backgrounds. During her down time, she enjoys reading, dancing, and cooking with her family.

Laura Vaughn (she/her) is a PhD candidate in the Educational Leadership and Policy Studies Department at Florida State University. She is a graduate assistant with the Leadership Learning Research Center, where she teaches in the undergraduate leadership certificate program and works with the alumni research project. Her fields of interest are exploring the intersections of international students and leadership, along with international student development and engagement.